Meet Me In The Kitchen

A Timeless Collection of
Kitchen-tested recipes!

by Bevelyn Blair

Published by: Blair of Columbus, Inc.

Additional copies of
MEET ME IN THE KITCHEN
may be obtained by addressing
BLAIR OF COLUMBUS, INC.
P. O. Box 7852
Columbus, Georgia 31908

First printing, 1990, 10,000 copies

Library of Congress Catalog Number: 90-81706
ISBN:0-9613709-1-2

Printed by: Columbus Productions, Inc.
Artwork by: Carol Crocker

Manufactured in the United States of America

FOREWORD

I acquired from my parents a very deep appreciation for good food. Mealtime was always a happy time at our home. It was a time of togetherness and gave me a sense of belonging. Maybe this is the reason I developed a "love affair" with the kitchen. I began helping in the kitchen when I was a young girl. This led me to an intense interest in home economics in an effort to expand my horizons. When I began cooking for my own family, I tried new recipes every week. I read cookbooks, swapped recipes with friends and family members, attended cooking schools. All of us remember special moments that sparkle up our lives—one of mine was when I baked my very first cake for my daughter's first birthday. It was perfect! There were other special moments, of course...preparing my son's favorite dishes, tuna casserole and eggplant fritters. In 1978, I organized a cookbook and had 100 copies printed for family and friends. This was called *Our Family Cookbook*. Then, in 1984, my sister, Joanne Walker, and I published my cookbook, *Country Cakes*. Now, finally, here we have published all of the recipes in *Our Family Cookbook*, plus many, many other recipes—a collection of over 35 years. All of them have been tested and used over and over again. I hope you will enjoy *Meet Me In The Kitchen!*

Bevelyn Blair,
Author/Editor

Books by Bevelyn Blair

Country Cakes

Meet Me In The Kitchen

DEDICATION

This book is dedicated to
JAMES WALKER, III,
for helping me turn a dream into reality,
and
JOANNE WALDING WALKER,
my sister and best friend.

ACKNOWLEDGMENTS

Putting together a cookbook of any kind is no small task. You first gather all of the recipes that you have accumulated and then begin the tremendous undertaking of sorting them out. You stop and start again many times. You want to give up but something inside you spurs you on. Then on and on you proceed until there is no turning back. You tackle each obstacle as it arises. You remember each recipe as you type the manuscript. You laugh...you cry...some of the recipes belonged to a favorite relative who is no longer here. I wish to acknowledge my many friends, family members and acquaintances for the recipes shared with me through the years. I may have changed some of them in the process of trying them out and for that I take full responsibility.

Bevelyn Blair

TABLE OF CONTENTS

Appetizers
and Beverages

Canapés are tiny open-faced sandwiches. Use your imagination to create a variety of canapés to be eaten with the fingers...crisp crackers, potato chips, toasted breads or miniature cutouts of bread toasted on one side with fillings of savory spreads. Serve with an assortment of hors d'oeuvres and chilled juices or vegetable cocktails.

CAVIAR CANAPÉS

10 large rounds of
  white bread
1 (3-ounce) package
  cream cheese,
  softened
Mayonnaise
3 tablespoons caviar

1/2 teaspoon lemon juice,
  freshly squeezed
1 tablespoon onion,
  finely chopped
1 hard boiled egg
Parsley

Toast bread rounds on one side. Beat cream cheese until softened; add mayonnaise to right spreading consistency. Spread on bread rounds, then spread on the caviar sprinkled with lemon juice. Top caviar with onion, then with sieved egg white, ending with sieved egg yolk. Garnish with parsley, if desired.

Easy to make!

CHEESE-CHUTNEY CANAPÉ SPREAD

1 (8-ounce) package
  cream cheese,
  softened
1/2 cup chutney

1 teaspoon curry powder
1/4 teaspoon dry ground
  mustard
1/4 cup almonds, chopped

Beat cream cheese until smooth; add remaining ingredients and blend well. Serve with assorted crackers.

CHEESE-CHUTNEY MOLD

1 (8-ounce) package
  cream
  cheese, softened
1 (8-ounce) package
  sharp Cheddar
  cheese, softened
1 teaspoon curry powder

2 tablespoons cooking
  sherry
1 cup chutney
Green onions, finely
  chopped
Assorted crackers

Beat cream cheese and Cheddar cheese until mixed well; add curry and sherry. Grease a 9-inch pie pan and fill with mixture. Chill in refrigerator. Remove from pan before serving and top with the chutney and onion. Best served at room temperature with an assortment of crackers.

CHEESE BALL

1 pound sharp cheese,
  grated
4 ounces blue cheese
12 ounces cream cheese
  softened
1 tablespoon
  Worcestershire
  sauce

1/2 teaspoon ground red
  pepper
1/2 teaspoon garlic
  salt
1 cup pecans, chopped
  fine, divided
1/2 cup chopped parsley

Beat the sharp cheese until soft and smooth. Add the blue cheese and cream cheese, blending thoroughly. Now add the Worcestershire sauce, red pepper, garlic salt and 1/2 cup of the pecans. Combine remaining 1/2 cup pecans with the parsley and roll ball in the mixture. Refrigerate until ready to serve. Serve with assorted crackers.

Delicious and will make a hit at your next party!

CRABMEAT CANAPÉS

1 (6-1/4 ounce) can
  crabmeat, flaked
  fine or 1-1/2 cups
  fresh cooked or
  frozen crabmeat

1/4 cup mayonnaise
1/4 cup pickled onion,
  finely chopped
Crackers
Sharp cheese, grated

Remove cartilage from crabmeat and flake fine. Stir in mayonnaise and onion. Spread on crisp crackers and top with cheese. Place under broiler until cheese melts. Serve warm. Good with tomato juice cocktail.

Delightful!

DATE CANAPÉ SPREAD

1 (8-ounce) package
  dates, finely cut
1 (8-ounce) package
  cream cheese,
  softened
1/2 cup celery, finely
  cut

1/2 cup walnuts, chopped
1 tablespoon mayonnaise
Crisp crackers and toast
  rounds

Combine all ingredients and blend together until of spreadable consistency; add additional mayonnaise, if necessary. Serve on crackers and toast rounds.

You will want to serve these often!

LIVER PATÉ NO. 1

4 tablespoons butter,
  divided
1/4 cup onion, finely
  chopped
1 clove garlic, crushed
1/2 pound chicken livers

1/2 teaspoon salt
1/4 teaspoon ground black
  pepper
1/8 teaspoon ground thyme
1 tablespoon cooking sherry

Melt 1 tablespoon butter; sauté onion and garlic until softened. Add livers and increase heat to low; sauté livers for 5 minutes. Place in blender and blend until smooth; add remaining butter until mixed well. Add seasonings and sherry. Spoon mixture into a mold. Refrigerate until set. Serve with melba toast.

LIVER PATÉ NO. 2

1-1/2 pounds chicken livers
1 medium onion, chopped
3/4 pound butter, melted
2 teaspoons salt
1/2 teaspoon ground
  nutmeg

2 teaspoons dry ground
  mustard
1/4 teaspoon ground cloves
1/4 teaspoon hot sauce

Place livers in a large saucepan and add water to cover; bring to a boil and simmer for around 20 minutes uncovered. Drain livers well and place in blender along with onion; blend until smooth. Add rest of ingredients and stir to mix well. Spoon mixture into a one-quart mold. Refrigerate until set. When ready to serve, place mold in hot water for a few seconds; turn onto serving dish. Good with toasted bread.

SARDINE CANAPÉS

Toasted bread strips
Butter, softened
Sardines, well drained
Lemon juice, freshly
  squeezed

1 tablespoon prepared
  mustard
1/2 cup sharp cheese,
  grated
Stuffed olive slices

Toast bread strips on one side and spread thinly with softened butter. Lay 1 or 2 sardines on untoasted side of each bread strip. Squeeze lemon juice over fish. Combine the mustard and cheese and place 1 teaspoonful on each canapé. Lay in a shallow baking pan and bake at 450 degrees until cheese melts and browns. Garnish with olive slices. Serve immediately.

Calling all sardine-lovers!

MUSHROOM CANAPÉS

24 large fresh mushrooms   1 pound sausage

Quickly clean mushrooms by washing gently in cold water. Trim the stem ends and save for soup or gravy. Stuff the caps with sausage. Broil on lower rack for around 20 minutes. Serve on thin toast rounds.

OLIVE CANAPÉS

4-1/2 ounces ripe
  olives, chopped
1/4 cup green onion,
  chopped fine
1 cup sharp cheese, grated

4 tablespoons mayonnaise
1/8 teaspoon salt
1/4 teaspoon curry powder
Toast rounds

Blend together first six ingredients. Spread on the rounds and heat in a 350 degree oven until canapés are hot. Serve immediately.

Worth the effort!

PEANUT BUTTER

1 cup salted cocktail
  peanuts (skins off)

1 tablespoon peanut oil
1/2 teaspoon salt

Place all ingredients in an electric blender and blend until mixture is spreadable, adding more oil if necessary. Blend for several minutes. Store in a tightly covered glass jar. Stir before using. Good on crackers and makes delicious sandwiches.

Try this just once and you will again!

SHRIMP CANAPÉ SPREAD

1/2 cup butter, softened
1 (3-ounce) package cream
  cheese, softened
1 (4-1/2-ounce) can tiny
  shrimp, well drained
2 teaspoons lemon juice,
  freshly squeezed

1/2 teaspoon onion salt
1/4 teaspoon paprika
Dash ground red pepper
Assorted crackers

Place all ingredients, except crackers, in blender or food processor and blend until smooth. Chill for several hours. Allow to soften when ready to serve and spread on crackers.

Compliments will be forthcoming!

PINEAPPLE CHEESE BALL

2 (8-ounce) packages
cream cheese,
softened
1 (8-1/4 ounce) can
crushed pineapple,
drained
3 tablespoons onion,
grated

1/2 teaspoon seasoned
salt
2 cups pecans, chopped
fine, equally
divided
Cherries and pineapple
slices, for garnish
(if desired)

Beat cream cheese until smooth and creamy; gradually add the pineapple and beat until smooth. Add onion, salt and 1 cup pecans. Refrigerate until chilled, then form into a ball and roll in remaining pecans. Place on an attractive serving plate and surround with pineapple slices and cherries with stems for garnish. Serve with assorted crackers.

Surprisingly good!

STRAWBERRY-CHEESE RING

1 (16 ounce) package
Cheddar cheese,
grated
1 cup mayonnaise
1/2 cup onion, grated

1/8 teaspoon ground red
pepper
1 cup pecans, chopped
Strawberry preserves

Beat cheese until smooth, blend in mayonnaise, then onion and pepper. Stir in pecans. Spoon into ring mold and chill. Serve with strawberry preserves.

TUNA CANAPÉS

1 (6-1/2-ounce) can tuna,
drained and flaked
3/4 cup stuffed olives,
finely chopped
1 tablespoon prepared
mustard

Mayonnaise
1 hard boiled egg
Toast rounds and crisp
crackers

Drain tuna and flake fine. Mix well with olives, mustard and enough mayonnaise for spreading. Spread on toast rounds and crisp crackers. Top with sieved egg yolk, followed with sieved egg white.

Delicious and a snap to make!

Cocktails are appetizers served as a first course of a meal and may be liquid or a semi-liquid.

APPLE COCKTAIL

2 apples, unpared and
  shredded
1 cup pineapple juice

1 cup miniature
  marshmallows
1/2 cup shredded coconut

Combine all ingredients and refrigerate until cold. Serve in sherbets.

CRANBERRY COCKTAIL

4 cups cranberries
4 cups water

2/3 cup granulated sugar

Combine cranberries and water and bring to a boil. Reduce heat and cook for 5 minutes. Strain cranberries and water through a cheesecloth; return to heat and bring to a boil. Add the sugar and cook for 2 minutes longer. Cool mixture and then refrigerate to chill thoroughly. Serve immediately.

FRUIT COCKTAIL

2 cups fruit cocktail,
  canned

1 cup banana slices
1 cup unpared apple, cubed

Refrigerate fruit cocktail until thoroughly chilled. When ready to serve, fold in fresh fruit and spoon into sherbet dishes.

MELON BALL COCKTAIL

2 cups cantaloupe balls
2 cups watermelon balls

2 cups ginger ale
Mint leaves, optional

Refrigerate cantaloupe and watermelon until ice cold. Scoop out balls and mix with ginger ale. Put into a glass jar with screw top and seal tightly. Refrigerate until chilled thoroughly. Serve in cocktail glasses. Garnish with mint, if desired.

STRAWBERRY COCKTAIL

1 pint fresh
  strawberries, cut up
1 large banana, cubed
1 cup crushed pineapple,
  with syrup

1 tablespoon granulated
  sugar

Combine all ingredients well and chill thoroughly before serving. Spoon into sherbet dishes.

PEACH COCKTAIL

2 cups ripe peaches,
  sliced and chilled
1 cup orange juice,
  freshly squeezed
  and chilled

1 teaspoon granulated
  sugar, or to taste
Mint leaves

Pare and slice peaches; spoon into sherbet glasses and pour on orange juice. Sprinkle with sugar. Garnish with mint, if desired, and serve immediately.

CRABMEAT-AVOCADO COCKTAIL

2 medium avocado
3 tablespoons lemon
  juice, freshly
  squeezed
1/2 cup catsup
1/4 teaspoon Tabasco
  sauce
1/4 teaspoon salt
1 (6-1/2-ounce) can
  crabmeat,
  flaked fine

3/4 cup celery, finely
  chopped
1 tablespoon green pepper,
  finely chopped
1/8 teaspoon ground black
  pepper
Lettuce leaves

Cut avocados in half, remove seeds, pare and dice. Add lemon juice. Combine with catsup, sauce, salt, crabmeat, celery, green pepper and black pepper; toss lightly. Line cocktail glasses with lettuce leaves and spoon mixture into glasses.

SHRIMP COCKTAIL

Sauce:
2 tablespoons catsup
1-1/2 teaspoons lemon
  juice, freshly
  squeezed
1/4 teaspoon salt
3 drops Tabasco sauce

1 teaspoon prepared
  horseradish
1/4 teaspoon
  Worcestershire
  sauce

Measure ingredients into a glass jar; stir well and cover. Chill thoroughly before serving.

Lettuce leaves
2 cups boiled shrimp
1/2 cup celery, finely
  diced

Lemon wedges
Crackers

Just before serving, line sherbet glasses with lettuce leaves.

Arrange shrimp in each glass and spoon celery in the center. Spoon sauce over shrimp and celery. Serve with lemon wedges and crackers.

CUCUMBER COCKTAIL

1 cup cucumber, pared
    and diced
1 teaspoon granulated
    sugar
1/2 teaspoon salt
1/8 teaspoon ground
    black pepper

1/4 teaspoon onion juice
1-1/2 teaspoons lemon
    juice, freshly
    squeezed
1/3 cup sour cream
Lettuce leaves
Parsley, optional

Combine cucumber with sugar, salt, pepper, onion juice and lemon juice. Fold into sour cream. Cover and place in refrigerator until thoroughly chilled. When ready to serve, line sherbet glasses with lettuce leaves. Spoon cucumber mixture in and garnish with parsley, if desired.

VEGETABLE COCKTAIL

1-1/2 cups vegetable
    juice cocktail
1-1/2 cups buttermilk

Dash of Tabasco sauce
1/8 teaspoon salt

Combine the juice and buttermilk. Mix well; add sauce and salt. Stir to blend. Serve immediately.

Dips are sauces or soft mixtures into which food may be dipped. The consistency should be thick enough not to drip. The mixture should be chilled and highly seasoned and served with crackers, potato chips, corn chips, pretzels, or vegetables. Turn mixture into an attractive bowl and place on a large serving tray. Arrange an assortment of crackers, etc. around the bowl.

CLAM DIP

1 (8-ounce) package
    cream cheese,
    softened
1 (6-1/2-ounce) can
    minced clams, drain
    and reserve juice
1-1/2 teaspoons onion,
    grated

1/2 teaspoon
    Worcestershire
    sauce
1 tablespoon reserved
    clam juice
Hot sauce to taste

Cream cheese until smooth; add minced clams, onion, Worcestershire sauce and clam juice; beat thoroughly. Add hot sauce to taste and beat with a fork. Serve with assorted crackers.

ARTICHOKE DIP

1 cup artichoke hearts,
  chopped
1 cup grated Parmesan
  cheese
1 cup mayonnaise
1/2 cup green onions,
  chopped

1 teaspoon parsley,
  chopped
1/2 teaspoon garlic salt
1/2 teaspoon ground
  white pepper
Paprika

Combine all ingredients, except paprika, and toss lightly. Spoon into a 1-1/2 quart baking dish and sprinkle with the paprika. Bake at 350 degrees for 25 minutes. Serve with raw vegetables and assorted crackers.

Delicious mix!

BROCCOLI-CHEESE DIP

1 cup onion, chopped
1 cup celery, chopped
1 cup mushrooms, chopped
2 tablespoons butter,
  melted
1 (10-ounce) package
  frozen broccoli,
  cooked and drained

2 (10-3/4-ounce) cans
  cream of mushroom
  soup
1 (8-ounce) package
  garlic cheese

Sauté onion, celery and mushrooms in the butter until tender. Cook and drain broccoli thoroughly. Combine the first mixture with the broccoli and soup in top of double boiler. Add cheese and cook until the cheese is melted. Transfer to a chafing dish when ready to serve. Good with waffle potato chips and corn chips.

You and your guests will enjoy this luscious mix!

CUCUMBER DIP

1 large cucumber,
  unpared, grated
1 (8-ounce) package
  cream cheese,
  softened

1 (8-ounce) carton sour
  cream
1 tablespoon mayonnaise
1/4 teaspoon salt
2 green onions, minced

Grate the cucumber into a blender or food processor and blend until smooth. Drain all liquid. Beat cream cheese until light and smooth; add sour cream and other ingredients, blending well. Chill thoroughly before serving. Serve with a variety of crackers and potato chips.

Delightful!

CRABMEAT DIP

4 tablespoons butter or
   margarine, melted
2 tablespoons all-purpose
   flour
1 pound crabmeat
2 tablespoons prepared
   horseradish
1 tablespoon lemon juice,
   freshly squeezed
1 tablespoon parsley,
   chopped

1 tablespoon dry ground
   mustard
1 cup whole milk
3/4 cup Cheddar cheese,
   grated
2 or 3 drops Tabasco sauce
1/2 cup bread crumbs,
   buttered lightly
Toast rounds

Blend together the butter and flour until smooth. Combine with next 8 ingredients. Spoon into a buttered dish and sprinkle with the crumbs. Bake at 400 degrees for just 20 minutes. Serve with toast rounds.

SEAFOOD DIP

1 (5-ounce) can shrimp,
   chopped fine
4 anchovy fillets,
   chopped fine
1/2 cup parsley,
   chopped fine
1 slice of onion,
   chopped fine
1 clove garlic, chopped
   fine
1-1/2 cups mayonnaise

1/4 cup whipping cream,
   unwhipped
2 tablespoons lemon
   juice, freshly
   squeezed
1 teaspoon white vinegar
Salt
Ground black pepper
Assorted chips and
   crisp crackers

Combine the shrimp, fillets, parsley, onion and garlic; mix well. Add mayonnaise and blend in cream, juice, vinegar and salt and pepper to taste. Chill thoroughly and serve with assorted chips and crackers.

This is really delicious!

ONION DIP

2 (8-ounce) cartons
   sour cream
2 tablespoons onion,
   grated

1 tablespoon pimiento,
   chopped fine
1/2 teaspoon salt

Blend all ingredients together thoroughly. Refrigerate and chill before serving. Delicious with crackers and potato chips.

SPINACH DIP

1 (10-ounce) package
    frozen chopped
    spinach
1 (8-ounce) package
    cream cheese,
    softened

1 (8-ounce) carton sour cream
1/3 cup onion, grated
1/4 cup Worcestershire sauce
1/2 teaspoon salt

Thaw and drain all water from spinach. Mix cream cheese and sour cream in blender. Add the spinach, onion, Worcestershire sauce and salt; blend until smooth. Chill for several hours in the refrigerator before serving. Good served with raw vegetables or with potato chips.

Serve often!

RAW VEGETABLE DIP

1 (8-ounce) carton
    sour cream
1 cup mayonnaise
1/2 teaspoon
    Worcestershire
    sauce
1/2 teaspoon lemon-pepper
    seasoning
1 teaspoon dry ground
    mustard

2 teaspoons grated onion
1/2 teaspoon chopped
    chives
1 teaspoon prepared
    horseradish
1/2 cup pecans, finely
    chopped

Blend together all ingredients. Chill for several hours or over-night. Serve with raw vegetables.

Delicious mix!

Hors d'oeuvres *are any of various foods served as appetizers. Hors d'oeuvres are similar to canapés in that the mixtures are highly flavored; however they differ from canapés in that the mixture is not spread on crackers or bread. Some mixtures are stuffed into fruits or vegetables; other mixtures are rolled into balls and broiled or fried. Some hors d'oeuvres are eaten from a pick. A large apple, grapefruit, or an eggplant will make an attractive pick holder.*

CHEESE CRISPIES

1 (8-ounce) package sharp
    cheese, grated
1/2 cup butter, softened
1 cup all-purpose flour

1/4 teaspoon ground red
    pepper
1-1/2 cups oven-toasted
    rice cereal

Combine all ingredients and blend well by hand. Form small balls and place on ungreased baking sheet. Press with dampened cookie press or fork. Bake at 325 degrees for around 15 minutes or until lightly browned.

CHEESE STRAWS NO. 1

1 pound New York sharp
  cheese, softened
1/2 cup butter, softened
2 cups all-purpose flour

1 teaspoon salt
1/4 teaspoon ground red
  pepper

Blend together with pastry blender the cheese and butter. Sift together the dry ingredients on top of the cheese-butter mixture and blend together thoroughly. Place in a pastry tube and squeeze onto an ungreased baking sheet. Bake at 350 degrees for about 10 minutes or until edges start to turn light brown.

CHEESE STRAWS NO. 2

1/2 cup butter
1 cup sharp cheese,
  grated
1 cup all-purpose flour

1 teaspoon salt
1/8 teaspoon ground red
  pepper
Whipping cream, unwhipped

Blend together with a pastry blender the butter, cheese, flour, salt and pepper. Add just enough cream to hold together. Roll out on a lightly floured surface. Cut in narrow strips and bake at 400 degrees until a delicate brown.

Appetizing!

CHEESE PUFFS

2 cups sharp cheese,
  grated
1/4 cup margarine or
  butter, softened
1 cup sifted all-purpose
  flour

1/2 teaspoon salt
1/2 teaspoon paprika
1/2 teaspoon dry ground
  mustard
Dash of ground red pepper

Blend together the cheese and butter. Sift all dry ingredients together and add to the butter-cheese mixture, blending well. Knead with hands and then form small balls (about one half inch). Place balls on ungreased baking sheet. Bake at 350 degrees for around 15-18 minutes until lightly browned. Remove immediately. These will stay fresh for a long time.

These cheese pastries make a wonderful addition to a party table!

BLACK-EYED SUSANS

1 pound sharp cheese
  grated
1 cup vegetable
  shortening
1 teaspoon salt
4 cups all-purpose flour
1/2 teaspoon ground red
  pepper

Pitted dates, halved
  lengthwise with
  scissors
Pecans, coarsely broken in
  fourths
Granulated sugar
Confectioners sugar

Cream cheese and shortening; add salt, flour and pepper; mix well. Chill for several hours in refrigerator. Form into 1-inch balls. Insert pecan pieces in date halves and wrap cheese mixture around to form a ball. Place on an ungreased baking sheet and bake at 275 degrees for around 15 minutes or until lightly browned. Remove and sprinkle immediately with granulated sugar; then roll in confectioners sugar.

CHEESE CORNFLAKE WAFERS

1 (8-ounce) package sharp
  Cheddar cheese,
  grated
1/2 cup butter, softened
1 cup all-purpose flour
1/4 teaspoon salt

1/4 teaspoon paprika
1/4 teaspoon Tabasco
  sauce
1-1/2 cups corn flakes
1 cup pecans, finely
  chopped

Cream the cheese and butter; add the sifted flour, salt and paprika, then the sauce, blending well. Add the corn flakes and pecans. Form 1-inch balls and press flat on an ungreased baking sheet. Bake at 350 degrees for around 15 minutes.

CHICKEN FINGERS WITH
SWEET SOUR SAUCE

6 chicken breast halves,
  boned and cut into
  1/2-inch strips
1 cup buttermilk
1 tablespoon lemon juice,
  freshly squeezed
1/2 teaspoon soy sauce
2 teaspoons Worcestershire
  sauce

1 teaspoon paprika
1/2 teaspoon salt
1/4 teaspoon ground black
  pepper
1 tablespoon onion,
  grated
3 cups breadcrumbs
1/4 cup sesame seed
1/2 cup butter, melted

Cut chicken into 1/2-inch strips and place in a flat marinating bowl. Combine the next 8 ingredients, blending well. Pour mixture over chicken strips. Cover and refrigerate for several hours or overnight. Drain chicken well and roll in bread crumbs and sesame seed combined. Arrange chicken in a greased, large oblong baking dish or pan. Drizzle melted butter over chicken. Serve with Sweet-Sour Sauce.

Sweet sour sauce:

1 cup red plum jam
1 tablespoon prepared
  horseradish
1 tablespoon prepared
  mustard

2 teaspoons lemon juice,
  freshly squeezed

Combine all ingredients and stir until well blended. Warm over low heat, stirring constantly. Serve with Chicken Fingers.

OLIVE BALLS

1 cup all-purpose flour,
  sifted
1 teaspoon dry ground
  mustard
1/4 teaspoon salt
1/2 cup Parmesan cheese,
  grated

1 cup water
1/2 cup butter
1/4 teaspoon hot sauce
4 large eggs
40 whole pimiento-stuffed
  olives

Sift together flour, mustard and salt; stir in cheese. Set aside. Heat water; add butter and hot sauce; simmer until butter melts. Remove from heat and add flour mixture all at once, beating until mixture forms a ball and leaves sides of pan. Beat in the eggs, one at a time, beating well after each addition. Drop by level table-spoonfuls onto lightly greased baking sheet. Press olive into center of each ball and wrap dough around each olive. Bake at 400 degrees for 20 to 25 minutes or until lightly browned and puffed. Serve hot.

OLIVE-CHEESE BALLS

2 cups sharp Cheddar
  cheese, grated
1-1/4 cups all-purpose
  flour

1/2 cup butter, melted
1 (2-ounce) jar pimiento
  stuffed olives

Mix the cheese and flour together until crumbly. Add butter and mix well with a fork. Now mix with hands like dough. Mold approximately 1 teaspoonful around each olive. Shape into ball. Bake 15 to 20 minutes at 400 degrees. Yield: 3 dozen.

Easy and good!

CHICKEN PUFFS

Filling:

1/4 cup mayonnaise
3/4 cup whipping cream,
  unwhipped
4 3/4 cups cooked
  chicken, minced
3/4 cup celery, finely
  chopped
2 whole pimientos,
  finely chopped
1 tablespoon onion,
  finely grated

1-1/2 tablespoons lemon
  juice, freshly
  squeezed
2 tablespoons capers,
  chopped
1/4 teaspoon salt
1/8 teaspoon ground black
  pepper

Blend together the mayonnaise and cream, stirring until smooth. Add remaining ingredients and mix well. Fill puffs and serve.

Puffs:

1 cup boiling water
1/2 cup butter
1 cup all-purpose flour,
  sifted

4 eggs, unbeaten

Bring water to a boil and add butter, stirring until melted. Reduce heat and add flour all at once, stirring constantly. Cook and stir until mixture thickens. Remove from heat. Add eggs, one at a time, beating vigorously after each addition, then beat until mixture is shiny and falls off spoon. Drop by 1/2 teaspoonfuls on baking sheet and shape in mounds. Bake at 425 degrees for around 20 minutes or until golden brown. Cool. When ready to serve, cut a slit in side of each puff and fill with chicken filling.
Yields: 6 dozen

You will receive raves when you serve these!

CORN CRISP WAFERS

1/2 cup corn meal, plain
1 teaspoon salt
3/4 cup boiling water

2 tablespoons butter,
  melted
Celery seed

Mix together the corn meal and salt; stir in the water and butter. Drop by teaspoonfuls onto a buttered baking pan; sprinkle with celery seed and bake at 425 degrees for around 8 minutes or until delicately browned. Remove to wire rack for 1 minute, then carefully remove with a wide spatula.

These are good with soups or salads.

FROSTED GRAPES

Grapes
Egg white, lightly
  beaten

Granulated sugar

Rinse grapes with cold water; drain on paper toweling until dry. Examine and snip out any damaged grapes. Separate into small clusters. Brush lightly with egg white. Roll in granulated sugar and place on a wire rack to air dry.

HONEY PECAN BALLS

1 cup butter, softened
1/4 cup honey
1/4 teaspoon salt
1 teaspoon grated orange
  rind
2 teaspoons pure vanilla
  extract

3 cups all-purpose flour
1 cup pecans, finely
  chopped
Confectioners sugar

Cream butter and honey; add salt, rind and vanilla, blending thoroughly. Gradually add flour until mixed well. Add nuts and stir until combined; form small balls. Place on ungreased baking sheet and bake at 300 degrees for around 20 minutes or until lightly browned. Roll in confectioners sugar while warm. Store in airtight container until served.

If you like the taste of honey, these are for you!

SPICED PECANS

1-1/3 cups pecan halves
1 cup granulated sugar
1 teaspoon ground ginger
1 teaspoon salt
1/2 teaspoon ground
  nutmeg

1/4 teaspoon ground
  cloves
1 large egg white
1 tablespoon cold water

Place pecans in a shallow pan; leave in 350 degree oven for 5 minutes. Remove immediately and set aside. Sift together the sugar, ginger, salt, nutmeg and cloves and set aside. Beat egg white until frothy with a fork, not stiff; then add the water and blend. Dip pecans in egg white mixture, then roll in sugar mixture. Sift leftover sugar mixture on cookie sheet; arrange pecans on sheet so they are not touching. Sift remaining sugar mixture over pecans. Bake at 275 degrees for 1 hour. Remove from baking sheet immediately and shake off excess sugar.

These are DEE-LISH!

ORANGE BALLS

1 (12-ounce) box vanilla
  wafers, finely
  crushed
1 (6-ounce) can frozen
  orange juice
  concentrate,
  undiluted
1 (16 ounce) box
  confectioners sugar,
  sifted

1/2 cup butter, melted
1 cup pecans, finely
  chopped
1 teaspoon pure vanilla
  extract
Grated coconut, canned
  or fresh

Combine all ingredients, except coconut. Blend together well. Form small balls and roll in coconut.

PEANUT BARS

1 loaf white bread
1 cup creamy peanut
  butter

1 cup vegetable oil

Trim off crusts and cut each bread slice into 4 strips. Spread strips on a baking sheet and crusts on a separate baking sheet. Place both in a 225 degree oven for 2 hours, then test for crispness. Roll the crusts into very fine crumbs. Combine the peanut butter and oil and mix well. Dip strips in this mixture, drain and roll in crumbs; a slotted spoon is helpful. Store in an air tight container. Will stay fresh for several weeks.

Easy to make and your guests will praise you!

PICKLED SHRIMP

3 pounds shrimp
1 quart water
1 teaspoon salt
2 medium onions, sliced

1 pint tarragon vinegar
12 peppercorns
2 bay leaves

Shuck and clean shrimp. Drop into boiling salted water. When water boils again, reduce heat, cover and simmer 5 to 10 minutes. Drain and cool. In a large glass bowl, alternate layers of shrimp and sliced onion. Combine vinegar, peppercorns and bay leaves; pour over the shrimp mixture. Place in refrigerator overnight, turning mixture over several times. Serve in same bowl with picks.

Who can resist these?

ROASTED PEANUTS

Shelled:

Place raw, shelled peanuts (with skins off) in a shallow baking pan one layer deep. Cook in oven at 350 degrees for around 15 to 20 minutes or until golden brown. Stir occasionally while cooking. Remove to a bowl; add butter and stir until coated, then salt to taste.

In the shell:

Place peanuts one layer deep in a shallow baking pan. Place in a 350 degree oven. Cook for 30 minutes, stirring occasionally, until roasted.

Top notch nutrition!

SAUSAGE BITS

3 cups prepared biscuit
  mix
1 pound hot ground
  sausage

8 ounces sharp cheese,
  grated

Combine all ingredients with your hands. Form into one-half inch balls. Place the balls on an ungreased baking sheet. Bake at 350 degrees for around 10 minutes or until lightly browned. Remove from baking sheet to cool. You may want to make these ahead of time as they freeze beautifully. Place them in a plastic freezer bag and reheat for serving. To reheat, place in a 400 degree oven for about 5 minutes.

Delicious for parties!

SPINACH BALLS

2 (10-ounce) packages
  frozen, chopped
  spinach
1 cup herb stuffing
3/4 cup melted margarine
6 eggs, slightly beaten

1/2 cup grated Parmesan
  cheese
2 small onions, minced
Salt, pepper and thyme
  to taste

Cook and drain spinach thoroughly. Combine all other ingredients and add to the spinach. Shape into balls, about one teaspoon each. Bake at 350 degrees for 20 minutes on a greased baking sheet. Remove at once and drain on paper towels. Serve hot! May be frozen for future use after baking. To reheat, place in a 400 degree oven for about 5 minutes.

Good and nutritious!

STUFFED CELERY

8 short celery ribs,
with tops
1 cup creamed cottage
cheese
1/3 cup blue cheese,
crumbled

1/3 cup walnuts, finely
chopped
1/2 teaspoon
Worcestershire sauce

Wash and trim celery ribs; chill in refrigerator or ice cold water while you prepare the filling. Combine cottage cheese, blue cheese, walnuts and Worcestershire sauce. Fill each celery rib and serve immediately.

Crunchy and good!

SUGARED PEANUTS

1 cup granulated sugar
1/2 cup water

2 cups peanuts, shelled
raw with skins on

Dissolve sugar in water over medium heat. Add peanuts and cook until peanuts sugar and are well coated. Stir often. Spread peanuts on ungreased baking sheet and bake at 300 degrees for around 30 minutes, stirring every 5 minutes until time is up. Serve or store in airtight container.

Don't try to resist these peanut goodies!

SUGARED PECANS

1 large egg white,
beaten
3/4 cup light brown sugar,
packed

1/2 teaspoon pure vanilla
extract
Pecan halves

Beat egg white until stiff. Gradually add the sugar until well blended, then stir in the vanilla. Dip pecan halves into mixture and place on a greased baking pan. Bake for 1-1/2 hours at 200 degrees, then turn oven off and leave in oven until cool.

TOASTED PECAN HALVES

3 cups pecans, halved
2 tablespoons butter,
melted

Salt

Place pecans in a baking pan in a 250 degree oven. Toast for around 30 minutes. Now add the butter and stir until pecans are greasy. Sprinkle generously with salt. Return pecans to oven and toast for 1 hour or until pecans are crisp and tasty.

You may want to make several recipes if you are having a party as these will not last long!

*A **Shrub** is made by adding cold fruit juice to iced water. A small scoop of sherbet or fruit ice is floated on top for additional flavor. Serve in small glasses with a spoon.*

CRANBERRY SHRUB

Chill sweetened cranberry juice thoroughly and float a scoop of orange sherbet on top. Pour into glasses and serve immediately.

GRAPEFRUIT SHRUB

Chill sweetened grapefruit juice thoroughly and float a scoop of lime sherbet on top. Pour into glasses and serve immediately.

ORANGE SHRUB

Chill freshly squeezed orange juice thoroughly and float a scoop of orange sherbet on top. Pour into glasses and serve immediately.

STRAWBERRY SHRUB

1-1/2 cups strawberries	*1/2 cup lemon juice*
1 cup water	*2 cups ice cold water*
1 cup granulated sugar	*1/2 pint strawberry ice*

Combine strawberries, water and sugar; simmer and stir for 8 minutes. Pour mixture through a fine sieve and rub through the pulp. Cover and refrigerate until thoroughly chilled. When ready to serve, add lemon juice and ice cold water. Pour into glasses. Float a scoop of strawberry ice on top.

Strawberry Ice:

1 cup granulated sugar	*1/8 teaspoon salt*
3 cups water	*2 large egg whites,*
1 cup strawberries,	* stiffly beaten*
* puréed*	
1/4 cup lemon juice,	
* freshly squeezed*	

Combine sugar and water and boil for 5 minutes. Cool completely. Add next 3 ingredients and mix well. Pour into refrigerator trays; freeze to a mush. Beat egg whites until stiff. Turn ice from freezing tray into a chilled bowl; add egg whites and beat hard then quickly return to refrigerator tray and freeze until firm.

Coffee starts the day for many adults; it is also essential for many social affairs. Learn to make good coffee!

HOT COFFEE

2 level tablespoons freshly ground coffee for each 1 cup of water. Serve piping hot, freshly brewed. Leftover coffee loses its flavor.

ICED COFFEE

Use 4 to 5 level tablespoons freshly ground coffee for each one cup of water. Pour coffee into glasses filled with ice. Do not use left over coffee.

Tea, an aromatic beverage prepared from tea leaves by infusion with boiling water. Always use a china, glass or pottery teapot for brewing tea; a metal pot will impart some of its own flavor.

FRENCH TEA

8 cups water
1 cup granulated sugar
2 cups orange juice,
  freshly squeezed
1/2 cup lemon juice,
  freshly squeezed
4 tea bags

Combine the water, sugar and juices; bring to a boil. Gently boil for around 5 minutes. Remove from heat and add the tea bags. Cover for 5 minutes. Remove top and serve hot or with ice.

Delightful!

ICED TEA

6 tea bags
2 cups boiling water
1 cup granulated sugar
5-1/2 cups water
1/2 cup lemon juice,
  freshly squeezed

Place tea bags in teapot and pour over the boiling water. Cover and let steep for 5 minutes. In a 1/2 gallon jug or tea pitcher, measure sugar. Pour the steeped tea into jug or pitcher and stir until sugar dissolves completely. Now fill jug or pitcher almost to the top with water and stir again. Stir in the juice and serve hot or over ice. Will keep in refrigerator if you want to make in advance.

Refreshing!

RUSSIAN TEA

1-1/2 cups granulated
  sugar
1 quart water
1 (3-inch) stick
  cinnamon
1 teaspoon whole cloves
1/2 teaspoon ground
  allspice
6 regular tea bags or
  6 teaspoons loose
  tea

1 cup orange juice,
  freshly squeezed
1/2 cup lemon juice,
  freshly squeezed
1 (12-ounce) can
  pineapple juice
Grated rind of 1 orange
Grated rind of 1 lemon

Combine sugar, water and spices; bring to a boil. Reduce heat and simmer, covered, for 10 minutes. Remove from heat; add tea, cover and let steep for 5 minutes. Strain mixture and combine with remaining ingredients. Serve while hot or reheat, but do not boil. Tea should be piping hot!

Fruit Drinks served cold are refreshing and nutritious. The various combinations are endless since fruit juices blend together in a delightful way.

GOOD FRUIT PUNCH

4 small tea bags
2 cups boiling water
2 cups granulated sugar
2 quarts water
2 cups pineapple juice

1 cup orange juice
1 cup lemon juice
2 quarts ginger ale
Lemon slices, for garnish
Cherries, for garnish

Place tea bags in a teapot and pour over the boiling water; steep for 5 minutes. Add sugar and dissolve completely, then add 2 quarts water and stir. Blend in juices. Just before serving, add ginger ale and garnish with lemon slices and cherries, if desired.

LEMONADE

1 quart water
1-1/2 cups granulated sugar

1-1/2 cups lemon juice,
  freshly squeezed

Combine water and sugar and bring to a boil; reduce heat to simmer and stir until sugar dissolves. Remove from heat and cool completely. Add juice and stir well. Serve over crushed ice at once.

BANANA-CRUSH PUNCH

4 cups granulated sugar
6 cups water
5 large ripe bananas,
    mashed
1/2 cup lemon juice,
    freshly squeezed

2-1/2 cups orange juice,
    freshly squeezed
4 cups pineapple juice
1 (28-ounce) bottle
    ginger ale, chilled

Combine sugar and water. Place over low heat and stir until sugar is completely dissolved; add bananas and juices, mixing well; cool. Place in freezer until mixture is firm. To serve, thaw until the mixture is mushy; pour in the ginger ale and serve while cold.

CREAMY PUNCH

1 (6-ounce) can frozen
    pink lemonade
    concentrate
1 (6-ounce) can frozen
    orange juice
    concentrate

4-1/2 cups water
1 pint pineapple sherbet
1 pint vanilla ice cream

Combine the juice concentrates with the water, stirring to blend well. Pour mixture into a punch bowl and gently fold in the sherbet and ice cream. Serve punch immediately.

THREE FRUIT PUNCH

1 (6-ounce) can frozen
    lemonade concentrate
1 (8-1/4-ounce) can
    crushed pineapple,
    in heavy syrup
1 (10-ounce) package
    frozen strawberries,
    in syrup, thawed

3 quarts ginger ale,
    chilled
Crushed ice

Combine lemonade concentrate, pineapple and strawberries in blender. Cover and turn on high speed until completely smooth. When ready to serve, combine with ginger ale. Fill a punch bowl with crushed ice and pour over the fruit mixture. Makes 1 gallon (32 servings).

Fruit mixture can be made in advance. Store in a covered jar and refrigerate. Combine with ginger ale just before serving time.

A beautiful pink punch and so delicious and refreshing!

LIME GELATIN PUNCH

3 (3-ounce) packages
lime gelatin dessert
2 cups hot water
6 cups granulated sugar
Juice of 3 dozen lemons
1 (1-quart 14-ounce) can
pineapple juice

2 or 3 drops green
food coloring
3 quarts ginger ale
Cherries, orange slices
and strawberries,
for garnish

Dissolve gelatin in hot water, stirring for several minutes. Add sugar and juices; stir to combine. When ready to serve, add coloring to mixture, then stir in the ginger ale. Place ice in punch bowl and pour mixture over ice. Garnish with cherries, orange slices and strawberries.

PINEAPPLE FRUIT PUNCH

3 quarts unsweetened
pineapple juice
Juice of 8 lemons
Juice of 3 limes
Juice of 8 oranges
2 cups granulated sugar

4 quarts ginger ale
2 quarts plain soda
water
Green food coloring,
optional

Combine juices and sugar and stir until sugar is completely dissolved. Chill thoroughly. Just before serving, add ginger ale and soda water. Tint a delicate green, if desired.

STRAWBERRY PUNCH

1 (1 quart 14-ounce)
can pineapple juice, chilled
1 (6-ounce) can frozen pink
lemonade concentrate
2-1/4 cups water

3/4 cup granulated
sugar
1 quart strawberry
ice cream
2 quarts ginger ale

Combine the juice, concentrate, water, and sugar in a punch bowl, stirring to blend well. Gently fold in the ice cream and stir in the ginger ale. Serve immediately. Will serve around 25.

Coolers are iced drinks and when served during the summer months are very refreshing!

BANANA COOLER

1 medium banana, mashed
2 cups chocolate milk or
   drink, cold

Whipping cream, whipped
   and sweetened

Combine banana and chocolate drink; beat with rotary beater. Serve while still very cold and garnish with whipping cream, if desired.

COLA COOLER

2/3 cup cola drink, cold
1 scoop vanilla ice
   cream

Fill glass 2/3 full with your favorite cola drink. Top with a scoop of ice cream. Do not stir; serve immediately with straw and spoon.

PINEAPPLE COOLER

2/3 cup pineapple juice
   chilled

1 scoop vanilla ice
   cream

Combine juice and ice cream; beat with a rotary beater until frothy. Serve immediately with straw and spoon.

ROOT BEER COOLER

1 cup chilled root beer
   equally divided
1 tablespoon whole milk

3 spoonfuls vanilla or
   chocolate ice cream

Mix 1/2 cup root beer and milk in a tall glass; add ice cream, then fill glass with remaining root beer. Serve with a straw and spoon.

Milk Shakes made at home are the best kind!

BANANA MILK SHAKE

1 cup whole milk, cold
1 ripe banana, mashed
1/3 cup orange juice,
   freshly squeezed

2 teaspoons granulated
   sugar
1 large scoop vanilla
   ice cream

Combine all ingredients. Beat with mixer or shake well. Serve at once. Makes 2 shakes.

Cool and refreshing!

CHOCOLATE MALTED MILK SHAKE

1/2 cup chocolate
  syrup, cold
1/4 cup malted milk
  powder

2 cups whole milk, cold
1 large scoop ice cream,
  vanilla or chocolate
Nutmeg

Combine the syrup, powder, milk and ice cream, beating or shaking until well mixed and frothy. Sprinkle with nutmeg and serve at once.

Great for a summertime pickup!

PEACH MILK SHAKE

1 cup peaches, chilled
  and mashed fine
2/3 cup whole milk, cold

2 drops almond extract
2 large scoops vanilla
  ice cream

Combine all ingredients. Beat or shake well. Serve at once. Makes 2 shakes.

Great shake!

***Sodas** are fun to make and fun to share with others!*

CHOCOLATE SODA

2 tablespoons Chocolate
  Sauce
2 tablespoons whipping
  cream, unwhipped

Carbonated water
2 spoonfuls vanilla
  ice cream

Measure chocolate sauce into a tall glass; add cream and mix well. Fill glass 2/3 full with carbonated water; stir lightly. Add ice cream and serve immediately with straw and spoon.

Chocolate Sauce:

3 squares unsweetened
  chocolate
1/2 cup whipping cream,
  unwhipped
3/4 cup granulated sugar

3 tablespoons butter
Dash salt
1 teaspoon pure vanilla
  extract

Melt chocolate and add cream; cook over low heat, stirring until smooth. Add sugar, butter and salt; cook over moderate heat, stirring constantly until thickened, around 3 minutes. Remove from heat and add vanilla. If mixture thickens, thin gradually with cream.

LEMON SODA

2 tablespoons white
  corn syrup
2 teaspoons lemon juice,
  freshly squeezed
1/8 teaspoon lemon
  extract

2 tablespoons whipping
  cream, unwhipped
Carbonated water
2 spoonfuls vanilla ice
  cream

Combine the syrup, juice and flavoring in a large glass; stir well. Add cream and mix thoroughly. Fill glass 2/3 full with carbonated water and lightly stir. Add the ice cream and serve immediately.

STRAWBERRY SODA

1/2 cup fresh
  strawberries,
  crushed
2 tablespoons granulated
  sugar
1/2 cup whipping cream,
  unwhipped

14 ounces ginger ale
1 pint vanilla ice cream
Whipping cream, whipped
  and sweetened,
  optional
Whole strawberries, optional

Combine strawberries and sugar; mix well. Measure 2 tablespoons of the mixture into each of 4 large glasses; add 2 tablespoons cream to each glass and stir. Fill each glass 2/3 full with ginger ale and stir to mix well. Add 2 spoonfuls ice cream to each glass and top with whipped cream and a whole strawberry, if desired. Serve with straws and spoons.

VANILLA SODA

2 tablespoons white
  corn syrup
1/4 teaspoon pure
  vanilla extract
2 tablespoons whipping
  cream, unwhipped

Carbonated water
2 spoonfuls vanilla
  ice cream

Measure syrup and flavoring into a tall glass; stir until blended. Add cream and mix well. Fill glass 2/3 full with carbonated water, stirring lightly. Add ice cream and serve immediately with a straw and spoon.

Hot Chocolate is especially good on a cold winter day!

HOT CHOCOLATE

1 square
  unsweetened
  chocolate
1 1/3 cups boiling
  water
1/2 cup granulated sugar

1 quart whole milk,
  scalded
1 teaspoon pure vanilla
  extract
Marshmallows or whipped
  cream

Melt chocolate and stir in the water until smooth. Add sugar and milk and heat for 5 minutes, stirring often. Add vanilla and whip with a hand beater for just 1 minute. Add a marshmallow or a spoon of whipped cream, if desired. Serve while very hot.

Appealing to everyone!

SPECIAL HOT CHOCOLATE

4 squares semi-sweet
  chocolate
1/4 cup white corn syrup
1 teaspoon pure vanilla
  extract

4 cups whole milk
1 (8-ounce) carton
  whipping cream,
  whipped

Melt chocolate in top of double boiler; add syrup, blending until smooth. Cover and cool mixture. Stir in vanilla. Heat milk to boiling point, but do not boil. Set aside. Beat cream until thickened; add chocolate mixture and beat until stiff. To serve, pour hot milk into a pitcher and fill cups. Spoon whipped cream mixture on top.

This is worth the effort when you want to serve something special!

*Serve some **eggnog** at Christmastime!*

EGGNOG NO. 1

4 large egg yolks,
  beaten
1/2 cup granulated sugar
3 cups cold milk
1 cup cold whipping
  cream, unwhipped

2 teaspoons pure vanilla
  extract
1/4 teaspoon salt
Ground nutmeg

Beat eggs for several minutes until very thick. Add sugar and beat in thoroughly. Stir in milk, cream, vanilla and salt. Serve immediately and sprinkle nutmeg in each glass.

EGGNOG NO. 2

2 dozen large egg yolks
2 quarts whipping cream,
  whipped
6 tablespoons granulated
  sugar

2 dozen egg whites
18 tablespoons granulated
  sugar
Grated nutmeg

Beat egg yolks for at least 20 minutes at medium speed, until stiff and fluffy. Whip cream until it stands in peaks; add 6 tablespoons sugar gradually until well blended. Fold egg yolk mixture into whipped cream. Beat egg whites until they are dry and have lost all their gloss before you begin adding the 18 tablespoons sugar. Add sugar, 1 tablespoon at a time, and continue beating for 10 minutes after all sugar has been added. Fold the beaten egg whites into the yolk mixture, continuing to blend with a folding motion until well mixed and smooth. Garnish with nutmeg when serving. Serve in goblets with an iced tea spoon. Do not compromise on the beating as this is the secret to the eggnog.

Breads

Biscuits served piping hot with butter are mouth-watering. They can be mixed in a few minutes and are well worth the extra trouble once in a while!

ANGEL BISCUITS

2-1/2 cups self rising
  flour
3 tablespoons
  granulated sugar
1/2 teaspoon baking
  soda
1/2 cup vegetable
  shortening

1 package active dry
  yeast
3 tablespoons warm
  water
1 cup buttermilk

Sift flour, sugar and soda together. Cut in shortening until it resembles crumbs. Dissolve yeast in warm water. Add buttermilk to flour mixture, then stir in yeast mixture. Stir well. Roll out dough to make biscuits. Cut with biscuit cutter or cut in any shape you desire. Bake at 375 degrees for around 20 minutes. Dough will keep in refrigerator about a week if well wrapped.

These angel biscuits taste heavenly!

BUTTERMILK BISCUITS

2 cups self-rising
  flour
1/4 cup vegetable
  shortening

1 cup buttermilk

Sift the flour and cut in shortening with a pastry blender or with your hands. Stir in buttermilk or work in with hands. Knead lightly on a well floured board or large bowl until dough pulls away from fork or hands. Pinch off dough and form biscuits lightly with hands; or roll out on floured surface and cut with floured biscuit cutter. If you pinch them off with your hands, flatten with hand or glass lightly. Bake on a greased baking sheet or pan at 450 degrees for around 12 to 15 minutes or until golden brown.

Homemade biscuits should be made more often— they are so easy to make!

SOUR CREAM BISCUITS

1/2 cup butter or
  margarine
1-1/2 cups self-rising
  flour

1 (8-ounce) carton
  sour cream

Cut butter or margarine into flour with a pastry blender or fork.

Blend in sour cream until well mixed. Drop into greased muffin tins by spoonfuls and bake at 425 degrees for 10 minutes or until golden brown.

Light and Delicious!

Scones are delicious served with hot tea or coffee!

SCONES NO. 1

1 cup self-rising
  flour, sifted
1/2 teaspoon salt
3 tablespoons lard
1 tablespoon granulated
  sugar

2 tablespoons currants
1 large egg, slightly
  beaten
1/4 cup whole milk, about
1 large egg, beaten

Sift together the flour and salt into a large bowl; rub in the lard with fingertips. Mix in the sugar and currants well. Stir in with a knife the egg and sufficient milk to make a soft dough. Handle lightly; knead, but do not over knead. Roll out to a thickness of about half an inch; cut in rounds with a scone cutter or pat out into rounds. Place on a greased baking sheet and brush over tops with beaten egg. Bake at 450 degrees for around 10 to 15 minutes. Serve hot.

SCONES NO. 2

1-3/4 cups all-purpose
  flour, sifted
3 teaspoons baking powder
1 teaspoon salt
1/4 cup granulated
  sugar
1/4 cup vegetable
  shortening
1/2 cup currants

1/2 cup whole milk
1 egg yolk, beaten
1 tablespoon whipping
  cream, unwhipped
2 tablespoons
  granulated sugar
  combined with
1/2 teaspoon ground
  cinnamon

Sift together the flour, baking powder, salt and sugar. Cut in shortening with a pastry blender. Stir in the currants. Add milk all at once and stir with a fork lightly. Divide dough into 6 equal portions and knead quickly and lightly; pat out into 1/4 inch rounds. Place on a greased baking sheet. Beat egg and add cream. Brush tops of scones with the mixture and sprinkle with the sugar-cinnamon mixture. Bake at 450 degrees for around 10 to 15 minutes. Serve hot.

Served with tea or coffee, scones are light and delightful!

Cornbread is especially good served with vegetables and soups!

ELEGANT CORN BREAD

2 large eggs
1 (8-ounce) carton
  sour cream
2 cups buttermilk
1/2 teaspoon baking
  soda

3 cups plain corn meal
2 teaspoons baking
  powder
1 teaspoon salt
2 tablespoons
  granulated sugar

Beat eggs; add sour cream, blending well. Combine the buttermilk and soda and add to the egg mixture. Sift together the meal, baking powder, salt and sugar; now add to the first mixture, beating thoroughly. Bake at 400 degrees for around 30 minutes or until done.

You will want to make this on special occasions!

CORN STICKS

1-1/2 cups plain corn
  meal
1/4 cup all-purpose
  flour
2 teaspoons baking
  powder
1-1/2 teaspoons salt
1/3 teaspoon baking
  soda, dissolved in 1
  tablespoon boiling water

1 cup buttermilk
2 tablespoons
  vegetable oil
2 large eggs, well
  beaten

Grease dry iron corn stick pans and place in 400 degree oven just before mixing batter. Sift together the meal, flour, baking powder and salt; dissolve the soda in boiling water and blend into the buttermilk. Add this mixture and oil to the dry ingredients. Add the eggs, blending thoroughly. Spoon into hot greased pans and bake at 400 degrees until golden brown; should take around 10 to 15 minutes.

These can be quickly made and are delicious with vegetables!

CRACKLING CORNBREAD

1 cup self-rising
  cornmeal
1/4 cup self-rising
  flour
1 tablespoon
  granulated sugar

3 large eggs, well
  beaten
1 cup buttermilk
1/2 cup vegetable oil
1 cup cracklings

Sift together cornmeal, flour and sugar; stir in eggs and buttermilk, mixing well. Add oil and combine; stir in cracklings. Pour into a greased heavy skillet; bake at 350 degrees for around 25 minutes.

NORTHEAST CORNBREAD

1 cup self-rising
   corn meal, sifted
3/4 cup all-purpose
   flour, sifted
1/2 teaspoon salt
4 teaspoons
   granulated sugar

1 cup whole milk
1 large egg, slightly
   beaten
2 tablespoons melted
   margarine

Combine the corn meal, flour, salt and sugar; add the milk, egg and melted margarine, mixing well. Pour mixture into a greased 9-inch baking pan. Bake at 425 degrees for around 20 minutes or until golden brown.

Easy, quick and so good!

Hush Puppies are usually served with fish, especially in the South. They are easy and quick to make, so try one of the recipes for a real treat!

HUSH PUPPIES NO. 1

3 cups plain corn
   meal, sifted
1 teaspoon salt
1/2 teaspoon baking
   soda
2 large eggs, slightly
   beaten

1 cup buttermilk
2 cups whole milk
1/2 cup onion, chopped
   fine
Hot oil

Sift together the corn meal, salt and soda. Beat eggs and gradually add the buttermilk and whole milk; add to the corn meal mixture and blend until mixed together. Stir in the onion. If possible, place in the refrigerator for 10 to 15 minutes. When ready, drop by tablespoonfuls into deep hot oil and cook until golden brown and crisp. Serve while hot.

Really good!

HUSH PUPPIES NO.2

1-3/4 cups corn meal
1/3 cup all-purpose
  flour
3 teaspoons baking
  powder
1 teaspoon salt
1/4 cup onion, finely
  chopped

1 large egg, slightly
  beaten
3/4 cup buttermilk
1/4 cup tomato juice
Vegetable shortening

Combine corn meal with sifted flour, baking powder and salt; stir thoroughly to mix. Add onion and stir. Beat egg; stir in buttermilk and tomato juice. Add to dry ingredients and beat until well blended. Mixture should be a thick drop batter. Dip teaspoon into hot melted shortening first and then into batter. Drop by teaspoonfuls into hot oil. Fry to golden brown on underside, flip over and brown until done all way through. Drain on paper toweling. Serve piping hot.

Fruit and Nut Breads *are nutritious and appealing in flavor. Try serving warm bread slices with butter or cream cheese!*

BANANA BREAD

1/2 cup vegetable oil
2-1/2 cups granulated
  sugar
4 large eggs
3-1/2 cups all-purpose
  flour

1/2 teaspoon salt
2 tablespoons baking
  soda
1 cup buttermilk
2 large bananas,
  puréed

Beat oil and sugar together until well blended. Add eggs, one at a time, beating well after each addition. Sift together the flour, salt and baking soda; add alternately with the buttermilk until blended. Purée the bananas and fold into the batter. Lightly oil or butter 2 large loaf pans and spoon in the batter. Bake at 350 degrees for around 1 hour or until the loaves test done with a cake tester. Cool for a few minutes on a cake rack and then turn out on rack.

Banana bread is always welcome!

BANANA LOAF

1/2 cup margarine,
  softened
3/4 cup granulated
  sugar
2 large eggs
3 large ripe bananas,
  mashed
2 cups all-purpose
  flour

1 teaspoon baking soda
1 cup pecans, chopped
  and dredged in
  flour
1 cup white raisins,
  dredged in flour

Cream margarine and sugar until well blended. Add eggs, one at a time, beating well after each addition. Mash bananas with a fork and add alternately with the sifted flour and baking soda. Add pecans and raisins and stir just until mixed. Spoon into a greased and floured loaf pan. Bake at 350 degrees for around 40 minutes or until loaf tests done with a cake tester.

BANANA-DATE-NUT BREAD

2 cups all-purpose
  flour
1 teaspoon baking soda
1 teaspoon salt
1/2 cup vegetable
  shortening
1 cup granulated sugar

2 large eggs
1 teaspoon pure vanilla
  extract
2 large or 3 small
  bananas, mashed
1/2 cup chopped pecans
1 cup chopped dates

Sift together the flour, baking soda and salt and set aside. Cream the vegetable shortening and sugar until well blended. Add eggs and flavoring and mix well. Blend in the mashed bananas. Add the flour mixture, pecans and dates, stirring to blend, but do not overbeat. Spoon the mixture into 3 greased and floured loaf pans. Bake at 350 degrees for around 45 minutes to 1 hour, or until tests done with a cake tester or straw. Cool for several minutes, then remove from pans.

Delicious and freezes well!

BANANA-PECAN BREAD

1 cup butter, softened
2 cups granulated sugar
4 large eggs
2 teaspoons pure
   vanilla extract
6 large or 8 small
   bananas, mashed

4 cups all-purpose
   flour
2 teaspoons baking soda
1 teaspoon salt
1/2 cup whole milk
2 cups pecans, chopped

Cream butter and sugar until light and fluffy. Add eggs, one at a time, beating well after each addition. Blend in vanilla and mashed bananas. Sift together the flour, baking soda and salt; add one half of the mixture to the creamed mixture thoroughly. Now add the milk and blend in; then add the rest of the dry ingredients. Stir in the pecans until blended throughout the batter. Spoon batter into 4 greased and floured loaf pans and bake at 350 degrees for around 55 minutes or until tests done.

Delightful flavor!

BLUEBERRY BREAD

5 cups all-purpose
   flour
1-1/2 cups granulated
   sugar
2 tablespoons baking
   powder
Dash salt
3/4 cup butter, do not
   soften
1-1/2 cups pecans,
   chopped

4 large eggs, slightly
   beaten
2 cups whole milk
2 teaspoons pure
   vanilla extract
3 cups blueberries,
   fresh or frozen
   (do not thaw)

Combine flour, sugar, baking powder and salt. Cut in butter to resemble fine crumbs. Stir in pecans. Beat eggs slightly, stir in milk and vanilla until well blended. Now stir into flour mixture and mix just until flour mixture is moistened. Gently fold in blueberries. Spoon batter evenly into a greased Bundt pan. Bake at 350 degrees for 1 hour and 20 minutes or until tests done with a cake tester. Remove to cake rack and cool for around 10 minutes. Remove from pan and store in refrigerator any leftovers.

Eat warm and serve with coffee or a warm drink ... your company will enjoy!

GINGERBREAD

1/2 cup vegetable
  shortening
1/2 cup granulated
  sugar
2 large eggs, separated
2-1/2 cups all-purpose
  flour
2 teaspoons baking
  soda
1 teaspoon ground
  cinnamon

1 teaspoon ground
  ginger
1/2 teaspoon ground
  cloves
1 cup molasses
1 cup boiling water
1 cup pecans, chopped
  (optional)

Cream shortening and sugar until light and fluffy. Add egg yolks and blend well. Sift together the dry ingredients and add alternately with the molasses and boiling water. Stir in the pecans, if used. Beat egg whites until stiff and fold into the creamed mixture well. Bake at 350 degrees for around 45 minutes. Good served while still warm, alone or with whipped cream.

Pleasing flavor and aroma!

ORANGE BREAD NO. 1

2 cups all-purpose
  flour
3/4 cup granulated
  sugar
1 teaspoon salt
1 teaspoon baking soda
1 large egg, beaten
1/4 cup butter, melted

1 cup orange juice,
  freshly squeezed
1 teaspoon orange rind,
  grated fine
1 teaspoon lemon rind,
  grated fine
1 cup pecans, chopped

Sift together the flour, sugar, salt and soda. Add the other ingredients, blending until well mixed. Spoon into a buttered loaf pan. Bake in a 350 degree oven for 45 to 50 minutes or until golden brown. Slice while warm and enjoy!

Keep one of these in the freezer for unexpected company!

ORANGE BREAD NO. 2

Rind preparation:

4 orange rinds, cut
  in strips
1 teaspoon baking soda
Water

1 cup granulated
  sugar
3/4 cup water

Remove all pulp from orange rinds and cut in strips; place rinds and soda in a small saucepan; cover with water and boil 2 minutes. Drain and rinse well. Return to saucepan; add sugar and 3/4 cup water. Cook until tender. Let cool and chop medium fine.

Bread:

1/4 cup butter,
  softened
1 cup granulated sugar
2 large eggs
3 cups all-purpose
  flour

3 teaspoons baking
  powder
1/4 teaspoon salt
1 cup pecans, chopped

Cream butter, gradually adding sugar until well blended. Add eggs, one at a time, beating well after each addition. Sift together the flour, baking powder and salt; add to creamed mixture. Stir in pecans and rind. Mix thoroughly. Spoon into a greased and floured loaf pan and bake at 350 degrees for 1 hour.

So good sliced, toasted and buttered!

PUMPKIN BREAD

2 cups granulated
  sugar
4 large eggs
1 teaspoon ground
  nutmeg
1 teaspoon ground
  cinnamon
1-1/2 teaspoons salt

1 cup vegetable oil
1 (16-ounce) can
  pumpkin
2/3 cup water
2 teaspoons baking
  soda
3 cups sifted
  all-purpose flour

Blend together the sugar, eggs, spices, salt and oil. Then stir in the pumpkin, water, baking soda and sifted flour, blending well. Fill three greased and floured 1 pound coffee cans 1/2 full of batter. You may also use loaf pans. Bake in 350 degree oven for around 50-55 minutes. Test for doneness before removing from cans or loaf pans by inserting a straw or metal tester. Let cool for a few minutes before removing from cans or pans. This is good alone or with cream cheese.

The flavor is outstanding!

STRAWBERRY BREAD

3 cups all-purpose
  flour, sifted
1 teaspoon salt
1/2 teaspoon cream of
  tartar
1/2 teaspoon baking
  soda
2 cups granulated
  sugar
1 cup butter, softened

1 teaspoon pure
  vanilla extract
1/2 teaspoon lemon
  juice, freshly
  squeezed
4 large eggs
1 cup strawberry
  preserves
1/2 cup buttermilk
1 cup pecans, chopped

Combine flour, salt, cream of tartar and baking soda; set aside. Beat sugar, butter, vanilla and lemon juice until light and fluffy. Add eggs, one at a time, beating well after each addition. Add preserves and buttermilk alternately with the dry ingredients, mixing just until blended. Stir in pecans. Spoon batter into 2 greased 9 x 5 x 3-inch loaf pans. Bake at 350 degrees for around 55 minutes or until loaves test done. Cool for 10 minutes. Remove from pans to cooling racks. Yield: 2 loaves.

Delicious!

SWEET POTATO BREAD

1 cup vegetable oil
3 cups granulated
  sugar
4 large eggs, well
  beaten
2 cups sweet potatoes,
  cooked and mashed
3-1/2 cups all-purpose
  flour
2 teaspoons baking soda
1 teaspoon baking
  powder

2 teaspoons salt
1 teaspoon ground
  allspice
1 teaspoon ground
  cinnamon
1 teaspoon ground
  nutmeg
2/3 cup whole milk
2 cups chopped pecans

Combine the oil, sugar and beaten eggs, mixing well. Blend in the sweet potatoes. Sift together the dry ingredients and add alternately with the milk. Add the pecans, blending into the batter. Grease and flour 4 loaf pans and spoon batter equally into the pans. Bake at 350 degrees for around 50 to 60 minutes or until done. Let stand for around 10 minutes before removing from pans.

Nutritious and tasty!

Muffins should be mixed quickly and should not be over-beaten. Make muffins for breakfast and enjoy!

APPLE MUFFINS

1 large egg, beaten
1 cup whole milk
1/3 cup butter, melted
2 cups all-purpose
  flour
1/4 teaspoon salt
4 teaspoons baking
  powder

1/2 cup granulated
  sugar
1/4 teaspoon ground
  cinnamon
1/4 teaspoon ground
  nutmeg
1 cup apple, chopped
  fine

Beat egg; add milk and butter. Sift together the dry ingredients; add to egg mixture blending just until dry ingredients are moistened. Fold in the apple. Fill greased muffin tins 2/3 full and bake in a 425 degree oven for around 25 minutes or until golden brown.

Tasty muffins!

BANANA-NUT-BRAN MUFFINS

2 cups oat bran
1 teaspoon ground
  cinnamon
1/2 cup light brown
  sugar, firmly
  packed
1/2 teaspoon salt
2 teaspoons baking
  powder
1-1/4 cups milk, whole,
  lowfat or skim

2 whole eggs, slightly
  beaten (or 2 egg
  whites, slightly
  beaten)
1/4 cup honey
2 tablespoons vegetable
  oil
1 medium-size, ripe
  banana, mashed
1/2 cup pecans, chopped

Combine the dry ingredients; add milk, eggs or egg whites, honey and oil; mix until dry ingredients are moistened. Lightly fold in mashed banana and pecans. Line muffin pans with paper baking cups; fill cups almost to top; bake in a 425 degree oven for around 15 minutes or until muffins are golden brown. Serve hot, either plain or with margarine. Muffins keep well in refrigerator wrapped in foil, or they may be frozen successfully.

BLUEBERRY MUFFINS

1/2 cup butter or
  margarine,
  softened
1 cup granulated
  sugar
2 large eggs
2 cups all-purpose
  flour, sifted
2 teaspoons baking
  powder

1/2 teaspoon salt
1/2 cup whole milk
1 teaspoon pure vanilla
  extract
2-1/2 cups blueberries
Granulated sugar, for
  tops

Cream the butter or margarine; add sugar gradually and beat until light and fluffy. Add eggs, one at a time, beating well after each addition. Sift together the flour, baking powder and salt. Add alternately with the milk and vanilla, beginning and ending with the flour mixture. Crush 1/2 cup berries and add to batter. Fold remaining whole berries into batter and spoon into a 12 cup greased muffin pan. Sprinkle with sugar. Bake at 375 degrees for 30 minutes, or until muffins test done with a cake tester. Cool in pans for 5 minutes, then turn onto wire rack.

These are great! Serve warm with butter for a special breakfast...

SWEET POTATO MUFFINS

1/2 cup granulated
  sugar
1 tablespoon light
  brown sugar,
  packed
2-1/2 cups all-purpose
  flour
2-1/2 teaspoons baking
  powder
1/2 teaspoon salt
2 eggs, slightly
  beaten

1 cup whole milk
1/4 cup butter or
  margarine, melted
1-1/2 cups cooked sweet
  potatoes, mashed
1/2 cup pecans, chopped
1/4 cup granulated
  sugar
1/2 teaspoon ground
  cinnamon

Combine the sugars and sifted flour, baking powder and salt, stirring until blended. Add the eggs, milk, butter or margarine, potatoes and pecans; stir and mix until all ingredients are moistened. Spoon into buttered muffin tins. Combine the 1/4 cup sugar and cinnamon and sprinkle over each muffin. Bake at 425 degrees for around 25 minutes or until muffins test done with a cake tester.

RAISIN-NUT-BRAN MUFFINS

2 cups oat bran
1/2 cup light brown
  sugar, firmly
  packed
1/2 teaspoon salt
2 teaspoons baking
  powder
1-1/4 cups milk, whole,
  lowfat or skim

2 whole eggs, slightly
  beaten (or 2 egg
  whites, slightly
  beaten)
1/4 cup honey
2 tablespoons
  vegetable oil
1/2 cup raisins
1/2 cup pecans, chopped

Combine the dry ingredients; add milk, eggs or egg whites, honey and oil; mix until dry ingredients are moistened. Lightly fold in raisins and pecans. Line muffin pans with paper baking cups; fill cups almost to top; bake in a 425 degree oven for around 15 minutes or until muffins are golden brown. Serve hot either plain or with margarine. Wrap in foil any leftover muffins; refrigerate or freeze.

Pancakes, French Toast and Waffles *Delicate and delicious recipes for special breakfasts!*

PANCAKES

2 eggs, slightly beaten
1-3/4 cups whole milk
2 tablespoons butter,
  melted
2 cups all-purpose
  flour

3 teaspoons baking
  powder
1/2 teaspoon salt
2 teaspoons granulated
  sugar

Beat eggs slightly; stir in milk and butter. Sift flour, baking powder, salt and sugar together. Add to egg mixture and blend lightly. Batter should be lumpy for light pancakes. Spoon onto lightly greased griddle and brown on both sides. Serve at once while still hot.

Good!

FRENCH TOAST

2 eggs, well beaten
Pinch of salt
2 teaspoons granulated
  sugar

1 cup whole milk
6 slices bread
Butter or margarine

Beat the eggs; add salt, sugar and milk; blend well. Dip bread into the mixture, coating both sides well. Melt a small amount of butter or margarine and brown the bread slices on both sides. Remove to serving platter and serve hot.

WAFFLES

2 large eggs
1-1/4 cups whole milk
6 tablespoons butter, melted
1-3/4 cups all-purpose flour, sifted

3 teaspoons baking powder
1 teaspoon salt
1 teaspoon granulated sugar

Beat eggs until frothy; add milk and melted butter. Beat until well blended. Sift together the flour, baking powder, salt and sugar. Add to the egg mixture and blend. Bake in hot waffle iron. Serve hot with melted butter and syrup.

Can be whipped up in a few minutes!

MORAVIAN SUGAR CAKE

2 cups potato water (water in which potatoes have been cooked)
1/2 cup granulated sugar
1 egg, beaten
1 package dry yeast, dissolved in 1/4 cup lukewarm water

2 teaspoons salt
2 cups all-purpose flour
1/2 cup vegetable shortening, melted
3 cups all-purpose flour, about
Butter
Light brown sugar
Ground cinnamon

Combine potato water, sugar, egg, yeast mixture, salt and 2 cups flour. Beat well. Cover and let rise until double in size. Now add shortening and amount of flour to produce a soft dough. Knead until dough drops cleanly from hands. Cover and let double in size again. With floured hands, pat dough into 3 greased 9-inch baking pans; let rise to top of pans. With floured fingers, punch holes in dough in rows. Place 1 teaspoon butter in each hole; sprinkle with brown sugar all over top and dust with cinnamon. Bake at 400 degrees for 20 minutes or until browned. Remove from pans while still hot; cool on a wire rack until ready to serve.

This is a delicious coffee cake and is perfect for freezing. Just "pop" one in the oven on Christmas morning while you open your packages. Afterwards, everyone can have coffee and cake!

Rolls The aroma and tempting taste of homemade bread is well worth the effort once in a while!

EASY ROLLS

1/2 cup vegetable
  shortening
1/3 cup granulated
  sugar
1/2 cup boiling water
1 egg, slightly beaten

1 package yeast
1/2 cup warm water
3 cups all-purpose
  flour, unsifted
1/2 teaspoon salt

Cream together the shortening and sugar; add the boiling water and stir until mixture is dissolved. Add the egg and blend in well. Dissolve the yeast in the warm water and add this to the mixture until blended. Stir in the flour and salt until mixed well. Cover and refrigerate overnight. When ready to make out the rolls, start about 3 to 4 hours before since it takes about this amount of time for the rolls to rise. Sprinkle waxed paper or a pastry cloth lightly with flour and roll out about 1/2 inch thick. Using a biscuit cutter, cut like biscuits. Place on a baking sheet and when they rise, bake at 400 degrees until brown.

These are so easy to make and worth the effort!

DELICIOUS DINNER ROLLS

1 cup whole milk,
  scalded
1/2 cup butter
1 teaspoon salt
1/4 cup granulated
  sugar

1/2 cup warm water
2 packages yeast
2 large eggs, slightly
  beaten
5-1/4 cups unsifted
  all-purpose flour

Scald milk, then add butter, salt and sugar; set aside to cool. Heat water to warm; add yeast and stir to dissolve. Add the milk mixture, eggs and 2 cups of the flour; beat until smooth. Stir in enough of the remaining flour to make a soft dough; turn out on a lightly floured board and knead until smooth and elastic. Knead for 8 to 10 minutes. Place dough in a greased bowl, turn to grease on all sides. Cover and let rise in warm place until double, about 30 minutes. Punch down and turn out on floured surface. Pinch off dough and shape as desired. Bake at 400 degrees for 12 to 15 minutes or until golden brown.

Doughnuts *Surprise someone with homemade doughnuts!*

DOUGHNUTS NO. 1

2 eggs, well beaten
1 cup granulated sugar
2 tablespoons vegetable
  oil
1 (8-ounce) carton sour
  cream
4 cups all-purpose flour

1 teaspoon baking soda
1 teaspoon salt
1/4 teaspoon ground
  cinnamon
1/2 teaspoon ground
  nutmeg
Confectioners sugar

Beat eggs; gradually add sugar until blended. Stir in the oil and then sour cream. Sift together the flour, soda, salt, cinnamon and nutmeg. Add to the egg mixture and beat well. Refrigerate until chilled. Turn out on a floured surface. Roll 1/4 inch thick and cut with a floured doughnut cutter. Fry in deep fat heated to 375 degrees, turning once. Drain and then sprinkle with confectioners sugar.

DOUGHNUTS NO. 2

1 large egg, beaten
1 cup granulated sugar
1 cup whole milk
3 cups all-purpose
  flour
4 teaspoons baking
  powder

1/2 teaspoon salt
1/2 teaspoon ground
  nutmeg
Granulated sugar

Beat egg; blend in sugar and then add the milk. Sift together the dry ingredients and beat into the egg mixture. Drop by spoonfuls into 375 degree hot fat, turning once. Drain on paper towels. Roll in granulated sugar when cooled.

Try your luck at making doughnuts ... it's fun!

Popovers are easy to make and a joy to serve and taste. Batter must be beaten vigorously (there is no danger of overbeating).

POPOVERS

1 cup all-purpose flour
1/2 teaspoon salt
2 teaspoon granulated
  sugar

1 cup whole milk
2 large eggs, beaten
1 tablespoon butter,
  melted

Sift together the dry ingredients and set aside. Combine milk, eggs and butter, add to flour mixture, then beat in mixer bowl for several minutes. Quickly pour batter into very hot muffin pans, filling about half full. Bake at 475 degrees for 12 minutes; reduce heat to 350 degrees and bake 15 minutes longer. Two or three minutes before end of baking time, pierce popovers with a very sharp skewer. Serve immediately.

Cakes, Fillings, Frostings, Icings

*Baking **cakes** can be fun and rewarding in many ways. Can you imagine a birthday, an anniversary or any important celebration without a cake? If you've never made a homemade cake, begin today!*

LEMON CHIFFON CAKE

2-1/4 cups cake flour
3 teaspoons baking
   powder
1 teaspoon salt
1-1/2 cups granulated
   sugar
1/2 cup vegetable oil
5 large egg yolks

3/4 cup <u>cold</u> water
2 teaspoons lemon rind,
   freshly grated
1 cup egg whites
   (around 8 large
   eggs)
1/2 teaspoon cream of
   tartar

Sift together the flour, baking powder, salt and sugar. Make a well in center and pour in the oil, egg yolks, water and rind. Beat until smooth and well blended for at least 2 minutes. Beat egg whites and cream of tartar until stiff; fold creamed mixture gently into whites 1/2 cup at a time; do not beat. Pour into ungreased 10-inch tube pan and bake at 325 degrees for 50 minutes; increase heat to 350 degrees and bake for around 15 additional minutes or until cake springs back when lightly touched. Invert at once over large funnel, or bottle, if pan does not stand on tube or side supports. When just cool, loosen cake from sides of pan and remove.

GOLDEN OLD FASHIONED FRUIT CAKE

4 cups cake flour
1/2 teaspoon baking
   powder
1-1/2 teaspoons salt
1-1/2 teaspoons ground
   cinnamon
1 teaspoon ground nutmeg
1-1/2 pounds pecans,
   chopped
3/4 pound candied
   pineapple, chopped

3/4 pound candied
   cherries, chopped
1 pound box golden
   raisins
1 cup butter, softened
2-1/4 cups granulated
   sugar
6 large eggs
3 tablespoons rum

Sift all dry ingredients together. Combine the pecans and fruit; add to the dry ingredients and set aside. Cream the butter until light and fluffy. Gradually add the sugar, blending well. Add eggs, one at a time, beating well after each addition. Stir in the rum. Now add the dry ingredients mixture until mixed in thoroughly. Spoon into a greased and floured 10-inch tube pan and bake at 275 degrees for 3 hours. You may also line the pan with brown paper to prevent sticking.

Be sure to bake this cake for the Christmas Holidays ... it is well worth the effort!

PERFECT CAKE

Layers:

1 cup butter, softened
2 cups granulated sugar
5 large eggs
1 teaspoon pure vanilla
  extract
3-1/2 cups cake flour,
  sifted

3 teaspoons baking
  powder
1/2 teaspoon salt
1 cup whole milk

Cream butter until light and fluffy. Gradually add the sugar, beating well. Add the eggs, one at a time, beating well after each addition. Blend in the vanilla. Sift together the flour, baking powder and salt and add alternately with the milk, beginning and ending with the flour mixture. Grease and flour 3 or 4 9-inch cake pans and spoon batter into pans. Bake at 350 degrees for 30-35 minutes or until cakes test done with a cake tester. Remove to cake racks to cool for several minutes. Remove from pans and continue cooling on racks while you make the Perfect Cake Icing.

Icing:

2 cups granulated sugar
1 cup water
1/4 cup white corn
  syrup
3 egg whites, stiffly
  beaten
1 teaspoon pure vanilla
  extract
2 cups coconut, grated
  (fresh or frozen)

1 (8-1/4-ounce) can
  crushed pineapple,
  well drained
1 (6-ounce) jar
  maraschino cherries,
  cut in small pieces
1 cup pecans, chopped

Combine the sugar, water and syrup; bring to a boil, stirring, and then cook, without stirring, until mixture spins a thread. Beat egg whites until stiff, but not dry. Pour syrup in a thin stream over whites, while beating the whites constantly, until mixture is stiff enough to hold its shape. Blend in the vanilla and then gently fold in the coconut, pineapple, cherries and pecans. Spread icing immediately over the layers, on top and sides.

A wonderful addition to a Christmas table!

BLACKBERRY CAKE

Cake:

1 cup butter, softened
2 cups granulated sugar
3 large eggs
3 cups cake flour
2 teaspoons baking soda
1/2 teaspoon salt
1 teaspoon ground
  allspice
1 teaspoon ground
  cinnamon
1 teaspoon ground nutmeg
2/3 cup buttermilk
2 cups blackberries,
  with juice

Cream the butter until light and fluffy. Gradually add the sugar, mixing well. Add eggs, one at a time, beating well after each addition. Sift together the dry ingredients and add alternately with the buttermilk, beginning and ending with the flour mixture. Fold in the blackberries and juice. Grease and flour a 9 x 13 inch pan. Spoon batter into pan and bake at 350 degrees for around 40 minutes or until cake tests done. Cool and frost cake with Cream Cheese Frosting. Also good with caramel frosting.

Cream Cheese Frosting:

1 (8-ounce) package
  cream cheese,
  softened
1/2 cup butter, softened
1 (16-ounce) box
  confectioners sugar
2 teaspoons pure
  vanilla extract
1 cup pecans, chopped

Beat the cream cheese and butter until well combined. Add the confectioners sugar and vanilla, blending until mixture is smooth. Stir in the pecans. Spread on cooled cake.

Bake and enjoy!

CHOCOLATE SHORT CAKE

Cake:

1/2 cup butter
1/8 cup vegetable
  shortening
1 cup water
4 tablespoons cocoa
1/2 teaspoon salt
2 cups all-purpose
  flour
2 cups granulated sugar
1/2 cup buttermilk
1 teaspoon baking soda
2 large eggs
1 teaspoon pure
  vanilla extract

Combine the butter, shortening, water, cocoa and salt in large saucepan; bring to rapid boil. Remove from heat and set aside. Sift together the flour and sugar; add to the cocoa mixture, stirring well to mix. (Do not use an electric mixer at all.) Combine the buttermilk and soda; add this mixture, eggs and vanilla until well blended. Pour into a greased and floured 9 x 12-inch oblong pan. Bake at 350 degrees for around 30 minutes or until cake tests done with a cake tester. While cake is baking, make the Chocolate Frosting and spread over the cake while hot.

Chocolate Frosting:

1/2 cup butter
6 tablespoons whole
  milk
4 tablespoons cocoa
1 (1-pound) box
  confectioners sugar

1 teaspoon pure
  vanilla extract
1 cup pecans, chopped

Combine the butter, milk and cocoa in medium saucepan; bring to a boil and immediately add the sugar. Beat until well blended. Add the vanilla and pecans. Spread on cake while hot.

NUT AND DATE CAKE

1 cup granulated sugar
1 cup all-purpose flour
1 pound pitted dates,
  cut up

1 pound pecans, chopped
4 large eggs, beaten
1 teaspoon pure
  vanilla extract

Combine the sugar and flour; dredge the dates and pecans in the mixture. Beat eggs until light; add vanilla, then mix with the date and nut mixture until well blended. Line a loaf pan with brown paper; pack mixture tightly in pan and bake at 350 degrees for 1-1/2 hours or until cake tests done.

NUT AND RAISIN CAKE

1/2 cup pecans, chopped
1/2 cup raisins, chopped
Flour to dredge
1/2 cup softened butter
1 cup granulated sugar

3 large eggs
2 cups cake flour
1/2 cup whole milk
1 teaspoon pure
  vanilla extract

Dredge pecans and raisins in small amount of flour; set aside. Cream butter until light and fluffy, gradually adding sugar until well blended. Add eggs, one at a time, beating well after each addition. Sift the flour and add alternately with the milk and vanilla until well blended. Stir in the pecans and raisins. Bake in a lightly greased and floured loaf pan at 350 degrees for around 1 hour or until cake tests done with a cake tester.

ORANGE-DATE CAKE

Cake:

1 cup butter, softened
2 cups granulated sugar
1/2 cup buttermilk
1 teaspoon baking soda
3-1/2 cups cake flour
4 large eggs
1 cup moist coconut,
   fresh or frozen

3 tablespoons grated
   orange rind
1 (8-ounce) package
   chopped dates
1 cup pecans, chopped

Cream butter until light and fluffy. Gradually add sugar until well mixed. Blend buttermilk and soda together and add to creamed mixture. Sift the flour and add alternately with the eggs, beating well after each addition. Stir in the coconut, rind, dates and pecans. Spoon into a greased and floured 10-inch tube pan and bake at 300 degrees for about 1-1/2 hours or until cake tests done with a cake tester. Pour icing over cake while warm and still in pan. Let cake remain in pan until cool, then remove to serve.

Icing:

2 cups granulated sugar
1 cup orange juice,
   freshly squeezed

4 tablespoons orange
   rind

Combine all ingredients and bring to a boil; reduce heat and simmer to a light syrup. Do not over cook; mixture should be thin. Pour over warm cake.

APPLE POUND CAKE

Cake:

1-1/2 cups vegetable oil
2 cups granulated sugar
4 large eggs
2 teaspoons pure
   vanilla extract
3 cups cake flour
1/2 teaspoon salt

1 teaspoon baking soda
1 teaspoon ground
   cinnamon
4 cups apple, chopped
   fine
1 cup pecans, chopped

Beat the oil and sugar until well blended. Add eggs, one at a time, beating well after each addition. Stir in the vanilla. Sift together the flour, salt, soda and cinnamon; blend in thoroughly. Fold in the apple and pecans. May be baked in a 10-inch tube pan or oblong baking pan. Grease and flour pan and spoon in the batter. Bake at 325 degrees if you use a tube pan and 350 degrees if you use an oblong pan. Bake for around 1 hour and 15 minutes in the tube pan or around 1 hour in the oblong pan or until the cake tests done with a cake tester. Serve plain or with Coconut Glaze. Great served warm!

Coconut Glaze:

1/2 cup confectioners
   sugar, sifted
1 teaspoon butter,
   softened
1 teaspoon white corn
   syrup

4 teaspoons whipping
   cream, unwhipped
1/2 cup coconut, grated

Combine all ingredients and beat to blend. Drizzle over top of cake.

The flavor is outstanding!

WALDORF CHOCOLATE CAKE

Cake:

1 cup butter, softened
2 cups granulated sugar
3 large eggs
4 squares semi-sweet
   chocolate, melted
2-1/2 cups cake flour
2 teaspoons baking
   powder

Dash salt
1-1/4 cups whole milk
2 teaspoons pure
   vanilla extract
1/2 cup pecans, chopped

Cream butter until smooth; gradually add sugar until blended. Add eggs, one at a time, beating well after each addition. Add melted chocolate. Sift together the flour, baking powder and salt and add alternately with the milk and vanilla until combined. Stir in the nuts. Spoon into a greased and floured 10-inch tube pan and bake at 350 degrees for around 45 minutes or until cake tests done. Cool on cake rack for 5 minutes before removing from pan. Let cool and then ice cake.

Chocolate Icing:

1/2 cup butter, melted
2 squares semi-sweet
   chocolate, melted
1-1/2 cups confectioners
   sugar
1 large egg, beaten

1 teaspoon pure
   vanilla extract
1 tablespoon lemon
   juice, freshly squeezed
1/2 cup pecans, chopped

Melt butter and chocolate in small saucepan; let cool. Add sugar, egg, vanilla and lemon juice; blend thoroughly. Spread icing over cooled cake and sprinkle pecans all over.

PRUNE CAKE

Cake:

1 cup vegetable oil
1-1/2 cups granulated
  sugar
3 large eggs
2 cups all-purpose flour
1 teaspoon baking soda
1/2 teaspoon salt
1 teaspoon ground
  allspice
1 teaspoon ground
  cinnamon

1 teaspoon ground
  nutmeg
1 cup buttermilk
1 teaspoon pure
  vanilla extract
1 cup cooked prunes,
  finely chopped
1 cup pecans, chopped

Beat the oil and sugar until thoroughly mixed. Add eggs, one at a time, beating well after each addition. Sift together the dry ingredients and add alternately with the buttermilk and vanilla. Fold in the prunes and pecans. Pour into a 13 x 9-inch greased and floured pan. Bake at 325 degrees for 1 hour, or until cake tests done with a cake tester. Pour Buttermilk Icing over hot cake; cool in the pan. Cut in squares and serve with sweetened whipped cream, if desired.

Buttermilk Icing:

1/4 cup butter, melted
1 cup granulated sugar
1/2 cup buttermilk
1/4 teaspoon baking soda

1 tablespoon white
  corn syrup
1 teaspoon pure
  vanilla extract

Melt butter in large saucepan; add sugar, buttermilk and soda combined, syrup and flavoring. Bring to a boil, stirring; cook over low heat for around 20 minutes, stirring occasionally. Pour over hot cake.

BLACK WALNUT POUND CAKE

1 cup butter, softened
1/2 cup vegetable
  shortening
3 cups granulated sugar
5 large eggs
1 teaspoon black walnut
  extract
1 square semi-sweet
  chocolate, melted

3 cups cake flour,
  sifted
1/2 teaspoon baking
  powder
1/2 teaspoon salt
5 tablespoons cocoa
1 cup half and half
1/2 cup black walnuts,
  finely chopped

Cream butter and shortening until well blended. Gradually add sugar until thoroughly mixed. Add eggs, one at a time, beating well after each addition. Blend in the flavoring and melted chocolate. Sift together the flour, baking powder, salt and cocoa; add alternately with the half and half, beginning and ending with the flour mixture. Fold in the nuts. Spoon mixture into a well greased 10-inch tube pan and bake at 325 degrees for 1 hour and 15 minutes or until cake tests done with a cake tester. Cool for several minutes on cake rack before removing from pan. Delicious warm ... served with a caramel glaze, or plain.

Different and delightfully delicious!

CHOCOLATE POUND CAKE

Cake:

1 cup butter, softened
1/4 cup vegetable
  shortening
3 cups granulated sugar
5 large eggs
3 cups cake flour,
  sifted
1/2 teaspoon baking
  powder

1/2 teaspoon salt
4 heaping tablespoons
  cocoa powder
1 cup whole milk
1 tablespoon pure
  vanilla extract

Cream butter and shortening until light and fluffy. Gradually add the sugar, beating well. Add eggs, one at a time, beating well after each addition. Sift together the flour, baking powder, salt and cocoa; add alternately with the milk and vanilla, beginning and ending with the flour mixture. Spoon into a greased 10-inch tube pan and bake at 325 degrees for 1 hour and 40 minutes or until cake tests done with a cake tester. Remove to cake rack and cool for 10 minutes before removing to cake plate. Cool completely; spread Chocolate Icing all over cake.

Chocolate Icing:

2 ounces German's sweet
  chocolate
1/2 cup butter
1 (1-pound) box
  confectioners
  sugar, sifted

Evaporated milk

Melt chocolate and butter, stirring to blend. Let cool. Sift sugar and add to chocolate mixture. Add enough milk to thin icing for spreading.

Delightfully delicious! Good for any occasion and also nice for a Groom's Cake .. garnished with fresh green grapes or as is.

BROWN SUGAR POUND CAKE

1 cup margarine,
  softened
1/2 cup vegetable
  shortening
1 cup granulated sugar
1 (16-ounce) box light
  brown sugar
5 large eggs
3 cups cake flour

1/2 teaspoon baking
  powder
1 cup whole milk
1 teaspoon pure
  vanilla extract
1 cup pecans, chopped
  and dredged in small
  amount of flour

Cream the margarine and shortening well. Gradually add the sugars, beating well. Add eggs, one at a time, beating well after each addition. Sift together the flour and baking powder; add alternately with the milk and vanilla. Dredge the pecans in flour and fold into the creamed mixture. Spoon into a greased and floured 10-inch tube pan; bake at 325 degrees for around 1-1/2 hours or until cake tests done with a cake tester. Cool for 5 minutes before removing from pan.

BUTTERMILK POUND CAKE

Cake:

1-1/2 cups vegetable
  shortening
2-1/2 cups granulated
  sugar
4 large eggs
1 tablespoon lemon
  extract

3-1/2 cups cake flour
1/2 teaspoon baking soda
1/2 teaspoon salt
1 cup buttermilk

Cream shortening until smooth; gradually add sugar and cream thoroughly. Add eggs, one at a time, beating well after each addition. Blend in the flavoring. Sift together the flour, baking soda and salt; add alternately with the buttermilk, beginning and ending with the flour. Spoon batter into a greased and floured 10-inch tube pan. Bake at 300 degrees for around 1 hour and 20 minutes or until cake tests done. Cool for around 5 minutes; remove from pan and pour over Glaze.

Glaze:

1 cup granulated sugar
2 tablespoons water

Juice and grated rind
  of 2 lemons

Combine all ingredients and bring to a boil. Pour over warm cake and serve while still warm.

GREAT POUND CAKE

1 pound butter, softened
3 cups granulated sugar
10 large eggs, separated
4 cups cake flour,
  sifted
1/2 teaspoon salt

2 teaspoons lemon
  flavoring or
2 teaspoons pure
  vanilla extract
1/2 cup whipping cream,
  unwhipped

Cream butter until light and fluffy. Gradually add the sugar, beating until well mixed. Add egg yolks, one at a time, beating well after each addition. Sift the flour and salt 3 times; add alternately with the flavoring and cream until well blended. Beat egg whites until stiff but not dry, and fold into the creamed mixture. Grease and line a 10-inch tube pan with waxed paper. Spoon in the mixture and bake at 300 degrees for around 1-1/2 hours or until cake tests done with a cake tester.

The taste is great!

LEMON POUND CAKE

Cake:

1/2 cup butter, softened
1/2 cup vegetable
  shortening
2 cups granulated sugar
3 large eggs
3 cups cake flour
1/2 teaspoon baking soda

1/8 teaspoon salt
1 cup buttermilk
1 teaspoon lemon juice,
  freshly squeezed
1 teaspoon lemon rind,
  packed

Cream the butter and shortening until light and fluffy. Gradually add the sugar until well blended. Add eggs, one at a time, beating well after each addition. Sift together the flour, soda and salt; add alternately with the buttermilk, juice and rind; beat until creamed well. Pour into a greased 10-inch tube pan and bake at 325 degrees for around 1 hour and 15 minutes or until cake tests done with a cake tester. Cool in pan on cake rack for around 10 minutes; remove to rack to cool. Spread the Lemon Icing over top and on sides of cake.

Lemon Icing:

1/2 cup butter, softened
1 (16 ounce) box
  confectioners sugar

Juice and rind of
  2 medium lemons

Cream butter; gradually add the sugar and mix well. Blend in the juice and rind, beating until smooth.

COCONUT POUND CAKE

1 cup butter, softened
1/2 cup vegetable
  shortening
2-1/2 cups granulated
  sugar
5 large egg yolks
3-1/2 cups cake flour
1/8 teaspoon salt
1 teaspoon baking
  powder

1 cup whole milk
1 teaspoon pure
  coconut extract
1 (7-ounce) package
  frozen coconut,
  thawed or 1 cup
  fresh coconut,
  finely grated
5 large egg whites,
  stiffly beaten

Cream butter and shortening until light and fluffy; gradually add sugar until well blended. Add egg yolks, one at a time, beating well after each addition. Sift together the flour, salt and baking powder; add alternately with the milk and flavoring, beating until blended thoroughly. Fold in the coconut and then the stiffly beaten egg whites by hand. Spoon into a greased and floured 10-inch tube pan. Bake at 325 degrees for 1 hour and 15 minutes or until cake tests done with a cake tester. Cool in pan on cake rack for 10 minutes, then turn out on rack to complete cooling.

OLD FASHIONED POUND CAKE

Cake:

1 pound butter,
  softened
2 cups granulated sugar
8 large eggs
3-1/4 cups cake flour

1/2 teaspoon salt
2 teaspoons pure
  vanilla extract
2 teaspoons almond
  extract

Cream butter well; add sugar gradually, beating until light and fluffy. Add eggs, one at a time, beating well after each addition. Sift together the flour and salt; add alternately with the flavorings. Beat for around 10 minutes. Spoon batter into a greased and floured 10-inch tube pan. Bake at 325 degrees for 1 hour and 15 minutes or until cake tests done with a cake tester. Cool on cake rack for 10 minutes before removing from pan. For Rum Cake, omit vanilla and almond extracts and use Rum Glaze.

Rum Glaze:

1/2 cup butter, melted
1/4 cup water

1 cup granulated sugar
1/2 cup rum

Melt butter in a saucepan. Stir in water and sugar; let come to a boil and boil for 5 minutes, stirring constantly. Stir in rum. Place cake on a serving plate and brush glaze evenly over the top.

SOUR CREAM COCONUT POUND CAKE

Cake:

1 cup butter, softened
1/2 cup vegetable
  shortening
3 cups granulated sugar
6 large eggs
3 cups cake flour
1 (8-ounce) carton sour
  cream, mixed with
  1/4 teaspoon
  baking soda

1 tablespoon whole milk
1 tablespoon pure
  coconut extract
1-1/3 cups flaked
  coconut

Cream butter and shortening until light and fluffy. Gradually add sugar and mix thoroughly. Add eggs, one at a time, beating well after each addition. Sift flour 3 times and add alternately with the sour cream-soda mixture; add the milk and flavoring and blend well. Stir in the coconut. Spoon into a greased 10-inch tube pan and bake at 325 degrees for 1 hour and 20 minutes or until cake tests done with a cake tester. Cool in pan on cake rack for 10 minutes. Turn out and complete cooling on cake rack. Spread frosting on cooled cake.

Frosting:

1 (16-ounce) box
  confectioners sugar
1/2 cup butter, melted
1/4 cup evaporated milk,
  about

1 teaspoon pure
  vanilla extract
1/2 cup flaked coconut

Combine sugar and butter until blended. Add milk and flavoring and blend to desired consistency. Stir in coconut; blend well. Spread on cooled cake.

PECAN SUGAR CAKE

1 (16-ounce) package
  light brown sugar
6 large egg whites,
  unbeaten

2 cups self-rising flour
1 teaspoon baking powder
3 cups pecans, chopped

Blend together the sugar and egg whites until creamy. Sift the flour and baking powder; add to the creamed mixture, blending well. Fold in the pecans. Spoon mixture into an ungreased 10-inch tube pan and bake for around 1 hour or until cake tests done with a cake tester. Cool for 10 to 15 minutes on cake rack before removing from pan.

PINEAPPLE POUND CAKE

Cake:

1 (8-ounce) can crushed
pineapple, in
heavy syrup
1 cup butter, softened
1/2 cup vegetable
shortening
3 cups granulated sugar
5 large eggs
1 tablespoon pure
vanilla extract

1 teaspoon lemon
extract
3 cups cake flour,
sifted
1/2 teaspoon baking
powder
Dash salt
1 cup whole milk

Drain pineapple and reserve juice for glaze; set aside. Cream the butter and shortening until light and fluffy. Gradually add the sugar until thoroughly mixed. Add eggs, one at a time, beating well after each addition. Stir in the flavorings. Sift together the flour, baking powder and salt; add alternately with the milk until blended. Fold in the pineapple. Spoon mixture into a 10-inch greased and floured tube pan and bake at 350 degrees for around 1-1/2 hours, or until cake tests done with a cake tester. Cool in pan on cake rack for about 20 minutes before turning out on cake rack. Drizzle with the Pineapple Glaze while warm.

Pineapple Glaze:

2 tablespoons butter,
softened
1 cup confectioners
sugar, sifted

1-1/2 tablespoons
pineapple syrup
1 teaspoon white
corn syrup

Cream butter, then add sugar and syrup alternately, a little at a time, stirring until smooth after each addition. Stir in the corn syrup. When smooth, drizzle over cake and let stand until set before cutting.

PRUNE POUND CAKE

Cake:

1 pound butter, softened
2 cups granulated sugar
6 large eggs
2 teaspoons grated
lemon rind
3-1/2 cups cake flour
1 teaspoon baking powder
1/2 teaspoon salt

2 tablespoons whipping
cream, unwhipped
1-1/2 cups pitted prunes,
finely cut
1-1/2 cups walnuts,
chopped
1/4 cup cake flour,
for dredging

Cream butter until light and fluffy; gradually add the sugar until well blended. Add eggs, one at a time, beating well after each addition. Sift together the flour, baking powder and salt; add alternately with the cream until well mixed. Dredge the prunes and walnuts in the flour, coating well. Stir into batter until blended. Lightly grease a 10-inch tube pan or Bundt pan and spoon batter into the pan. Bake at 350 degrees for around 1 hour or until cake tests done with a cake tester. Cool on cake rack for 10 minutes before removing to rack to cool. Pour glaze over cooled cake and let drizzle down sides.

Glaze:

1/4 cup confectioners
  sugar, packed and
  sifted

1/2 teaspoon pure
  vanilla extract
1 tablespoon whole milk

Beat sugar, vanilla and milk until smooth. If glaze is too thick, gradually add additional milk to give right consistency.

RUM POUND CAKE

Cake:

1 cup butter, softened
2 cups granulated sugar
6 large eggs
2 tablespoons rum
  flavoring

3 cups cake flour
1/4 teaspoon baking soda
1 (8-ounce) carton sour
  cream

Cream butter until light and fluffy. Gradually add sugar, mixing thoroughly. Add eggs, one at a time, beating well after each addition. Blend in the flavoring. Sift together the flour and baking soda and add alternately with the sour cream, beginning and ending with the flour mixture. Spoon into a greased 10-inch tube pan and bake at 325 degrees for 1 hour and 15 minutes or until cake tests done with a cake tester. To enhance the flavor, drizzle icing over warm cake. (You may also change the flavoring for a different twist.)

Icing:

1-1/2 cups confectioners
  sugar, sifted
2-1/2 tablespoons
  boiling water
1 teaspoon butter,
  softened

1 teaspoon pure
  vanilla extract
1 tablespoon white
  corn syrup

Measure sugar into a large mixer bowl. Melt the butter in boiling water and add to the sugar along with the vanilla, blending. Beat in the syrup until smooth. Thin with additional hot water, if necessary. Drizzle at once over warm cake.

WHITE POUND CAKE

Cake:

1 cup butter, softened
1 (16 ounce) box
  confectioners
  sugar, sifted
4 cups cake flour
1 teaspoon baking
  powder

1/2 cup whipping cream,
  unwhipped
2 teaspoons pure
  vanilla extract
12 large egg whites,
  beaten

Cream butter until light and fluffy; add sugar gradually and beat until thoroughly blended. Sift together the flour and baking powder 3 times; add to the creamed mixture alternately with the cream and vanilla, beginning and ending with the flour mixture. Beat egg whites until stiff, but not dry. Add whites to the batter and beat for around 15 to 20 minutes. This is necessary. Spoon mixture into a lightly greased 10-inch tube pan and bake for 1-1/2 hours at 325 degrees or until the cake tests done with a cake tester. Remove to cake rack and cool for several minutes before removing to cake rack to cool. Good plain or with White Icing.

White Icing:

2-1/2 cups granulated
  sugar
1/2 cup white
  corn syrup
1/2 cup water

2 large egg whites
Dash salt
1 teaspoon pure
  vanilla extract

Combine sugar, syrup and water in large saucepan; stir and bring to a boil. Cook, without stirring, until syrup spins a thread. Beat egg whites and salt until stiff. Slowly pour the hot syrup in a thin stream over the whites, beating constantly until thick; blend in vanilla and spread immediately over cake.

SOUR CREAM POUND CAKE

1/2 pound butter,
  softened
3 cups confectioners
  sugar, sifted
6 large eggs
3 cups cake flour

1/4 teaspoon baking soda
1/4 teaspoon salt
1 (8-ounce) carton sour
  cream
1 teaspoon pure
  vanilla extract

Cream the butter well; add the sifted sugar gradually, beating until thoroughly mixed and fluffy. Add eggs, one at a time, beating well after each addition. Sift together 3 times the flour, baking powder and salt. Add alternately with the sour cream and vanilla, creaming well. Spoon into a greased 10-inch tube pan and bake at 350 degrees for 1-1/2 hours or until cake tests done with a cake tester. Do not open the oven door during baking time until cake is almost done.

RICH CREAM POUND CAKE

1/2 cup butter, softened
1/2 cup margarine,
  softened
2 cups granulated sugar
6 large eggs
2 teaspoons pure
  vanilla extract

3 cups cake flour,
  sifted
1 (8-ounce) carton
  whipping cream,
  unwhipped

Cream the butter and margarine well. Gradually add the sugar and beat for 10 minutes. Add eggs, one at a time, beating well after each addition. Stir in the vanilla. Sift the flour, measure and re-sift 3 times. Add alternately with the cream until thoroughly blended. Spoon into a lightly greased 10-inch tube pan and bake at 300 degrees for 1 hour and 15 minutes or until cake tests done with a cake tester.

RAISIN POUND CAKE

1 cup butter, softened
1-1/2 cups granulated
  sugar
4 large eggs
1/4 teaspoon grated
  lemon rind
3 teaspoons lemon juice,
  freshly squeezed

2-1/4 cups cake flour
1/4 teaspoon baking
  powder
1 cup raisins, dredged
  in small amount
  of flour

Cream butter until softened; gradually add sugar and beat until light and fluffy. Add eggs, one at a time, beating well after each addition. Add lemon rind and juice; blend well. Sift together the flour and baking powder; add to the creamed mixture, beating thoroughly. Stir in raisins. Pour into a greased and floured 9 x 5 x 3-inch loaf pan. Bake at 300 degrees for around 1 hour and 20 minutes or until cake tests done.

Good warm or cold!

STRAWBERRY POUND CAKE

Cake:

1-1/2 cups butter,
  softened
2-1/2 cups granulated
  sugar
1 (3-ounce) package
  strawberry gelatin
  dessert
6 large egg yolks
3-1/2 cups cake flour

1/2 cup whipping cream,
  unwhipped
6 large egg whites,
  stiffly beaten
3 tablespoons
  granulated sugar
1/2 cup fresh
  strawberries,
  cut up

Cream the butter until soft and fluffy; gradually add the 2-1/2 cups sugar and gelatin until blended thoroughly. Add egg yolks, one at a time, beating well after each addition. Sift flour 3 times and add alternately with the cream until blended well. Beat egg whites until frothy and gradually add the 3 tablespoons sugar until stiff. Beat in 1 large spoonful of egg whites with electric beaters, then fold in remaining egg whites and strawberries. Spoon mixture into a lightly greased 10-inch tube pan. Bake at 300 degrees for 1-1/2 hours or until cake tests done with a cake tester or straw. Top with Strawberry Glaze.

Strawberry Glaze:

1 cup confectioners sugar
1 tablespoon butter, softened
3 tablespoons strawberries,
  puréed or finely mashed

1 teaspoon whipping cream,
  unwhipped

Combine all ingredients and beat with mixer beaters until blended thoroughly. Spoon over warm cake and let drizzle down sides.

BANANA CAKE

1/4 pound butter, softened
1-1/2 cups granulated
  sugar
3 large eggs
2 cups all-purpose flour
1/2 teaspoon baking
  powder

1/2 teaspoon baking soda
1 teaspoon pure
  vanilla extract
1/4 cup whole milk
4 ripe bananas, mashed

Cream butter and sugar until light and fluffy; add eggs, one at a time, beating well after each addition. Sift together the flour, baking powder and soda; add alternately with the vanilla and milk. Blend in the mashed banana. Spoon into a greased and floured 9-inch square baking pan. Bake in a 350 degree oven for around 1 hour or until cake tests done.

ORANGE CHEESECAKE

Crust and topping:

1-1/2 cups graham
  cracker crumbs

1/3 cup butter, melted
1/3 cup granulated sugar

Combine all ingredients, blending well. Press 1-3/4 cups crumb mixture evenly on bottom of a buttered 9-inch springform pan. Reserve remaining crumb mixture for top.

Filling:

3 (8-ounce) packages
  cream cheese,
  softened
1 cup granulated sugar,
  divided

Grated rind and juice
  of 1 large orange
4 large egg whites

Beat cream cheese until light and fluffy. Add 1/2 cup of the sugar and beat in thoroughly. Add rind and juice, blending well. Beat egg whites until stiff; add remaining sugar gradually and beat until shiny. Fold into cheese mixture. Spoon into crumb crust. Sprinkle reserved crumbs on top. Bake at 325 degrees for 45 to 50 minutes. Cool and then chill in refrigerator for several hours or overnight.

PINEAPPLE CHEESECAKE

1 (9-inch) graham
  cracker crust
1 (3-ounce) package
  lemon gelatin
  dessert
1 cup boiling water
1 (8-ounce) package
  cream cheese,
  softened
3/4 cup granulated
  sugar

1 (8-ounce) can crushed
  pineapple, in heavy
  syrup (add water to
  syrup to make 1 cup
  liquid)
1 cup evaporated milk,
  well chilled
2 tablespoons lemon
  juice, freshly
  squeezed

Prepare crust and set aside. Place gelatin in boiling water and stir for several minutes until gelatin is completely dissolved. Beat cream cheese until creamy; gradually add sugar until blended. Now add the pineapple, liquid and gelatin; place in refrigerator to chill. Beat chilled milk until fluffy; add lemon juice and whip until stiff. Fold into chilled gelatin mixture. Refrigerate until mixture mounds when dropped from a spoon; around 15-20 minutes. Spoon into crust and refrigerate for several hours until firm enough to cut.

JAPANESE FRUIT CAKE

Layers:

1 cup butter, softened
2 cups granulated sugar
4 large eggs
1 teaspoon pure vanilla
 extract
3 cups cake flour,
 sifted
1/4 teaspoon salt
3 teaspoons baking
 powder

1 cup, plus
 2 tablespoons
 milk
1 teaspoon ground
 allspice
1 teaspoon ground
 cinnamon
1/4 teaspoon ground
 cloves
1/4 pound white raisins,
 cut up

Cream the butter until soft and fluffy; gradually add the sugar until thoroughly blended. Add the eggs, one at a time, beating well after each addition. Stir in the vanilla. Sift together the flour, salt and baking powder; add alternately with the milk, beginning and ending with the flour mixture. Divide the batter in half and add to one half of the batter the allspice, cinnamon, cloves and raisins. Grease and flour 4 9-inch cake pans. Spoon the first half of batter into two of the pans and the second half into the other two pans. Bake at 350 degrees for around 30 to 35 minutes or until the cakes test done with a cake tester. Cool; remove and spread filling between layers.

Filling:

2 tablespoons
 cornstarch
1/2 cup cold water
2 cups granulated sugar
1 cup boiling water
Juice of two lemons

Grated rind of one
 lemon
1 small coconut, grated
 or 1 (12-ounce)
 package frozen
 coconut

Dissolve the cornstarch in cold water. Set aside. Combine the other ingredients and bring to a boil. Add the cornstarch mixture and cook, stirring constantly, until mixture drops from the spoon in one lump. Cool and then spread between the layers. Frost the top and sides with the Seven Minute Frosting.

Seven Minute Frosting:

2 egg whites
1/4 teaspoon cream of
 tartar
Dash salt
1-1/2 cups granulated
 sugar

5 tablespoons cold water
1 teaspoon pure vanilla
 extract
3 teaspoons white corn
 syrup

Place first 5 ingredients in top of double boiler, then cook over boiling water. Beat with an electric hand beater for 7 minutes or until icing stands in stiff peaks. Remove from heat and place in a pan of cold water. Add vanilla and syrup, then continue beating until shiny. Spread on cake immediately.

WHITE CHOCOLATE CAKE

Cake:

1/4 pound white
   chocolate
1/2 cup boiling water
1 cup butter, softened
2 cups granulated sugar
4 large egg yolks
1 teaspoon pure vanilla
   extract

2-1/2 cups cake flour
1 teaspoon baking soda
1 cup buttermilk
4 large egg whites
1 cup pecans or almonds,
   chopped
1 cup flaked coconut

Combine chocolate and water in small saucepan; stir until melted; cool. Beat butter until creamed well, gradually adding the sugar until mixed thoroughly. Add egg yolks, one at a time, beating well after each addition. Blend in vanilla. Sift together the flour and soda; add alternately with the buttermilk. Beat egg whites until stiff but not dry. Fold into the creamed mixture; gently stir in the nuts and coconut. Spoon into 3 9-inch greased and floured cake pans and bake at 350 degrees for around 30 to 35 minutes or until cakes test done with a cake tester. Remove pans to cake racks and let cool for around 5 minutes; remove from pans and let cool completely on cake racks before frosting.

Frosting:

1 (12-ounce) can
   evaporated milk
1 cup granulated sugar
1/4 cup butter
3 large egg yolks, slightly
   beaten

1 teaspoon pure vanilla
   extract
1-1/3 cups flaked
   coconut
1-1/2 cups pecans,
   chopped

Pour milk into a large saucepan; add sugar and butter; bring to a boil, stirring constantly. Blend a small amount of the hot mixture into the egg yolks; beat rapidly to prevent curdling. Add vanilla and stir into the cooked mixture; cook, stirring, over low heat until thickened, around 15 minutes. Remove from heat and stir in coconut and nuts. Beat until blended and spread in between layers and on top and sides.

LANE CAKE

Layers:

2/3 cup butter, softened
1-3/4 cups granulated
  sugar
3 cups cake flour,
  sifted
3 teaspoons baking powder

1/2 teaspoon salt
1 cup whole milk
1 teaspoon pure vanilla
  extract
5 large egg whites

Cream butter until light and fluffy. Gradually add the sugar until blended well. Sift together the flour, baking powder and salt; add alternately with the milk and vanilla, beginning and ending with the flour mixture. Beat the egg whites until stiff but not dry. Beat in one large spoonful with the electric mixer and then fold in the rest until blended. Grease and flour 3 9-inch cake pans and spoon batter into the pans. Bake at 350 degrees for 30 to 35 minutes or until the cakes test done with a cake tester. Remove to cake racks to cool for several minutes before removing from pans.

Filling:

8 large egg yolks, well
  beaten
1/2 cup butter
1 cup granulated sugar
1 cup coconut, grated,
  fresh or frozen

1 cup pecans, chopped
1 cup white raisins,
  cut fine

Combine beaten egg yolks, butter and sugar; cook in double boiler until mixture is thickened. Add the coconut, pecans and raisins, blending well. Spread between cooled cake layers.

White Icing:

3 cups granulated sugar
1-1/3 cups water
2 tablespoons white
  corn syrup
3 large egg whites

1/8 teaspoon salt
1/8 teaspoon cream of
  tartar
1-1/2 teaspoons pure
  vanilla extract

Combine the sugar, water and syrup; cook and stir until mixture begins to boil. Then boil, stirring only occasionally, until syrup spins a thread. While syrup is boiling, beat egg whites, salt and cream of tartar until stiff but not dry; add the hot syrup in a very thin stream, beating constantly, until thick. Now add the vanilla and stir in well. Immediately spread over the top and sides of cake.

This cake brings back nostalgic Christmas memories ... the taste is rich and well worth the effort at least once a year!

CHOCOLATE SOUR CREAM COFFEE CAKE

1/2 pound butter, softened
1 cup granulated sugar
2 large eggs
2 cups all-purpose flour
1 teaspoon baking powder
1 teaspoon baking soda
1/4 teaspoon salt
1 teaspoon pure vanilla
  extract

1 (8-ounce) carton sour
  cream
1/4 cup light brown
  sugar, firmly packed
1 teaspoon ground
  cinnamon
1 square grated semi-
  sweet chocolate

Cream butter until fluffy. Gradually add sugar, blending well. Now add eggs, one at a time, beating well after each addition. Sift together the flour, baking powder, soda and salt; add alternately with the vanilla and sour cream. Combine the brown sugar, cinnamon and grated chocolate and set aside. Grease and flour a 9-inch square pan. Spoon one half of the batter into the pan, then add the sugar-cinnamon mixture. Spoon the rest of the batter over top. Bake at 350 degrees for around 45 minutes or until done.

Delicious!

CRANBERRY SOUR CREAM COFFEE CAKE

Cake:
2 cups self-rising flour
1 cup granulated sugar
2 large eggs, well
  beaten
1 (8-ounce) carton sour
  cream

2 teaspoons grated
  orange rind
1 cup cranberry sauce

Sift flour and sugar together; set aside. Blend together the eggs, sour cream and rind; add all at once to flour mixture; mix until smooth. Spoon half the batter into a buttered 9 x 9-inch baking pan. Spread cranberry sauce over batter; spoon remaining batter on top. Sprinkle topping over batter and bake at 350 degrees for around 45 minutes or until golden brown.

Topping:
3 tablespoons all-
  purpose flour
1 teaspoon ground
  cinnamon

1/3 cup light brown
  sugar, packed
2 tablespoons butter,
  softened

Combine flour, cinnamon and sugar. Cut in butter with a pastry blender or fork until mixture is coarse and crumbles. Sprinkle over top of batter.

LEMON CHEESECAKE

Crust:

4 ounces butter, melted

1-1/2 cups graham
cracker crumbs

3 tablespoons
granulated sugar

Melt butter in small saucepan; remove from heat, add crumbs and sugar, blending well. Spread crumbs into square or oblong glass dish pressing firmly with hand. Set aside and prepare the filling.

Filling:

1 (3-ounce) package
lemon gelatin
dessert

1 cup boiling water

1 (8-ounce) package
cream cheese,
softened

1 cup granulated sugar

1 teaspoon lemon
extract

1 (12-ounce) can
evaporated milk,
chilled and whipped

3/4 cup graham cracker
crumbs

Blend together the gelatin and boiling water; stir for several minutes until gelatin is completely dissolved. Set aside to cool. Beat cream cheese until light and fluffy. Gradually add the sugar until creamy. Add flavoring and blend. Add the gelatin and milk and blend in thoroughly. Spoon gently into crust. Sprinkle the top evenly with 3/4 cup plain graham cracker crumbs. Refrigerate until well chilled before serving. Cut into squares to serve, if desired.

A very light and delicious cheesecake; especially good during the summer ... no baking necessary!

LEMON CHEESE LAYER CAKE

Layers:

1 cup butter, softened

2 cups granulated sugar

5 large eggs

1 teaspoon pure vanilla
extract

3-1/2 cups cake flour,
sifted

3 teaspoons baking
powder

1/4 teaspoon salt

1 cup whole milk

Cream the butter until soft and fluffy. Gradually add the sugar until well mixed. Add eggs, one at a time, beating well after each addition. Blend in the vanilla. Sift together the flour, baking powder and salt; add alternately with the milk, beginning and ending with the flour mixture. Spoon into 4 9-inch greased and floured cake pans. Bake at 350 degrees for around 30 to 35 minutes or until tests done with a cake tester. Remove to cake racks and cool for several minutes before removing from pans. While layers are cooling, cook the filling and then spread in between layers and on top and sides.

Filling:

5 large egg yolks
1 cup granulated sugar,
  plus 2 tablespoons
1/2 cup butter, softened

Juice of 3 medium-size
  lemons
Grated rind of 1/2 lemon

Beat egg yolks; gradually add sugar, mixing well. Beat in the butter until creamy; then add juice and rind, blending. Transfer mixture to top of double boiler and cook over boiling water until slightly thickened. Cool in pan. Spread over layers and on top and sides of cake. You may also top with Seven Minute Frosting for variation.

This cake will prove to be one of the great cakes of all time!

LEMON FRUIT CAKE

1 pound butter, softened
1 (16-ounce) box light
  brown sugar
6 large egg yolks
2 cups all-purpose
  flour
1 teaspoon baking
  powder
1 (1-1/2-ounce) bottle
  lemon extract

4 cups pecans, chopped
1/2 pound candied
  cherries, chopped
1/2 pound mixed fruit,
  chopped
1/2 pound candied
  pineapple, chopped
2 cups all-purpose flour
6 large egg whites,
  stiffly beaten

Cream butter until light and fluffy; gradually add the sugar beating well. Add egg yolks, one at a time, beating well after each addition. Sift together 2 cups flour and baking powder; add alternately with the lemon extract beginning and ending with the flour mixture. Place pecans and fruit in large bowl and mix with 2 cups flour. Add this mixture to the creamed mixture and combine thoroughly. Beat the egg whites until stiff but still moist. Fold into the batter. Grease and flour a 10-inch or larger tube pan; spoon in the batter. Cover and refrigerate overnight or at least 12 hours. Bake at 250 degrees for around 3 hours or until golden brown. Let cool completely before removing from pan.

You will need a strong right arm to mix the cake but it is well worth the effort!

CARROT LAYER CAKE

Cake:

1-1/2 cups vegetable
  oil
2 cups granulated sugar
4 large eggs
2-1/2 cups cake flour,
  sifted
1 teaspoon baking soda

1/4 teaspoon salt
1 teaspoon baking
  powder
1 teaspoon ground
  cinnamon
2 cups carrots, finely
  grated

Beat oil and sugar until well blended. Add eggs, one at a time, beating well after each addition. Sift together the dry ingredients and add gradually until mixed thoroughly. Fold in the grated carrots and mix well. Grease and flour 3 or 4 9-inch cake pans. Spoon batter into pans and bake in a 350 degree oven for around 50 to 60 minutes or until layers pull away from sides and are tested for doneness with a cake tester. Remove to cake racks and cool for several minutes before removing from pans. Cool and then frost with Cream Cheese Frosting.

Cream Cheese Frosting:

1/2 cup butter, softened
1 (8-ounce) package
  cream cheese, softened
1 pound box
  confectioners sugar

1 teaspoon pure vanilla
  extract
1 cup pecans, chopped

Cream butter and cream cheese until light and fluffy. Add sugar and blend in thoroughly. Stir in vanilla until smooth and creamy; add the pecans and mix well. Frost in between cake layers and on top and sides.

Outstanding flavor!

SOUR CREAM COFFEE CAKE

Cake:

1 cup butter, softened
2 cups granulated sugar
2 large eggs
2 cups cake flour
1 teaspoon baking powder
1/4 teaspoon salt

1 (8-ounce) carton sour
  cream
1 teaspoon pure vanilla
  extract
Confectioners sugar

Grease and flour a Bundt pan and set aside. Cream butter and sugar until well blended; add eggs and beat thoroughly. Sift together the dry ingredients and add alternately with the sour cream; stir in the vanilla. Spoon 1/2 of the batter into the prepared pan; sprinkle over this 1/2 of the topping. Add rest of batter and top with remaining topping ingredients. Bake at 350 degrees for around 1 hour or until cake tests done. Cool 5 to 10 minutes before removing from pan. Sprinkle while still warm with confectioners sugar, if desired.

Topping:

2 tablespoons
  granulated sugar
1/2 teaspoon ground
  cinnamon

1 cup pecans, finely
  chopped

· Combine all ingredients; mix until well blended.

FLUFFY CHOCOLATE CAKE

Cake:

2 cups light brown
  sugar, packed and
  divided
1 cup buttermilk,
  divided
3 squares unsweetened
  chocolate

1/2 cup butter, softened
3 large eggs
1 teaspoon pure vanilla
  extract
2 cups cake flour
1/4 teaspoon salt
1 teaspoon baking soda

Heat 1 cup sugar, 1/2 cup buttermilk and the chocolate in small saucepan, stirring just until chocolate melts; cool. Cream the butter, gradually adding the remaining sugar until well blended. Add eggs, one at a time, beating well after each addition. Add the chocolate mixture and vanilla and beat until mixed thoroughly. Sift together the dry ingredients and add alternately with remaining buttermilk, blending well. Spoon into 2 greased and floured 9-inch baking pans. Bake at 350 degrees for around 30 minutes or until cakes test done with a cake tester. Cool in pans on a cake rack for several minutes before removing to complete cooling. Ice with Fluffy Chocolate Icing.

Fluffy Chocolate Icing:

2 large egg whites
1-1/2 cups granulated
  sugar
5 tablespoons cold water
1 tablespoon white
  corn syrup

1 teaspoon pure vanilla
  extract
2 ounces unsweetened
  chocolate, melted

Combine egg whites, sugar, water and syrup in top of double boiler; beat over boiling water for 7 minutes until stiff; cool. Add vanilla and gently stir in melted chocolate. Spread between layers, on top and sides of cake immediately.

14 CARAT CAKE

Cake:

1-1/2 cups vegetable oil
2 cups granulated sugar
4 large eggs
2-1/2 cups cake flour,
  sifted
2 teaspoons baking
  powder
1-1/2 teaspoons baking
  soda

1-1/2 teaspoons salt
2 teaspoons ground
  cinnamon
2 cups carrots, finely
  grated
1 (8-ounce) can crushed
  pineapple, well
  drained
1-1/2 cups pecans, chopped

Beat the oil and sugar until well mixed; add eggs, one at a time, beating well after each addition. Sift together the dry ingredients. Add the flour mixture to the creamed mixture, beating until well blended. Add the carrots, pineapple and pecans, stirring to combine thoroughly. Spoon into 3 9-inch greased and floured cake pans. Bake at 350 degrees for around 35 to 40 minutes or until tests done. Cool completely and then spread frosting between layers and on top and sides.

Cream Cheese Frosting:

1/2 cup butter, softened
1 (8-ounce) package
  cream cheese,
  softened

1 teaspoon pure vanilla
  extract
1 (16-ounce) box
  confectioners sugar

Cream the butter and cream cheese; blend in the vanilla. Add the confectioners sugar and beat until smooth.

SPICE CAKE NO. 1

Cake:

2 cups all-purpose
  flour, unsifted
1 teaspoon baking powder
1 teaspoon baking soda
Dash salt
1/2 teaspoon ground
  allspice
1/4 teaspoon ground
  nutmeg
1 teaspoon grated
  orange rind

1 cup butter, softened
1-1/2 cups granulated
  sugar
2 large eggs
1 teaspoon pure vanilla
  extract
1/2 cup orange juice,
  freshly squeezed
1/2 cup whole milk

Combine the flour, baking powder, soda, salt, spices and rind; set aside. Cream the butter well, gradually adding the sugar until thoroughly mixed. Add eggs, one at a time, beating well after each addition: stir in the vanilla and juice. Add the flour mixture alternately with the milk, beating just until well blended. Spoon into 2 greased and floured 8-inch baking pans. Bake at 350 degrees for around 30 minutes or until cakes test done with a cake tester. Cool on cake racks for 10 minutes, then remove from pans to cool completely before frosting.

Frosting:

1 (3-ounce) package
  cream cheese,
  softened
2 cups confectioners
  sugar, packed
1-1/2 tablespoons
  orange juice,
  freshly squeezed

1/2 teaspoon grated
  orange rind
1/4 teaspoon ground
  nutmeg

Beat the cream cheese until smooth; gradually add the sugar until blended. Add orange juice, rind and nutmeg; beat until thoroughly mixed. Spread in between layers and on top layer.

APPLE CARROT CAKE

2/3 cup butter, softened
1 cup granulated sugar
2 large eggs, beaten
1-1/4 cups all-purpose
  flour
1 teaspoon baking soda
1 teaspoon baking
  powder
1 teaspoon ground
  cinnamon
1/2 teaspoon ground
  nutmeg

1/2 teaspoon salt
1 cup carrots, finely
  grated
1/2 cup apple, finely
  grated
3 tablespoons orange
  juice, freshly
  squeezed
1/2 cup pecans, chopped
Confectioners sugar,
  for garnish

Cream butter and gradually add the sugar until thoroughly blended. Add eggs, one at a time, beating well after each addition. Sift together the dry ingredients and stir into the creamed mixture well. Stir in the carrots, apple, juice and pecans. Spoon into a greased and floured 8-inch square baking pan. Bake at 325 degrees for around 50 minutes or until cake tests done with a cake tester. Cool completely on a cake rack, then sprinkle with sifted confectioners sugar. Cut into squares.

PINEAPPLE CAKE

Cake:

1 cup butter, softened
2 cups granulated sugar
5 large eggs
1 teaspoon pure vanilla
  extract

3-1/2 cups cake flour
3 teaspoons baking
  powder
1/2 teaspoon salt
1 cup whole milk

Cream butter until light and fluffy; add sugar gradually, beating well. Add eggs, one at a time, beating well after each addition. Blend in the vanilla. Sift together the flour, baking powder and salt; add alternately with the milk, beginning and ending with the flour mixture. Grease and flour 3 or 4 9-inch cake pans. Spoon the mixture into the prepared pans. Bake at 350 degrees for around 30 to 35 minutes or until cakes test done and are golden brown. Cool on wire racks for around 5 minutes. Remove from pans and continue to cool on the wire racks until you are ready to fill and frost the cake.

Pineapple Filling and Frosting:

1-1/2 cups granulated
  sugar
4 tablespoons all-
  purpose flour,
  sifted

6 large egg yolks
3/4 cup butter, melted
1 (20-ounce) can crushed
  pineapple, well
  drained.

Combine all ingredients in top of double boiler; cook over hot water until thickened. Cool and spread on cooled layers, top and sides.

Wonderful flavor!

BLACK WALNUT CAKE NO. 1

3/4 cup butter, softened
2 cups granulated sugar
4 large eggs
3 cups cake flour
1 teaspoon baking powder

1 cup whole milk
1 teaspoon pure
  vanilla extract
2 cups black walnuts,
  chopped fine

Cream the butter until light and fluffy. Gradually add the sugar until thoroughly blended. Add the eggs, one at a time, beating well after each addition. Sift together the flour and baking powder; add alternately with the milk and vanilla until well blended. Stir in the walnuts. Grease a Bundt pan or 2 loaf pans and spoon in the mixture. Bake at 350 degrees for around 1 hour or until tests done with a cake tester.

The aroma is unforgettable!

VANILLA CAKE

Layers:

1 cup butter, softened	3 teaspoons baking
2 cups granulated sugar	powder
5 large eggs	1 tablespoon pure
3 cups cake flour,	vanilla extract
sifted	1 cup whole milk

Cream butter until light and fluffy; add sugar gradually, beating well. Add eggs, one at a time, beating well after each addition. Sift together the flour and baking powder; add alternately with the flavoring and milk, beginning and ending with the flour mixture. Grease and flour 4 9-inch baking pans and spoon in the mixture. Bake at 350 degrees for around 30 minutes or until layers test done with a cake tester. Leave in pans on cake rack for several minutes and then remove to racks to cool. Spread with Cream Nut Filling.

Cream Nut Filling:

2-3/4 cups granulated	1 teaspoon white
sugar	corn syrup
1 (12-ounce) can	1 cup pecans, chopped
evaporated milk	fine
1 (6 ounce) can	
evaporated milk	

Combine the sugar, milk and syrup; cook, stirring until thickened. Add the pecans. When layers are cool, spread each layer with the cooled filling.

Creamy and good!

APPLE CHIP CAKE

1-1/2 cups vegetable oil	1 teaspoon baking soda
2 cups granulated sugar	1 tablespoon ground
2 large eggs	cinnamon
2 teaspoons pure	1/2 teaspoon salt
vanilla extract	3 cups apple, chopped
3 cups cake flour,	or cubed
measure before	1 cup pecans, chopped
sifting	

Beat oil and sugar until blended well. Add eggs, one at a time, beating well after each addition. Add vanilla and stir to blend. Sift together the flour, soda, cinnamon and salt. Add to creamed mixture and mix well. Fold in apple and pecans. Spoon into a greased and floured 10-inch tube pan and bake at 300 degrees for around 1-1/2 hours or until cake tests done with a cake tester.

SPICE CAKE NO. 2

Cake:

1/2 cup butter, softened
1 cup granulated sugar
1/2 cup light brown
  sugar, packed
2 large eggs
1 teaspoon pure vanilla
  extract
1/2 teaspoon pure
  lemon extract
2-1/2 cups cake flour
1 teaspoon baking
  powder

1 teaspoon baking soda
1 teaspoon ground
  cinnamon
1/4 teaspoon ground
  ginger
1/4 teaspoon ground
  cloves
1 teaspoon ground
  nutmeg
1-1/4 cups buttermilk

Cream butter until light and fluffy; gradually add sugars until well blended. Add eggs, one at a time, beating well after each addition. Stir in flavorings. Sift together the flour, baking powder, soda and spices. Add alternately with buttermilk, blending thoroughly. Spoon into 2 greased and floured 9-inch cake pans. Bake at 350 degrees for around 30 minutes or until cakes test done with a cake tester. Cool on cake racks for around 5 minutes, then turn out on cake racks to complete cooling. Frost.

Frosting:

2 large egg whites
1-1/2 cups light brown
  sugar, packed
1/3 cup cold water
1 tablespoon white
  corn syrup

1/2 teaspoon salt
1 teaspoon pure
  vanilla extract

Combine all ingredients in top of double boiler; beat for 1 minute, then beat over boiling water for around 7 minutes or until peaks form. Remove from heat and continue beating, if necessary, to reach spreading consistency.

BLACK WALNUT CAKE NO. 2

1/2 cup butter, softened
2 cups light brown
   sugar, well packed
3 egg yolks, lightly
   beaten
2 cups cake flour
1/2 teaspoon salt
3 teaspoons baking
   powder

1 cup whole milk
1 teaspoon pure
   vanilla extract
1 cup black walnuts,
   finely chopped
3 egg whites, stiffly
   beaten

Cream butter and sugar until well blended; add egg yolks and mix well. Sift together the dry ingredients and add alternately with the milk and vanilla. Stir in the walnuts. Fold in the egg whites. Pour into a greased 10-inch tube pan and bake at 350 degrees for around 45 minutes or until cake tests done.

APPLE CAKE

4 apples, pared
   and diced
5 tablespoons granulated
   sugar
2 teaspoons ground
   cinnamon
1 cup vegetable oil
2 cups granulated sugar
4 large eggs

3 cups cake flour
1 teaspoon salt
3 teaspoons baking
   powder
2-1/2 teaspoons pure
   vanilla extract
1/4 cup freshly squeezed
   orange juice
1 cup walnuts, chopped

Mix together the apples, sugar and cinnamon; set aside. Blend together the oil and sugar; add the eggs, one at a time, beating well after each addition. Sift together the flour, salt and baking powder and add alternately with the vanilla and orange juice. Stir in the walnuts. Grease and flour a 10-inch tube pan. Spoon the batter alternately with the apple mixture, beginning and ending with the batter. Bake at 350 degrees for around 1-1/2 hours or until cake tests done.

Delicious served as coffee cake, or as cake for dessert!

Candy and Cookies

Candy is a source of quick energy and is sometimes needed during extremely strenuous days. Yes, there is a place for candy in our diets as long as it does not interfere with regular meals. So, make a batch of good homemade candy and satisfy a "sweet tooth" once in a while!

CANDY STRAWBERRIES

1 (6-ounce) package
   strawberry gelatin
   dessert
1 cup pecans, ground
1 cup coconut, ground
3/4 cup sweetened
   condensed milk

1/2 teaspoon pure vanilla
   extract
Red sugar crystals
Slivered almonds
Green food coloring

Combine the gelatin, pecans, coconut, milk and flavoring until well blended. Shape into strawberries and chill thoroughly for several hours. Roll in sugar crystals until coated well. Tint slivered almonds a delicate green; use for stems and leaves of strawberries.

These are not only pretty but taste good!

CARAMELS

2 cups granulated sugar
1-3/4 cups dark corn
   syrup
1 cup butter
2 cups whipping cream
   (divided)

1 teaspoon pure vanilla
   extract
1 cup pecans, chopped

Combine sugar, syrup, butter and 1 cup cream. Stir until mixture begins to boil. Add rest of cream very slowly and continue to boil. Cook until mixture forms a hard ball when dropped into cold water. This cooking process will take between 45 minutes to 1 hour. Slowly stir in vanilla and pecans, but do not beat the mixture. Turn into buttered 13 x 9 x 3/4-inch pan. Completely cool and then cut into small cubes; wrap in waxed paper or plastic wrap.

Yummy!

PEANUT BRITTLE

2 cups granulated sugar
1 cup white corn syrup
1/2 cup hot water

1/2 teaspoon salt
2-1/2 cups raw peanuts
1 tablespoon baking soda

Combine the sugar, syrup, water and salt in large saucepan. Bring to a rolling boil and then add the peanuts; cook slowly until peanuts are a golden brown and syrup spins a thread. If using a candy thermometer, remove from heat when syrup reaches 293 degrees. Add baking soda and beat rapidly. Pour on a buttered baking sheet; spread to 1/4 inch thickness. When cooled, break into pieces. Store in airtight container lined with waxed paper.

Make some for yourself and for gifts!

CHOCOLATE FUDGE

4 cups granulated sugar
1 (12-ounce) can evaporated
  milk
1/2 cup butter
1 (8-ounce) package semi-sweet
  chocolate chips

1 (8-ounce) package
  marshmallows
1 teaspoon pure vanilla extract
1 cup pecans, chopped

Combine the sugar, milk and butter in large saucepan. Bring to a boil and cook to soft ball stage, stirring frequently to prevent burning. Remove from heat and add the chocolate chips, marshmallows and vanilla. Beat until thickened. Add the pecans, blending well. Pour into a buttered pan. Let cool and cut into squares.

Rich and very good!

CREAMY CHOCOLATE FUDGE

2 cups granulated sugar
1 cup water
1 cup sweetened condensed
  milk
3 squares unsweetened
  chocolate, cut in small
  pieces

2 teaspoons pure vanilla
  extract
1 cup pecans, chopped

Combine sugar and water in a large saucepan and bring to a boil, stirring constantly. Add milk and cook over low heat until mixture forms a firm ball in cold water, stirring constantly to prevent scorching. Remove from heat and add chocolate pieces. Stir until chocolate dissolves completely, then add the vanilla and pecans. Beat until thick and creamy. Pour into buttered dish. When cooled, cut in squares.

Easy to make and flavorful!

DIVINITY-NUT FUDGE

2-1/2 cups granulated sugar
1/2 cup white corn syrup
1/2 cup water
1/4 teaspoon salt
2 large egg whites
1 teaspoon pure vanilla extract

1 cup pecans or walnuts,
  chopped
Candied cherry halves,
  optional
Pecan or walnut halves,
  optional

Combine the sugar, syrup, water and salt in large saucepan; cook over medium heat, stirring constantly, until mixture comes to a boil. Reduce heat and cook, without stirring, until temperature reaches 265 degrees on a candy thermometer. While syrup is cooking, beat egg whites in a large mixer bowl until stiff and shiny (not dry). Pour syrup in a thin stream over egg whites while beating constantly at high speed. Beat until mixture begins to lose its gloss; stir in vanilla and nuts. Drop by teaspoonfuls onto waxed paper. For pastel candies, add a few drops of food coloring along with the vanilla. Garnish with pecan or walnut halves or candied cherry halves, if desired.

A real treat!

DREAM BALLS

1/2 cup butter, softened
2 pounds confectioners sugar
1 (14-ounce) can sweetened
  condensed milk
2 cups pecans, chopped
1/4 pound parafin wax

4 squares unsweetened
  chocolate or
1 (12-ounce) package semi-
  sweet chocolate chips,
  melted

Mix together the butter, sugar, milk and pecans. Grease hands with butter and make into balls. Chill thoroughly. Melt parafin in double boiler; add melted chocolate and blend. Using toothpick to hold candy balls, dip each ball into hot chocolate mixture. Place on waxed paper to cool.

Better than any candy you can buy!

PECAN LOG ROLL

1 cup whipping cream,
   unwhipped
2 cups granulated sugar
1 cup light brown sugar, packed
1/8 teaspoon salt

1/2 cup white corn syrup
Confectioners sugar
1 cup pecans, chopped
1/2 cup pecans, chopped very
   fine

Combine the cream, sugars, salt and syrup in a large saucepan. Bring to a boil and cook to hard boil stage, 250° to 265° on candy thermometer. When dropped in cup of cold water will form a ball that remains brittle when removed from water. Cool to room temperature and beat until creamy. Turn onto surface dusted with confectioners sugar and add 1 cup chopped pecans. Knead until firm enough to roll, blending in pecans. Shape into roll and cover outside with the finely chopped pecans. Let cool until hardened. Slice with a sharp knife to serve.

Delicious candy!

PENUCHE

1-3/4 cups light brown sugar,
   packed
1 tablespoon white corn syrup
1 tablespoon butter

3/4 cup evaporated milk
1/4 cup water
1 teaspoon pure vanilla extract
1 cup pecans, chopped

Combine sugar, syrup, butter, milk and water in a large saucepan. Cook to soft ball stage, stirring constantly. Cool and beat until thickened. Add vanilla and nuts and turn into a buttered pan. Refrigerate and then cut into squares when cooled completely.

Creamy and good!

POTATO CANDY

1 medium white potato, boiled
   and peeled
1 pound confectioners sugar

1/2 teaspoon pure vanilla
   extract
Peanut butter, creamy

Beat cooked potato in small mixer bowl until all lumps are gone. Add sugar and vanilla until blended. If mixture is too stiff, add 1 teaspoon milk. Roll out on lightly floured surface; spread with peanut butter. Roll up like jelly roll and cut into circles.

Good flavor!

PEANUT BUTTER BALLS

1-1/2 cups crunchy peanut
  butter
2 cups butter
1 teaspoon pure vanilla extract
2-1/2 pounds confectioners
  sugar

1 (4-ounce) cake parafin wax
1 (12-ounce) package semi-
  sweet chocolate morsels

Melt peanut butter and butter in large saucepan over low heat. Remove from heat and stir in vanilla. Add sugar and mix well. Shape into 1-inch balls. Melt chocolate and parafin over low heat. Dip each ball with a toothpick into chocolate mixture and cool on waxed paper. Reheat chocolate if it thickens.

Better than store bought candy!

PRALINES

1 cup light brown sugar, packed
2 cups granulated sugar
3 tablespoons white corn syrup
3/4 cup evaporated milk

1/2 cup water
2 teaspoons maple syrup
1 cup pecans, chopped
Pecan halves

Combine sugars, corn syrup, milk, water and maple syrup in a large saucepan; cook to soft ball stage, stirring frequently. Remove from heat and cool slightly. Add chopped pecans and beat until stiff; drop from spoon onto buttered waxed paper, making patties. Press pecan halves into top of each praline. Wrap in waxed paper until ready to serve.

Delicious candy!

TOFFEE

1/2 cup butter
2/3 cup light brown sugar,
  packed

1 cup pecans, chopped
1/2 cup chocolate or
  butterscotch chips

Butter a 9 x 9 x 2-inch dish and set aside. Melt butter in medium saucepan and add brown sugar; stir until dissolved. Bring to a boil over medium heat and boil for around 7 minutes, stirring constantly. Keep heat high enough to maintain a boil but do not burn. Spread pecans in buttered dish; pour cooked mixture over pecans. Sprinkle chips over mixture and cover pan to soften chips, then spread chips out evenly over top. Cut into squares while slightly soft. When prepared properly this will be fairly brittle.

A snap to make!

Cookies are by definition small, sweet, usually flat cakes. *Cookies* are not defined as nostalgic, but who among us does not remember making **cookies** as a child, or watching someone in the kitchen make our favorite recipe of **cookies**. The aroma is heavenly. Make some **cookies** for someone today!

BUTTER COOKIES NO. 1

1 cup butter, softened
1 cup granulated sugar
2 large egg yolks
1 teaspoon pure vanilla extract

2-1/2 cups all-purpose flour
1 ounce semi-sweet chocolate
(melted)

Cream butter thoroughly in large mixer bowl; add sugar and continue beating until light and fluffy. Add egg yolks, one at a time, beating well after each addition. Blend in the vanilla and beat well. Stir in flour and mix thoroughly. Remove half the dough for plain cookies. Blend chocolate into other half. Make small round balls and press with a fork, fingers or cookie press onto ungreased baking sheet. Bake at 400 degrees for around 10 minutes. Makes around 4 dozen cookies. Add nuts, if desired.

Easy and so delicious!

BUTTER COOKIES NO. 2

1-1/2 cups butter, softened
2 cups granulated sugar
2 large eggs
4 cups all-purpose flour

3 teaspoons baking powder
2 teaspoons pure vanilla extract
1 cup pecans, chopped

Cream butter in large mixer bowl until light and fluffy. Gradually beat in the sugar, blending well. Add the eggs, one at a time, beating well after each addition. Sift together the flour and baking powder; add alternately with the vanilla. Stir in the pecans until blended throughout the batter. Roll in waxed paper and place in refrigerator overnight. When ready to bake, cut in slices and place on ungreased baking sheet; bake for 10 to 12 minutes in 350 degree oven until browned. Cool; then remove from baking sheet to cookie tin or serving plate.

Good!

BUTTER CRISPS

1/2 cup butter, softened
1 cup granulated sugar
1 large egg yolk
2 teaspoons pure vanilla extract

2 cups all-purpose flour, sifted
1 large egg white, slightly
   beaten
1 cup pecans, chopped

Cream the butter and sugar in a large mixer bowl; beat in the egg yolk until blended; stir in the vanilla. Add the flour and beat until mixture is combined well. Lightly grease 2 large shallow pans with sides. Spread batter in pans; layers will be thin. Lightly beat egg white until frothy; spread over top, then evenly sprinkle pecans. Bake at 250 degrees for around 45 minutes to 1 hour. Cut in small pieces.

Crisp and delicious!

BUTTERSCOTCH-OATMEAL CRISPS

2-1/4 cups all-purpose flour
1 teaspoon baking soda
1 teaspoon salt
1 cup butter, softened
1 cup granulated sugar
1 cup light brown sugar, packed

2 large eggs
1 teaspoon pure vanilla extract
3 cups quick oats
1 cup pecans, chopped
   or 1 cup flaked coconut

Sift together the flour, soda and salt; set aside. Cream the butter until light and fluffy. Gradually add the sugars until well blended. Add eggs, one at a time, beating well after each addition. Stir in the vanilla. Blend in the dry ingredients gradually until thoroughly mixed. Stir in the oats and pecans or coconut. Chill in the bowl for 1 hour. Remove from refrigerator and divide dough in half. Shape into rolls, 1-1/2 inches in diameter. Wrap in aluminum foil. Chill at least 2 hours or overnight. When ready to bake, cut into slices around 1/4 inch thick and place on a greased baking sheet. Bake at 350 degrees for 10 to 12 minutes; remove from pan immediately.

Crisp and good!

PEANUT BUTTER COOKIES

1/4 cup butter, softened
1/4 cup vegetable shortening
1/2 cup creamy peanut butter
1/2 cup granulated sugar
1/2 cup light brown sugar,
   packed

l large egg, slightly beaten
1-1/2 cups all-purpose flour
1/4 teaspoon salt
1/2 teaspoon baking powder
3/4 teaspoon baking soda

Cream the butter, shortening and peanut butter in large mixer bowl; add the sugars and beat well; add egg and beat until combined. Sift together the dry ingredients and blend into creamed mixture. Chill dough in refrigerator. Roll into 1-1/4 inch balls. Place 3 inches apart on lightly greased baking sheet. Flatten with fork crisscross style. Dip fork in flour to prevent sticking. Bake at 375 degrees for around 10 to 12 minutes.

Nutritious and good!

PECAN MACAROONS

1 large egg white
1 cup dark brown sugar, packed

1 teaspoon pure vanilla extract
2 cups pecans, chopped fine

Beat egg white until stiff; add sugar, vanilla and pecans, blending well. Drop by teaspoonfuls onto a greased baking sheet and bake at 275 degrees for around 20 minutes.

These won't last long!

PRALINE SQUARES

30 graham cracker squares
1 cup butter, melted
1 cup light brown sugar, packed

1 cup pecans, chopped

Place graham cracker squares on ungreased baking sheet. Melt butter and mix in sugar until dissolved. Stir in pecans. Spread mixture on crackers. Bake at 350 degrees for 10 minutes. Cool for at least 30 minutes and cut or break into bite size pieces.

Quick and easy!

OLD FASHIONED TEA CAKES

1 cup butter, softened
2 cups granulated sugar
2 large eggs

1 teaspoon pure vanilla extract
Dash of salt
All-purpose flour, sifted

Cream butter until light and fluffy; gradually add sugar until well blended. Add eggs, one at a time, beating well after each addition. Add the vanilla and salt; blend well. Stir in enough flour, gradually, to make a medium stiff dough. Roll dough out on a lightly floured surface about 1/4 inch thick. Cut with a cookie cutter. Bake at 350 degrees for around 15 minutes or until lightly browned. Watch carefully!

SUGAR COOKIES

2 large eggs
1 cup butter, melted
4 cups all-purpose flour
1-1/2 cups granulated sugar
1/3 teaspoon baking soda

1 teaspoon salt
3 teaspoons baking powder
2 tablespoons heavy cream
1 teaspoon pure vanilla extract

Beat the eggs in a large mixer bowl; add melted butter, blending well. Sift together the flour, sugar, soda, salt, and baking powder; add to the butter-egg mixture, blending well. Add the cream and vanilla. Place in refrigerator for several hours until cold. Roll out on a floured board or cloth in thin layer and cut into desired shapes. Lift these out with a spatula onto an ungreased baking sheet. Place in a 325 degree oven and then reduce heat to 300 degrees. Bake for 15 minutes or until done. Remove from pan immediately and sprinkle with red or green granulated sugar if desired, or just plain granulated sugar.

Delicious cookies and can be made into any shape!

DROP SUGAR COOKIES

1/2 cup butter, softened
1/2 cup vegetable shortening
1 cup granulated sugar
1 large egg
1 teaspoon pure vanilla extract
or 1 teaspoon lemon extract

2-1/2 cups all-purpose flour,
sifted
1/2 teaspoon baking soda
2 tablespoons whole milk

Cream together the butter and shortening until light and fluffy. Gradually add the sugar, beating well. Beat in the egg and then add the flavoring. Sift together the flour and baking soda; add alternately with the milk until smooth. Drop by teaspoonfuls on greased baking sheet. Flatten with bottom of glass dipped in granulated sugar. Bake at 400 degrees for around 12 minutes or until brown around edges. Makes about 5 dozen cookies.

A memorable cookie!

TEA CAKES

1 cup butter, softened
1-1/2 cups granulated sugar
3 large eggs
3 cups all-purpose flour

3 teaspoons baking powder
1/2 teaspoon salt
1 tablespoon pure vanilla
extract

Cream together the butter and sugar; add eggs, one at a time, beating well after each addition. Blend in the sifted dry ingredients and then stir in the vanilla. Drop by tablespoonfuls onto a greased baking sheet. Bake at 375 degrees for 10 to 12 minutes or until golden brown.

OLD FASHIONED SUGAR COOKIES

1/2 cup vegetable shortening
1 cup granulated sugar
2 large eggs
2 cups all-purpose flour
1 teaspoon baking powder
1/2 teaspoon baking soda
1/2 teaspoon salt
2 tablespoons whole milk
1 teaspoon pure vanilla extract
1 teaspoon lemon extract or
   fresh lemon juice

Cream the shortening and then add the sugar gradually, beating until very light. Add eggs, one at a time, beating well after each addition. Sift together flour, baking powder, soda and salt. Add flour mixture and milk to first mixture and then stir in the flavorings. Dough will be stiff. Place by teaspoonfuls on ungreased baking sheet and flatten with the bottom of a glass dipped in granulated sugar. Bake at 375 degrees for around 8 to 10 minutes or until done.

Very tasty!

WEDDING COOKIES

1 cup butter, softened
6 tablespoons confectioners
   sugar
2 cups all-purpose flour,
   measure before sifting
2 teaspoons pure vanilla
   extract
2 cups pecans, chopped
Confectioners sugar

Cream butter until light and fluffy; add sugar and blend. Beat in flour, then vanilla. Stir in the pecans until mixed throughout. Form into crescent shapes using 1 teaspoonful batter. Place on ungreased cookie sheet and bake at 325 degrees until lightly browned; start checking at around 10 minutes. Remove from oven and slide off cookie sheet gently with a spatula onto waxed paper. Cool slightly and sift powdered sugar over cookies on all sides. Turn over gently until well covered. Store in airtight cookie tin until ready to serve.

These will melt in your mouth!

CARROT COOKIES

Cookies:

2/3 cup vegetable shortening
1 cup granulated sugar
2 cups cooked carrots, mashed
1 large egg, beaten
2 cups all-purpose flour

1-1/2 teaspoons baking soda
1/2 teaspoon baking powder
1/2 teaspoon pure lemon
extract
1 teaspoon pure vanilla extract

Cream shortening and sugar in large mixer bowl; add carrots and egg; beat until blended. Sift together the flour, soda and baking powder; stir into carrot mixture. Blend in the flavorings. Drop by teaspoonfuls onto a greased cookie sheet. Bake at 375 degrees for 10 minutes. When cooled, drizzle the frosting over cookies. Yields: 4 dozen cookies.

Frosting:

1-1/2 cups confectioners sugar, packed
Juice and grated rind of 1 orange

Combine and beat the sugar, juice and rind until blended and smooth. Drizzle over cookies when cooled.

CHERRY COOKIES

3/4 cup butter, softened
1/2 cup granulated sugar
1 teaspoon pure vanilla extract
2 tablespoons maraschino
cherry juice
2 cups all-purpose flour, sifted
2 teaspoons baking powder

1 teaspoon ground cinnamon
Dash salt
1/4 cup maraschino cherries,
chopped and well drained
1 cup coconut, grated or flaked
Maraschino cherry halves, well
drained

Cream the butter and sugar in large mixer bowl until well blended. Stir in the vanilla and cherry juice. Sift together the flour, baking powder, cinnamon and salt; add to the butter mixture, mixing well. Add the chopped cherries and coconut, blending in thoroughly. Shape into 1-inch balls and place on an ungreased baking sheet. Top each ball with a cherry half and bake at 375 degrees for around 15 minutes or until browned.

Delectable!

CHOCOLATE CREAM COOKIES

2 squares unsweetened
   chocolate
1-3/4 cups all-purpose flour
1/2 teaspoon baking soda
1/2 teaspoon salt
2/3 cup butter, softened

1-1/3 cups granulated sugar
1 teaspoon pure vanilla extract
1 large egg
1/2 cup sour cream
1/2 cup pecans, chopped

Melt chocolate in small saucepan and set aside to cool. Sift flour, baking soda and salt together; set aside. Cream the butter until light and fluffy; gradually add the sugar beating until well blended. Stir in the vanilla, then beat in the egg until well mixed. Add the cooled chocolate, then blend in the sour cream. Add the flour mixture, mixing well. Stir in the pecans. Drop by teaspoonfuls 2 inches apart onto greased baking sheet. Bake around 9 or 10 minutes or just until done. Remove immediately to cake rack for 2 or 3 minutes, then remove cookies to rack to cool completely. Serve or store in an air-tight cookie tin with waxed paper between layers.

Fine flavor!

CHOCOLATE-OATMEAL COOKIES

4 tablespoons butter, melted
2 cups granulated sugar
1/2 cup whole milk
5 tablespoons cocoa

3 cups quick oats
1 tablespoon pure vanilla
   extract

Melt butter in medium saucepan; add sugar and milk; bring to a boil. Cook, stirring, for 1 minute. Remove from heat and add cocoa, oats and vanilla, blending well. Drop by teaspoonfuls onto waxed paper; let set. Store in cookie tin.

CHURCH WINDOWS

1 (12-ounce) package chocolate
   morsels
1/2 cup butter
1 (10-1/2 -ounce) package
   miniature marshamallows,
   multicolored

1 cup pecans, finely chopped
Grated coconut

Melt chocolate and butter in large saucepan over low heat. Remove from heat and add marshmallows and pecans. Shape into 2 rolls 2 inches in diameter; roll in grated or flaked coconut. Refrigerate 6 to 8 hours or overnight. Slice into 1/2 inch slices.

Surprisingly good!

COCONUT-DATE BALLS

1 large egg, well beaten
1 cup granulated sugar
1 (8-ounce) box chopped dates
1 teaspoon pure vanilla extract
1 cup coconut, grated fresh or
    frozen

2-1/4 cups rice crispies
1 cup pecans, chopped fine
Confectioners sugar

Combine egg, sugar and dates in medium saucepan; cook over medium heat until dates are melted. Remove and add vanilla, coconut, rice crispies and pecans. Form small balls with hands and roll in confectioners sugar. Store in airtight container until ready to serve.

A wonderful addition to a Holiday table!

COCONUT SNACKS

8 slices white bread, slightly
    stale
1 cup sweetened condensed
    milk

1-1/2 cups coconut, grated
    fresh or frozen, thawed

Cut bread slices into 4 or 5 strips. Dip into milk, then into coconut; cover all sides. Place on a greased baking sheet and bake in a 325 degree oven for around 10 to 15 minutes or until lightly browned. Remove from pan immediately and place on a cake rack to cool. For variation, you may want to add ground pecans to the coconut or omit the coconut and use only the ground pecans or other nuts.

A quick snack!

CONGO BARS

2/3 cup butter
1 (1-pound) box light brown
    sugar
3 large eggs
2-2/3 cups all-purpose flour

2-1/2 teaspoons baking powder
1/2 teaspoon salt
1 cup semi-sweet chocolate
    chips
1 cup pecans, chopped

Melt butter in large saucepan; add sugar and blend well; cool. Beat in the eggs, one at a time, beating well after each addition. Sift together flour, baking powder and salt; add to the egg mixture. Stir in the chocolate chips and pecans, blending throughout the batter. Pour into a buttered baking pan and bake for 45 to 50 minutes at 350 degrees. Cool and cut into bars.

Rich and good!

CORNFLAKE MACAROONS

2 large egg whites
1 cup granulated sugar
2 cups cornflakes, crushed

1/2 cup pecans, chopped
1 cup flaked coconut
1 teaspoon pure vanilla extract

Beat egg whites until stiff but not dry. Fold in sugar very carefully. Now fold in cornflakes, pecans and coconut; add vanilla and blend. Drop by teaspoonfuls onto a greased baking sheet. Bake at 350 degrees for around 15 to 20 minutes. Remove from oven and place on a very damp towel. Moisture will make cookies turn loose easily.

Crunchy and good!

DATE-NUT BALLS OR FINGERS

1/2 cup butter
1 cup granulated sugar
1 (8-ounce) package pitted
    dates

1 cup rice crispies
1 cup pecans, chopped
1 teaspoon pure vanilla extract
Confectioners sugar, sifted

Melt butter in saucepan; add sugar and dates, stirring until sugar dissolves and dates are smoothly blended. Remove from heat; add rice crispies, pecans and vanilla. Form into finger shapes or balls. Roll in sifted confectioners sugar. Store in airtight container until ready to serve.

DATE-NUT COOKIES

1 cup butter, softened
1-1/2 cups granulated sugar
2 large eggs
3 cups all-purpose flour
1 tablespoon ground cinnamon
1 teaspoon ground cloves

1 teaspoon baking soda,
    dissolved in 2 tablespoons
    molasses
1 pound pitted dates, cut up
1 pound pecans, chopped
Flour

Cream butter in large mixer bowl; add sugar gradually, beating thoroughly. Add eggs, one at a time, beating well after each addition. Sift flour and spices together and then add to the creamed mixture. Add the baking soda and molasses. Dredge the dates and pecans in a small amount of flour, coating well. Blend into the creamed mixture. Drop by teaspoonfuls onto an ungreased baking sheet for around 15 minutes or until done.

You won't have any of these left over!

FRUIT BARS

2 cups pecans, chopped
1/2 cup butter, softened
1-1/2 cups light brown sugar,
    packed
2 large eggs

1 cup all-purpose flour
1 cup candied cherries, finely
    cut
1 cup chopped dates, finely cut

Lightly butter a 9 x 13-inch baking dish; spread pecans over bottom. Cream butter and sugar thoroughly. Add eggs, one at a time, alternating with the flour and beating well. Spread batter over the pecans. Spoon the finely cut cherries and dates over top of batter. Bake at 275 degrees for 1 hour or until done. Cool thoroughly and then cut into bite size pieces.

FUDGE DREAM CAKES

1 cup granulated sugar
2 tablespoons cocoa
1/2 cup butter, melted
2 large egg yolks, slightly
    beaten
1-1/2 cups pecans, finely
    chopped

3/4 cup all-purpose flour
2 large egg whites, stiffly
    beaten
Confectioners sugar

Grease and flour a square or oblong baking pan and set aside. Combine the sugar, cocoa, butter and egg yolks, mixing well. Add the pecans and flour, blending until smooth. Fold in the beaten egg whites. Pour into the prepared pan and bake at 350 degrees for around 30 minutes. Cut in squares and then roll in confectioners sugar.

OATMEAL COOKIES NO. 1

1 cup vegetable shortening
1 cup granulated sugar
1 cup light brown sugar,
    packed
1 teaspoon pure vanilla extract
2 large eggs

1-1/2 cups all-purpose flour,
    sifted
1 teaspoon baking soda
3 cups quick oats
1 cup pecans, chopped

Cream shortening; gradually add sugars, beating well. Stir in vanilla; add eggs, one at a time, beating well after each addition. Sift together the flour and soda; add to mixture, blending well. Stir in the oats and pecans; mix thoroughly. Drop by 1/2 teaspoonfuls onto an ungreased cookie sheet. Bake at 425 degrees for around 7 minutes; test for doneness.

OATMEAL COOKIES NO. 2

1 cup raisins
1/2 cup butter, softened
1 cup granulated sugar
1 egg
1-1/2 cups all-purpose flour
1 teaspoon baking soda
1/4 teaspoon salt

1 teaspoon ground cinnamon
1/2 teaspoon ground nutmeg
2/3 cup buttermilk
1-1/2 teaspoons pure vanilla
  extract
1-1/2 cups quick oats
1/2 cup pecans, chopped

Cover raisins with hot water in small saucepan and simmer for 10 minutes; drain raisins and set aside. Cream butter until fluffy; beat in sugar well. Add egg and continue beating thoroughly. Sift together the flour, soda, salt and spices; add alternately with the buttermilk and vanilla. Add the oats, pecans and raisins; blend throughout the batter. Drop by heaping teaspoonfuls onto greased baking sheet 2 inches apart. Bake for 10 to 12 minutes or until lightly browned. Cool one minute, then remove to cake racks to cool. Serve or store in air tight container with cover. Place waxed paper between layers.

Moist with excellent flavor!

OATMEAL TEACAKES

2-1/2 cups quick oats
1 teaspoon salt
4 tablespoons granulated
  sugar

1/4 cup butter, melted
1 (8-ounce) carton sour cream
Butter, melted
Quick oats

Mix together the oats, salt and sugar. Blend in the butter and mix well. Chill in refrigerator for several hours. Shape the dough into 1-inch balls and place on a lightly greased baking sheet. Flatten with bottom of glass dipped in melted butter, then oats. Bake at 375 degrees for 20 to 25 minutes.

Delicious for breakfast!

LACE COOKIES

2-1/4 cups quick oats
2-1/4 cups light brown sugar,
  packed
3 tablespoons all-purpose flour

1 teaspoon salt
1 cup butter, melted
1 egg, slightly beaten
1 teaspoon pure vanilla extract

Combine the oats, sugar, flour and salt; stir until mixed. Blend in the melted butter, egg and vanilla. Drop by teaspoonfuls onto a buttered baking sheet. Bake at 375 degrees for around 7 minutes or until golden brown.

These will be in high favor with all tasters!

HELLO DOLLIES

1/2 cup butter or margarine
1 cup graham cracker crumbs
1 (3-1/2 -ounce) can flaked
   coconut (1 cup)
1 (6-ounce) package semi-sweet
   chocolate chips
1 (6-ounce) package semi-sweet
   butterscotch chips
1 cup pecans, coarsely broken
1 (14-ounce) can sweetened
   condensed milk

Melt butter in a 13-1/2 x 8-1/2 inch pan. Layer rest of ingredients in order listed; spreading evenly over butter. Bake at 325 degrees for 25 to 35 minutes, or until golden brown. Cool and cut into bars.

A fun dessert!

LEMON BALLS

2-1/2 cups vanilla wafer
   crumbs, rolled fine
1 cup confectioners sugar
1 tablespoon instant coffee
   powder
1/4 cup lemon juice, freshly
   squeezed
1 teaspoon grated lemon rind
3 tablespoons white corn
   syrup
1 cup pecans, finely chopped
Confectioners sugar

Mix together the crumbs, 1 cup sugar, coffee, juice, rind, syrup and pecans. Blend well and shape into small balls. Roll in confectioners sugar. Store in a cookie tin or covered container until ready to serve.

Especially good for summertime parties!

Cereals, Eggs
and Cheese

Cereals include products derived from such grains as barley, corn, oats, rice and wheat. Some of these products are macaroni, noodles, white and wild rice, spaghetti, tapioca, corn meal, crackers and popped corn. Add variety to your breakfast, lunch or dinner menus by serving your family a new cereal dish soon!

BROWN RICE

1/2 cup butter or margarine
1 cup white rice
1 cup onion, chopped
2 (10 3/4-ounce) cans beef
  consommé

1 (4-ounce) can mushroom
  pieces

Melt butter or margarine in medium saucepan; add the rice and onion. Cook and stir until mixture browns, around 15 minutes. Add consommé and mushrooms. Spoon rice mixture into a buttered casserole dish. Bake at 300 degrees for around 1 hour or until set.

A delightful way to serve rice!

CRACKER JACKS

1/4 cup vegetable oil, hot
1 cup popping corn
2 cups granulated sugar
3/4 cup white corn syrup
1/4 teaspoon salt

2 cups raw peanuts, skins on
3 teaspoons baking soda
2 teaspoons pure vanilla
  extract
1 tablespoon butter

Heat oil in large saucepan and pop the popping corn; pour into a large mixing bowl. Combine the sugar, syrup, salt and peanuts; cook, stirring, until mixture comes to a boil. Cook to hard crack stage (300 degrees); syrup, when dropped into cold water, will separate and become hard and brittle. Remove from heat and quickly add the soda, vanilla, and butter. Beat rapidly and quickly pour over the popped corn, mixing until well coated. Turn out on a greased baking sheet to cool. Break into small pieces when completely cooled.

Nice to have on hand for small children!

CREAMY FETTUCINI NO. 1

1 (8-ounce) package fettucini
  noodles, cooked and drained
1/2 cup butter
1 (8-ounce) carton whipping
  cream, unwhipped

1/2 cup grated Parmesan
  cheese

Cook noodles by package directions and drain well. Return to saucepan and stir in butter until melted, without heat. Stir in cream and then cheese until blended. Serve immediately!

So delicious!

CREAMY FETTUCINI NO. 2

1 pound box fettucini noodles, cooked and drained
1 (8-ounce) carton sour cream
1/3 cup butter, melted
1/2 cup grated Parmesan cheese, grated

Cook noodles by package directions and drain well. Return to saucepan; add sour cream, butter and cheese. Stir until noodles are well blended. Serve immediately!

GRITS-EGG CASSEROLE

3/4 cup boiling water
1/3 cup quick grits
1/2 teaspoon salt
2 large eggs, well beaten
3/4 cup milk
1/4 teaspoon ground black pepper
1 cup Cheddar cheese, grated

Bring water to boil, stir in grits and salt; cover and simmer for 2 minutes. Remove from heat. Beat eggs, then stir in the milk and pepper. Add this mixture to the grits, beating in well. Return to heat and add cheese; stir until cheese melts. Spoon mixture into a buttered 8 X 8 X 2-inch baking dish. Bake at 350 degrees for around 15 minutes or until set. Serve hot!

You may want to serve this on special occasions when you have overnight guests...delicious anytime!

MACARONI AND CHEESE

1 cup macaroni
1 large egg, beaten
1 cup whole milk
1/2 teaspoon salt
1/8 teaspoon ground black pepper
2-1/2 cups sharp cheese, grated (divided)
4 tablespoons butter

Cook macaroni by directions on package; drain and set aside. beat egg; add milk, salt and pepper; add 2 cups cheese and pour into a greased casserole dish. Top with remaining cheese. Dot with butter. Bake at 350 degrees for around 30 minutes, or until lightly browned and bubbly hot.

PARMESAN NOODLES

1 (8-ounce) package egg
   noodles

1/4 cup butter
1 cup grated Parmesan cheese

Cook noodles by package directions. Drain thoroughly and stir in butter and cheese until blended. Serve while hot.

RICE AND TOMATOES

8 bacon slices
1 (14-1/2 -ounce) can whole
   tomatoes, mashed fine
1 teaspoon salt
1/2 teaspoon ground black
   pepper

1 cup whole milk
2 tablespoons all-purpose flour
2 cups hot cooked rice

Cook bacon in skillet until crisp. Drain, cool, crumble and set aside. Reserve 3 tablespoons drippings. Blend together the tomatoes, salt, pepper and milk. Brown flour in drippings, stirring constantly; add the tomato mixture and cook, stirring, until thickened. Serve over hot rice and top with crumbled bacon.

Extraordinarily good!

RICE LOAF

2 cups cooked rice
2 tablespoons butter, melted
1 cup dry breadcrumbs
3 tablespoons all-purpose flour
1/2 cup celery, finely cut
1/4 cup green pepper, finely
   cut

1-1/2 teaspoons salt
1/4 teaspoon ground black
   pepper
1 cup whole milk
2 cups pecans, chopped
1 large egg, beaten

Blend together all ingredients in large bowl, mixing thoroughly. Grease a 9 X 5 X 3-inch loaf pan and line with waxed paper. Pack pan with the mixture tightly and bake at 375 degrees for around 1 hour.

The taste will surprise you!

WILD RICE CASSEROLE

1/2 cup butter
1/2 pound mushrooms, sliced
1 cup wild rice
4 tablespoons chives, chopped

3 cups chicken broth
2 tablespoons butter
1/2 cup almonds, slivered

Melt butter in a large skillet; sauté mushrooms, stirring until lightly browned. Remove mushrooms and set aside. Add rice to butter; cook, stirring until rice turns yellow. Add the mushrooms and chives; spoon into a buttered casserole. Pour over the broth. Cover and bake at 325 degrees for around 1 hour. Melt the 2 tablespoons butter and lightly brown the almonds. Add to the baked casserole and lightly stir. Serve while piping hot.

RICE PILAFF

2-1/2 tablespoons butter,
    melted
1 cup raw white rice
2-1/2 cups beef consommé, hot
1/8 teaspoon garlic salt
1/8 teaspoon ground red
    pepper

1/8 teaspoon paprika
1/3 cup celery, finely chopped
1/2 cup carrots, finely chopped
1/3 cup parsley, finely chopped
1/2 cup green onion, finely
    chopped
1/2 cup pecans, chopped

Melt butter and brown rice in a skillet, stirring constantly. Heat consommé and add to rice. Blend in the garlic salt, red pepper and paprika. Spoon into a buttered casserole dish; cover and bake at 375 degrees for around 30 minutes. Remove and add the remaining ingredients, stirring to combine. Return to oven and bake additional 30 minutes.

SPANISH RICE

1 tablespoon butter or
    margarine, melted
1 cup onion, finely chopped
1 cup celery, finely chopped
1/2 cup green pepper, chopped
1 cup tomatoes, mashed

2 cups cooked rice
1 teaspoon oregano
1 teaspoon salt
1/2 teaspoon ground black
    pepper

Melt butter in large saucepan; add onion, celery and green pepper. Stir until lightly browned and tender. Add tomatoes, rice, oregano, salt and pepper. Mix well and spoon into a buttered casserole dish; bake, uncovered, at 350 degrees for 25 to 30 minutes.

Eggs should always be cooked at a low temperature; high heat will cause toughness. Eggs are easily digested and are one of the most widely used and valuable foods in cookery. Include eggs in your menu planning!

CHEESE EGGS

1 cup Cheddar cheese, grated
  and divided
4 large eggs, slightly beaten
1/4 teaspoon salt

1/8 teaspoon ground black
  pepper
3 tablespoons milk or half and
  half

Grease shallow baking dish and spread 1/2 cup grated cheese over bottom. Combine the eggs, salt, pepper and milk. Pour over cheese and top with remaining cheese. Bake at 350 degrees until eggs are set and cheese is lightly browned, around 8 to 10 minutes.

CURRIED EGGS

6 eggs, hard boiled
1/2 teaspoon prepared
  mustard
1/8 teaspoon salt
1/8 teaspoon ground black
  pepper
1/2 teaspoon white vinegar
2 tablespoons mayonnaise
1 teaspoon onion, finely
  chopped or grated
2-1/2 tablespoons all-purpose
  flour

1/4 cup butter, melted and-
  divided
1-1/4 cups whole milk
1 bouillon cube, chicken
  flavored
1/3 teaspoon curry powder
2 slices white bread, cubed
1 tablespoon onion, finely
  chopped or grated

Cut eggs in half lengthwise; carefully remove yolks and mash fine with a fork; add mustard, salt, pepper, vinegar, mayonnaise and the 1 teaspoon onion; mix well. Spoon lightly back into the egg white halves; arrange halves in bottom of a greased, shallow baking dish. Make a white sauce of the flour, 2-1/2 tablespoons of the melted butter, and the milk, then add the bouillon and curry. Spoon over the egg halves and set aside. Combine the bread cubes, onion and remaining 1-1/2 tablespoons melted butter, toss to coat bread cubes. Top egg halves with this mixture. Bake at 350 degrees for 15 minutes or until crumbs are toasted brown. Serve at once.

DEVILED EGGS

Eggs, hard boiled
Salt
Ground black pepper
Celery seed

Dry ground mustard
Mayonnaise
Ground red pepper

Hard boil the number of eggs you will need. Peel and cut lengthwise. Carefully scoop out the yolks into a small mixing bowl and mash with a fork. Season with salt, pepper, celery seed, and dry mustard to taste. Add enough mayonnaise to soften the mixture. Fill whites and sprinkle red pepper over them. Sweet pickle cut up in small pieces is also good with the mixture.

Who can resist deviled eggs?

SAUSAGE AND EGGS

1 pound ground sausage
2 cups sharp cheese, grated
6 slices white bread, quartered
6 large eggs, beaten

1 teaspoon salt
1 teaspoon dry ground
  mustard
2 cups whole milk

Brown sausage in large skillet and drain off grease. Place the browned sausage in a casserole dish. Add the grated cheese and place the bread over top of the cheese. Beat eggs well; add the salt and dry mustard, then the milk. Pour egg-milk mixture over the bread and place in the refrigerator overnight. Bake at 325 degrees for around 1 hour. Serve hot.

Tops in eating pleasure!

Cheese is one of our most important foods and is a nutritious milk product with a unique flavor that is tantalizing. The art of making cheese is believed to have been discovered by Asiatic tribes more than 4,000 years ago. The first dairy cows arrived in America in Jamestown in 1611. Today the United States ranks as the leading cheese-producing country and Wisconsin is the leading cheese-making state. Let's remember these historical facts today as we enjoy the cheese recipes!

QUICHE LORRAINE

1/2 pound bacon, (or 1/4
   pound diced ham)
1 tablespoon margarine
1/2 cup finely chopped onion
1/2 teaspoon dry ground
   mustard
3 eggs, slightly beaten
2 cups whipping cream
   (unwhipped) or half & half

1 teaspoon salt
1/2 pound Swiss cheese (small
   cubes)
1/2 teaspoon ground nutmeg
1/4 teaspoon ground red
   pepper
2 (9-inch) unbaked pie shells

Cook bacon until crisp; crumble and set aside. Melt magarine in saucepan, add onion and sauté until tender. Combine mustard, eggs, cream, salt, cheese, nutmeg and red pepper with the sautéed onion. Spoon into pie shells and bake for 10 minutes at 450 degrees. Reduce heat to 325 degrees and bake until firm (around 20 minutes). Cut in wedges, as you would a pie. Serves 12.

SPINACH QUICHE

2 (9-inch) deep dish pie shells
4 large eggs, beaten
2 cups half and half
1 teaspoon salt
1/4 teaspoon ground white
   pepper

2 tablespoons butter, melted
2 tablespoons green onion,
   minced
1 (10-ounce) package frozen
   chopped spinach, uncooked
1/4 teaspoon ground nutmeg

Bake pie shells in 350 degree oven for 6 to 8 minutes; do not brown. Remove and set aside to cool. Combine eggs, half and half, salt and pepper; mix well and set aside. Melt butter in a large skillet; add the onion and sauté, stirring constantly until tender. Stir into the creamed mixture along with the spinach, thawed and well drained. Blend in the nutmeg. Spoon into pie shells and bake at 425 degrees for 15 minutes; reduce heat to 325 degrees and continue baking for around 35 minutes or until set.

So good!

HAMBURGER QUICHE

1/2 pound ground beef
1/3 cup onion, chopped
1/2 cup whole milk
1 tablespoon cornstarch
1/2 cup mayonnaise

2 large eggs, slightly beaten
2 drops Tabasco sauce
1-1/2 cups Cheddar cheese,
   grated
1 (9-inch) pie shell, unbaked

Brown meat and onion in a large skillet, stirring constantly.

Drain and set aside. Blend together the milk and cornstarch until smooth. Add to meat mixture and stir in the remaining ingredients well. Spoon into pie shell and bake at 350 degrees for 35 to 40 minutes.

CHEESE FONDUE

2 cups whole milk, scalded
1/2 pound sharp American
  cheese, grated
1 tablespoon butter
1 teaspoon salt

1/8 teaspoon ground black
  pepper
3 large eggs, separated
4 slices toasted bread, cubed

Scald milk, remove from heat and stir in cheese, butter and seasonings until cheese melts. Beat egg yolks and slowly stir into milk mixture. Beat egg whites until stiff, then fold in cheese mixture lightly but thoroughly. Place toast cubes in a buttered baking dish. Pour cheese mixture over toast and bake at 350 degrees for 25 to 30 minutes.

CHEESE MOLD

2 tablespoons butter, melted
3 tablespoons all-purpose flour
1 cup whole milk
1/4 pound American cheese,
  grated
1/4 pound Swiss cheese,
  grated

1/2 teaspoon salt
1/8 teaspoon ground red
  pepper
4 large eggs, slightly beaten
1 cup soft bread crumbs

Melt butter in top of a double boiler and blend in flour. Add milk gradually and cook over hot water until mixture is smooth, stirring constantly. Add both the American and Swiss cheese and seasonings and cook until cheese is melted, stirring occasionally. Pour gradually over the beaten eggs and mix well. Fold in crumbs very lightly, but well, and pour into a greased 5-cup mold. Line mold with waxed paper. Set in a pan of hot water and bake at 350 degrees for 30 minutes. Turn out on a platter and fill center with buttered or creamed vegetables.

Desserts

Desserts are served at the end of a meal and make a perfect ending for a delicious meal. I am sure you will recall being told as a child to finish your meal first and then you could have your dessert. Prepare a special dessert to serve soon!

AMBROSIA NO. 1

3 large oranges
3 large Delicious apples
3 large bananas, well ripened
2 cups crushed pineapple, with
  heavy syrup

1/2 cup granulated sugar, or
  to taste
Strawberries or maraschino
  cherries, optional

Pare oranges and remove all white fiber and seeds. Cut crosswise into 1/4-inch slices and then cut into wedges. Pare apples and cut into small cubes; peel and cut bananas crosswise into 1/4-inch slices, then combine and mix well. Add the pineapple and sugar; stir until blended. Chill thoroughly and spoon into sherbets or glass dishes. Garnish with strawberries or cherries, if desired.

A special ending for a special meal!

AMBROSIA NO. 2

5 large oranges
1 cup coconut, grated fresh or
  canned, cut fine with
  kitchen shears

1/2 cup granulated sugar, or
  to taste

Pare oranges and remove all white fiber and seeds. Cut crosswise into 1/4-inch slices, then cut into wedges. Combine with the coconut and toss well. Add the sugar and stir until mixed thoroughly.

Good alone or served with plain cake.

APPLE PUFFS

1-1/2 cups all-purpose flour
1/8 teaspoon salt
1 teaspoon baking powder
3/4 cup granulated sugar
1 egg, beaten

2/3 cup whole milk
1-1/2 cups apple, chopped
  fine or grated
Vegetable oil

Sift together the flour, salt, baking powder and sugar; add the egg and milk; mix well. Batter should be stiff. Fold in the apple. Drop by spoonfuls into hot oil and cook until golden brown.

You will receive nothing but compliments here!

BAKED APPLE DUMPLING

5 medium-size tart apples
1/2 teaspoon salt
3 tablespoons cold water
1-1/2 cups all-purpose flour
3 teaspoons baking powder
1/4 teaspoon salt

5 tablespoons butter
1 large egg
1 cup whole milk, about
Ice cream or whipped cream,
  sweetened (optional)

Wash, pare and slice apples into a 1 quart buttered casserole. Mix the salt and water together and pour over apples. Sift the flour, baking powder and salt. Cut in butter until crumbly. Stir in the egg and then add enough milk to make a soft dough. Spread batter over the apples completely. Make several slits in top. Bake in 400 degree oven for about 25 to 30 minutes or until crust is browned and apples are tender. Delicious served warm as it comes from oven. Also good with ice cream or whipped and sweetened cream.

A tempting apple dish!

BANANA CREAM

3 large, ripe bananas, mashed
  fine
3/4 cup granulated sugar
1/4 cup lemon juice, freshly
  squeezed

1 (8-ounce) carton whipping
  cream, stiffly beaten
Salted peanuts, crushed

Combine bananas, sugar and juice; cook, stirring until mixture almost comes to a boil. Remove from heat and spoon into a bowl; chill in refrigerator, then fold in whipped cream. Spoon into sherbet dishes and top with a few peanuts.

BANANA FRITTERS

1 cup all-purpose flour
1 teaspoon baking powder
1/2 teaspoon salt
3 tablespoons granulated
  sugar
1 large egg
1/3 cup whole milk

1 teaspoon butter, melted
2 large ripe bananas
2 teaspoons lemon juice,
  freshly squeezed
1/2 cup confectioners sugar,
  sifted
Cooking oil

Sift together the flour, baking powder, salt and sugar. Set aside. Beat egg; add milk and butter, then add flour mixture and beat until smooth; set aside. Peel bananas and cut into small cubes. Sprinkle with lemon juice and sugar. Fold into batter. Heat oil and fry until golden brown, turning once. Serve while still hot.

BANANA PUDDING

3 large egg yolks, slightly
  beaten
1 cup granulated sugar
1 (12-ounce) can evaporated
  milk
1 teaspoon pure vanilla extract

3 medium-size bananas
Vanilla wafers
3 large egg whites
3 tablespoons granulated
  sugar

Combine egg yolks and sugar in a medium saucepan until well blended. Gradually add the milk and vanilla. Cook and stir over medium heat until mixture just begins to thicken; remove from heat immediately and set aside. In a glass casserole dish, layer the bananas and then the vanilla wafers in 2 layers. Spoon over the custard. Beat the egg whites until stiff; add sugar gradually, beating until shiny. Spoon over the entire top. Brown top quickly in a 350 degree oven; should take 4 or 5 minutes. Do not leave in oven too long as pudding will become too thick.

Easy and mouth watering!

BLUEBERRY COBBLER

1 cup granulated sugar
1 cup water
1 teaspoon lemon juice
1 quart fresh blueberries

1/2 cup butter
1 cup granulated sugar
1-1/2 cups self-rising flour

Combine sugar and water in a large bowl; stir to dissolve sugar; add juice and berries. Pour mixture into a 9 X 13-inch baking dish and set aside. Combine butter, sugar and flour; cut with a pastry blender until crumbly and well mixed. Spoon over the blueberry mixture. Bake at 350 degrees for around 30 minutes or until lightly browned and bubbly hot. Good served alone or with ice cream or whipped cream.

BLUEBERRY PUDDING

1/3 cup butter, softened
1/2 cup granulated sugar
2 large eggs
1 cup all-purpose flour

Milk
1 cup fresh blueberries
Flour

Cream butter and sugar well. Add eggs, one at a time, beating well after each addition. Add flour gradually until blended. Slowly add just enough milk to form a thick batter. Place berries in a shallow pan and sprinkle small amount of flour over them; roll to cover berries with flour, then stir into the batter gently. Spoon mixture into a greased 9-inch square pan. Bake at 350 degrees for around 30 minutes or until pudding is set. Serve with Sherry Sauce.

Sherry Sauce:

1/2 cup butter, softened
1/2 cup confectioners sugar
2 large egg yolks, beaten

1-1/2 cups granulated sugar
1/4 cup cooking sherry

Cream butter and gradually add confectioners sugar until blended; add egg yolks and blend thoroughly. Gradually add the granulated sugar and beat for around 8 to 10 minutes. Slowly add sherry until completely blended. Just before serving with pudding, beat again.

CHOCOLATE MINT BROWNIES

Brownies:

4 squares unsweetened
    chocolate, melted
1 cup butter, melted
2 cups granulated sugar
4 large eggs, slightly beaten

1 teaspoon pure vanilla extract
1 cup all-purpose flour
1/8 teaspoon salt
1 cup chopped pecans

Melt chocolate and butter together; add sugar and stir until blended. Slowly beat in the eggs; add remaining ingredients and stir just until moistened throughout. Spoon mixture into a greased 12 X 18-inch pan with sides; bake at 350 degrees for about 20 minutes. Cool and spread frosting over top. Top with glaze.

Frosting:

1/2 cup butter, softened
1 (16-ounce) package
    confectioners sugar
4 tablespoons whole milk

2 teaspoons peppermint
    extract
3 drops green food coloring

Beat butter until smooth; add sugar and blend, then add milk, peppermint flavoring and food coloring; beat until smooth. Spread on cold brownies. Chill in refrigerator and then top with glaze.

Glaze:

4 squares unsweetened
    chocolate, melted

4 tablespoons butter, melted
2/3 cup confectioners sugar

Melt chocolate and butter together; add sugar and beat until blended well. Cover cold brownies with glaze; refrigerate until glaze is set; cut into 1-inch squares.

BREAD PUDDING

Pudding:

1 loaf French bread
1 quart whole milk
3 large eggs
2 cups granulated sugar

2 tablespoons pure vanilla
  extract
1 cup raisins
3 tablespoons butter, melted

Soak bread in milk; crush with pastry blender until well mixed. Add eggs, sugar, vanilla and raisins and stir well to blend. Pour butter in bottom of a heavy baking pan. Spoon in the pudding mixture. Bake at 350 degrees until mixture is firm, around 30 minutes. Let cool completely; cube pudding and place in individual dessert dishes. Add sauce and heat under broiler just before serving time.

Whiskey Sauce:

1/2 cup butter, melted
1 cup granulated sugar

1 large egg, beaten
Whiskey, to taste

Melt butter in top of double boiler; add sugar and cook, stirring, until completely dissolved. Add beaten egg gradually, beating constantly so egg will not curdle. Let cool and add whiskey to taste.

CHOCOLATE MARBLE SQUARES

1 cup, plus 2 tablespoons all-
  purpose flour, sifted
1/2 teaspoon baking soda
1/2 teaspoon salt
1/2 cup butter, softened
6 tablespoons granulated
  sugar
6 tablespoons light brown
  sugar, packed

1/2 teaspoon pure vanilla
  extract
1/4 teaspoon water
1 large egg
1 cup pecans, chopped
1 cup (6-ounce package) semi-
  sweet chocolate morsels
Pecan halves

Sift together the flour, soda and salt; set aside. Blend together the butter, sugars, vanilla and water. Beat in the egg. Add flour mixture and mix well. Stir in pecans. Spread in a buttered glass baking dish. Sprinkle chocolate morsels over top of batter. Place in 375 degree oven for 1 minute. Remove and run knife through batter to marbleize. Decorate with pecan halves. Return to oven and continue to bake at 375 degrees for 12 to 14 minutes, or until done. Cool and cut into squares.

Hard to resist!

BROWNIES

Brownies:

1-1/2 squares unsweetened
    chocolate
1/2 cup vegetable shortening
1 cup granulated sugar

2 large eggs
3/4 cup self-rising flour
1 teaspoon pure vanilla extract
1 cup chopped pecans

Melt the chocolate and shortening in a small saucepan; set aside to cool. Combine the sugar and chocolate mixture, add the remaining ingredients, blending well. Spoon into a greased baking pan and bake for around 20 minutes. When cooled, spread with icing; let set, then cut into squares and remove from pan.

Icing:

1 square unsweetened
    chocolate
2 tablespoons butter or
    margarine

1/2 cup evaporated milk
2 cups confectioners sugar
1 teaspoon pure vanilla extract
Dash salt

Combine all ingredients and stir over medium heat until mixture comes to a boil. Remove and beat until thickened. Spread over brownies.

You won't regret making these brownies and your guests will come back for more!

RAISIN PUDDING

Pudding:

1 cup all-purpose flour
2/3 cup granulated sugar
2 teaspoons baking powder
1/4 teaspoon salt
3/4 cup sour cream
2 tablespoons vegetable oil

1 cup seedless raisins
1/2 cup pecans, chopped
3/4 cup light brown sugar,
    packed
1-1/2 cups hot water

Combine flour, sugar, baking powder, salt, sour cream and oil. Mix well. Stir in raisins and pecans. Spoon into an ungreased 9-inch baking pan. Combine brown sugar and hot water; pour over batter. Bake at 350 degrees for 50 to 60 minutes or until done. Spoon topping over warm pudding.

Topping:

1/2 cup whipped topping (or
    whipping cream, whipped)

1/2 cup sour cream

Combine both ingredients and spoon over pudding. Raisin sauce will be on bottom.

If you like raisins, you will enjoy this pudding!

CHERRY COBBLER

1/2 cup butter, softened
1 cup granulated sugar
2 large eggs
1 teaspoon pure vanilla extract
1-1/2 cups all-purpose flour
1 teaspoon baking powder
Dash salt
1 (21-ounce) can cherry pie
  filling

Cream butter, gradually adding sugar until fluffy. Add eggs, one at a time, beating well after each addition. Stir in flavoring. Sift together the flour, baking powder and salt. Gradually add to the creamed mixture and beat well. Reserve 1/2 cup batter. Spread the remaining batter in a buttered 8 X 8 X 2-inch baking pan. Spread cherry pie filling over batter. Drop reserved batter by teaspoonfuls around edge of pan and over filling. Bake at 350 degrees for around 1 hour; check for doneness about 10 minutes before the hour is up.

Wonderful served while warm with vanilla ice cream; also great when cold!

CHERRY MOUSSE

1 cup boiling water
1 (3-ounce) package cherry
  gelatin dessert
1/4 cup granulated sugar
1/4 cup orange liqueur
2 large egg whites
1-1/2 cups heavy cream,
  whipped
2 cups pitted and halved
  fresh, sweet cherries
  or 1 (17-ounce) package
  frozen, drained sweet
  cherries
Whole cherries for garnish
  (pitted)

Bring water to boiling point; dissolve gelatin and sugar in water, stirring until completely dissolved; let cool, then stir in liqueur. Place in refrigerator and chill until just slightly thickened. Beat egg whites until stiff; fold egg whites and whipped cream into gelatin mixture. Gently fold in the halved cherries. Turn into a 6 cup mold. Chill until firm. Unmold and garnish with the whole cherries.

A delicious treat!

CHERRY PUDDING

1 pint sour cherries, pitted
1 cup granulated sugar
2 tablespoons butter, softened
1/2 cup granulated sugar
1 cup all-purpose flour, sifted
1/4 teaspoon salt
2 teaspoons baking powder
1/2 cup whole milk
1 cup boiling water

Cover cherries with 1 cup sugar; stir and set aside. Cream butter and 1/2 cup sugar. Sift together the flour, salt and baking powder; add alternately with the milk until well blended. Spoon batter into a buttered casserole dish; add cherries and pour over the boiling water. Bake at 350 degrees for around 30 minutes. Batter will rise to top.

Wonderful taste!

PEACH PUDDING

Pudding:

2 cups peaches, cut up	1 cup whole milk
2 tablespoons butter, melted	2 teaspoons lemon juice,
3 tablespoons all-purpose flour	freshly squeezed
1/2 cup light brown sugar,	3 large eggs, well beaten
packed	2 tablespoons water

Pare and cut up peaches; blend until smooth in blender; set aside. Combine butter, flour, sugar, milk and juice; bring to a boil; remove from heat. Beat eggs and add water. Add to the flour mixture. Arrange peaches in a buttered casserole dish; pour batter over peaches. Top with meringue.

Meringue:

3 large egg whites	1/4 teaspoon pure vanilla
Dash salt	extract
4 tablespoons granulated	
sugar	

Beat the egg whites and salt until stiff; gradually add the sugar until shiny. Stir in the vanilla. Spread meringue over top of pudding. Bake at 350 degrees for around 12 to 15 minutes.

Tempting flavor!

PEACHES AND CREAM

1 (8-ounce) package	Lettuce leaves
cream cheese, softened	1 (16-ounce) can yellow
Reserved peach juice	cling peach halves, reserve
1 cup pecans, finely	juice
chopped	

Beat the cream cheese until soft and smooth; add enough peach juice to soften the cream cheese. Stir in the pecans. Arrange peach halves on a serving plate with lettuce leaves; top each peach half with the cream cheese mixture.

PEANUT BUTTER BROWNIES

1 cup vegetable shortening
1 cup peanut butter
3 cups granulated sugar
8 large eggs
1 tablespoon pure vanilla
  extract

8 ounces chocolate chips
2 cups all-purpose flour
2 teaspoons baking powder
1 teaspoon salt

Cream shortening and peanut butter thoroughly. Blend in sugar; then eggs and vanilla. Stir in chocolate chips. Sift together the remaining dry ingredients; add to chocolate mixture and mix just to blend. Pour batter into 3 greased 8 X 8 X 2-inch pans. Bake at 350 degrees for about 20 minutes. Cool slightly and cut into squares. Yields: 4 dozen 2 X 2-inch brownies.

Moist and delicious brownies!

PEANUT BUTTER ICE CREAM

4 large eggs
2-1/2 cups granulated sugar
2 (12-ounce) cans evaporated
  milk

1 (14-ounce) can sweetened
  condensed milk
1-1/2 cups peanut butter,
  crunchy or extra crunchy

Beat eggs until light and fluffy. Add sugar gradually, beating well after each addition. Stir in all of milk and then add the peanut butter, blending well. Pour mixture into freezer can and add milk to full line. Freeze.

If you like peanut butter then you will enjoy this delicious ice cream!

PEAR-BUTTERSCOTCH CRISP

1 (16-ounce) can pear halves,
  drained
1/2 cup light brown sugar,
  packed

1/2 cup all-purpose flour
1/4 teaspoon salt
1/4 teaspoon ground cinnamon
1/2 cup butter

Arrange pears, cut sides down, in a buttered pie plate. Mix sugar, flour, salt and cinnamon together; cut in butter with pastry blender or fork until crumbly. Sprinkle thickly over and around pears. Bake at 425 degrees for 15 to 20 minutes, or until crumbs are golden brown.

An elegant way to end a meal!

PECAN TASSIES

1 (3-ounce) package cream
  cheese, softened

1/2 cup butter, softenend
1 cup all-purpose flour, sifted

Blend together the cream cheese and butter; stir in flour. Place in refrigerator and chill for 1 hour. Shape into 2 dozen 1-inch balls; place in ungreased 1-3/4-inch muffin cups. Press dough with fingers against bottom and sides of cups. Prepare filling.

Filling:

1 large egg
3/4 cup light brown sugar,
  packed
1 tablespoon butter, softened

1 teaspoon pure vanilla extract
1 cup pecans, coarsely broken,
  (divided)

Beat together the egg, sugar, butter and vanilla just until smooth. Sprinkle 1/2 cup pecans in bottom of shells; add filling and then top with remaining 1/2 cup pecans. Bake at 325 degrees for around 25 minutes or until filling sets. Cool and then remove from muffin pans.

STEWED RED PLUMS

9 red plums, very ripe
3/4 cup granulated sugar

2/3 cup water

Wash plums and prick with a fork in several places. Heat sugar and water to boiling point; drop plums into hot syrup. Cover and gently boil for around 15 minutes or until plums are tender. Serve warm or cold.

STRAWBERRY ICE CREAM

1 quart very ripe strawberries,
  or 2 cups pureé
1-1/2 cups granulated sugar
1 tablespoon lemon juice,
  freshly squeezed
1/4 teaspoon salt

1 teaspoon unflavored gelatin
1 tablespoon cold water
1 (8-ounce) carton half and
  half
3 (8-ounce) cartons whipping
  cream, unwhipped

Wash and hull strawberries; pureé in blender. Add sugar, lemon juice and salt until combined well. Cover and place in refrigerator. Soften gelatin in the water. Scald the half and half, then add the gelatin and stir until dissolved. Cool the gelatin mixture. Combine with the strawberry mixture and add cream, blending well. Pour into freezer can and freeze according to directions.

Excellent ice cream!

PINEAPPLE CREAM

24 large marshmallows
2 cups crushed pineapple, in
  heavy syrup
1 cup whipping cream,
  whipped

1 tablespoon granulated sugar
Cherries with stems

Cut marshmallows with kitchen shears in small pieces into a large bowl. Pour over the pineapple and stir. Beat the cream until thickened; blend in the sugar thoroughly. Fold into pineapple mixture. Spoon into sherbet glasses and top with a cherry. Serve immediately.

Yummy!

PINK CRANBERRY FREEZE

2 (3-ounce) packages cream
  cheese, softened
2 tablespoons mayonnaise
2 tablepoons granulated sugar
1 (16-ounce) can whole
  cranberry sauce
1 (9-ounce) can crushed
  pineapple, undrained

1/2 cup pecans, chopped
1 (8-ounce) carton whipping
  cream, whipped
1/2 cup confectioners sugar
1 teaspoon pure vanilla extract

Beat cream cheese in large mixer bowl until soft and fluffy; blend in mayonnaise and sugar. Add fruit, pecans and then fold in whipped cream, sugar and vanilla. Spoon mixture into a loaf pan and freeze for 6 hours before serving.

STRAWBERRY PUDDING

Pudding:
1 cup dry white bread crumbs
3/4 cup whole milk
1-1/2 cups granulated sugar
2 tablespoons butter

2 large egg yolks
1 cup whole milk
1-1/2 cups fresh strawberries,
  mashed

Place crumbs in small bowl and pour over the 3/4 cup milk to soften the crumbs. Combine the sugar, butter and yolks; add crumb mixture and beat for 2 or 3 minutes. Add the 1 cup milk and strawberries. Gently stir until well mixed. Top with meringue.

Meringue:
2 large egg whites
Dash salt

1/4 cup granulated sugar

Beat the whites and salt until stiff, gradually add the sugar until stiff and shiny. Spread over top of pudding and bake in 350 degree oven for 12 to 15 minutes, or until golden brown.

Wonderful taste!

SWEET POTATO PUDDING NO. 1

4 cups grated raw sweet
  potato
1/2 cup granulated sugar
3/4 cup light brown sugar,
  packed
1/2 cup whipping cream,
  unwhipped

4 tablespoons butter, melted
1 teaspoon ground cinnamon
1/4 teaspoon ground nutmeg
1/4 teaspoon ground allspice

Combine all ingredients; mix until well blended. Spoon into a buttered casserole dish. Bake at 325 degrees for around 1 hour and 15 minutes or until pudding is set and lightly browned.

SWEET POTATO PUDDING NO. 2

3 cups sweet potatoes, cooked
  and mashed
1 cup granulated sugar
1/2 cup butter, melted
6 large egg yolks, well beaten
1 tablespoon lemon rind,
  grated

1/4 teaspoon ground nutmeg
1 cup orange juice, freshly
  squeezed
6 large egg whites, stiffly
  beaten
1/4 cup granulated sugar

Mash cooked sweet potatoes and press through a sieve to remove any strings. Add the 1 cup sugar and butter, blending well. Beat in the egg yolks, lemon rind, nutmeg and juice. Beat the egg whites until stiff but not dry. Fold gently into the potato mixture. Spoon into a large buttered casserole dish. Sprinkle with the 1/4 cup sugar and bake at 350 degrees for around 1 hour. Serve hot.

Plan to serve this dish soon!

STEWED PRUNES

1 pound dried prunes
Water

1/2 cup granulated sugar

Place prunes in a large saucepan and barely cover with water. Cover and cook over low heat, never boiling, until fruit is tender. Allow at least 30 to 40 minutes. Add sugar, if you want a syrupy mixture. Good served warm or cold. Refrigerate any unused portion.

SWEET POTATO PUDDING NO. 3

4 large sweet potatoes,
  uncooked
2 large eggs
1 cup molasses

1/2 cup whole milk
1/2 cup butter, melted
1 teaspoon ground allspice
1 teaspoon salt

Pare and grate potatoes; set aside. Beat eggs until smooth; add molasses, milk, butter, allspice and salt. Stir in potatoes. Spoon into a greased casserole dish and bake at 350 degrees for about 1-1/2 hours or until pudding begins to caramelize. Good with Lemon Sauce.

Lemon Sauce:

1/2 teaspoon grated lemon
  rind
3 tablespoons lemon juice,
  freshly squeezed
1 tablespoon cornstarch
3/4 cup granulated sugar

1/8 teaspoon salt
3/4 cup boiling water
1 large egg yolk, beaten
1 tablespoon butter

Combine rind and juice; set aside. Blend together the cornstarch, sugar and salt in top of double boiler; stir in the boiling water. Cook, stirring until mixture boils and begins to thicken. When mixture becomes clear, remove from heat and stir small amount of hot liquid into beaten egg yolk, then return to double boiler, stirring until well combined. Cook and stir for 2 or 3 additional minutes. Remove from heat and stir in the butter, lemon juice and rind. Serve warm over the pudding.

VANILLA ICE CREAM NO. 1

1-1/2 quarts whole milk
4 large eggs, beaten
2-1/2 cups granulated sugar
4 cups whipping cream,
  unwhipped

2 tablespoons pure vanilla
  extract
1/2 teaspoon salt

Scald milk and set aside to cool. Beat eggs in large mixer bowl until light and fluffy; gradually add the sugar, beating well after each addition, until mixture is very stiff. Stir in the milk. Return to heat and cook and stir for 2 minutes longer. Remove from heat and cool. Stir in cream, vanilla and salt thoroughly. Pour into a gallon freezer. Freeze according to your freezer directions. Makes 1 gallon.

Wonderful flavor!

VANILLA ICE CREAM NO. 2

4 large eggs
1 cup granulated sugar
1 (8-ounce) package whipping
cream, unwhipped
1 tablespoon pure vanilla
extract

1 (14-ounce) can condensed
milk
1-1/2 quarts whole milk

Beat eggs in large mixer bowl until light and fluffy; add the sugar and beat well. Then add the cream and vanilla beating just until combined. Pour mixture into freezer can. Add condensed milk and dairy milk to full line and stir well. Now freeze according to freezer directions.

Delicious!

SHERRY PUDDING

2 tablespoons unflavored
gelatin
1/2 cup whole milk
3 large eggs, separated
1/2 cup granulated sugar
2 cups whole milk

1/2 cup cooking sherry
1/8 teaspoon salt
1 (8-ounce) package whipping
cream, whipped
1 cup ladyfingers, broken into
pieces

Combine the gelatin and 1/2 cup milk; let stand for 5 minutes. Combine and cook the egg yolks, sugar and 2 cups milk over low heat until mixture thickens, stirring constantly. Remove from heat and stir in the dissolved gelatin and sherry; mix well and let cool. Beat egg whites and salt until stiff and shiny. Pour cooled custard mixture over whites; set aside. Whip cream until thickened; break ladyfingers into pieces. Fold the cream and ladyfingers into the custard mixture. Spoon into sherbet glasses or large mold and let chill in refrigerator before serving.

Don't skip this dessert!

STEWED APPLES

10 apples, medium
1 cup granulated sugar
1-1/4 cups water

1/4 cup white corn syrup
Dash of salt
1/4 teaspoon ground nutmeg

Pare and thinly slice apples. Combine sugar, water, syrup, salt and nutmeg; stir to mix well and place over low heat. Add apple and bring to boiling point; reduce heat, cover and simmer for around 20 minutes or until tender. Gently pour into serving bowl.

Good warm or cold!

STEWED PEACHES

6 ripe, juicy peaches
2/3 cup granulated sugar

2/3 cup water

Pare and thinly slice peaches. Combine sugar and water in a large saucepan; bring slowly to boiling point; reduce heat and simmer for several minutes. Drop peaches into hot syrup, cover and heat to boiling again. Simmer for around 10 additional minutes or until peaches are tender. Serve warm, plain or with milk or cream.

STEWED PEARS

5 medium pears, well ripened
1 cup granulated sugar
1-1/2 cups water

1 tablespoon lemon juice,
freshly squeezed

Wash, pare and thinly slice pears. Combine the sugar, water and juice; heat to boiling point. Drop pears into hot mixture; cover and simmer until pears are tender, around 10 minutes. Serve warm or cold.

CHOCOLATE PARTY DESSERT

1 large package chocolate
creme-filled cookies
1/2 gallon vanilla ice cream,
softened

Chocolate syrup
Whipped topping
1 cup chopped pecans

Break cookies into 4 pieces each; spread over bottom of a 9 X 11-inch glass dish. Spread softened ice cream over cookies. Drizzle chocolate syrup over ice cream. Spread whipped topping over syrup and add pecans, covering entire top. Cover with plastic wrap and place in freezer until ready to serve. Cut into squares and serve on dessert plates.

CHOCOLATE SQUARES

Cake:

2 cups all-purpose flour
2 cups granulated sugar
1/2 teaspoon salt
1/2 teaspoon ground cinnamon
4 teaspoons cocoa
1/2 cup vegetable oil

1/2 cup butter
1 cup water
2 large eggs
1/2 cup buttermilk
1 teaspoon baking soda

Sift together the flour, sugar, salt and cinnamon; set aside. Combine the cocoa, oil, butter and water and bring to a boil. Pour over dry ingredients and beat well. Add eggs, one at a time, beating well after each addition. Combine the buttermilk and soda; stir into the creamed mixture. Pour into a greased and floured 11 X 13-inch baking pan. Bake at 350 degrees for about 20 minutes. Leave in pan to cool. Spread Chocolate Icing over cake, let set then cut into squares.

Icing:

5 tablespoons cocoa
8 tablespoons evaporated milk
1/2 cup butter
1 (16-ounce) package
   confectioners sugar

1 teaspoon pure vanilla extract
1 cup pecans, chopped
   (optional)

Combine the cocoa, milk and butter; heat and stir to completely dissolve; add sugar and vanilla; blend until smooth. Fold in pecans, if desired. Spread on cooled cake and let icing set.

COCONUT PUDDING

3/4 cup granulated sugar
1/8 teaspoon salt
2 large eggs, slightly beaten
2 cups milk, scalded
1 cup coconut, finely shredded

4 tablespoons butter, melted
1/2 teaspoon pure vanilla
   extract
1-1/2 cups stale bread, cut into
   1/2-inch pieces

Combine sugar, salt and eggs, blending well. Gradually add milk until blended; then add coconut, butter and vanilla. Place stale bread in greased baking dish and pour over the milk mixture; place dish in pan of hot water. Bake at 350 degrees for around 50 minutes or until pudding is set. Good warm or refrigerate and serve chilled.

COFFEE CREAM

2 teaspoons instant coffee
1/2 cup boiling water
1/4 pound marshmallows
Dash of salt

1/8 teaspoon ground nutmeg
1 (8-ounce) carton whipping
   cream, whipped

Pour boiling water over coffee in large saucepan, add marshmallows, salt and nutmeg and stir over low heat until marshmallows are dissolved completely. Pour mixture into a bowl and chill in refrigerator until partially set. Whip cream until stiff; fold marshmallow mixture into the cream. Spoon into a serving dish and refrigerate until ready to serve.

CRANBERRY TORTE

Crust:

1-1/2 cups graham cracker
  crumbs
1/2 cup chopped pecans

1/4 cup granulated sugar
6 tablespoons margarine,
  melted

Combine crumbs, pecans, sugar and margarine well. Press into bottom and up sides of an 8-inch springform pan. Chill in refrigerator.

Filling:

1-1/2 cups ground cranberries
  (2 cups whole berries)
1 cup granulated sugar
2 large egg whites
1 tablespoon frozen orange
  juice concentrate

1 tablespoon pure vanilla
  extract
1/8 teaspoon salt
1 (8-ounce) carton whipping
  cream, whipped
Fresh orange slices

Combine cranberries and sugar; let stand for around 5 minutes. Add unbeaten egg whites, orange juice, vanilla and salt. Beat until stiff peaks form, 6 to 8 minutes. Whip cream until soft peaks form; gently fold into cranberry mixture. Spoon into crust. Freeze until firm.

To serve, remove torte from springform pan. Place on an attractive serving plate. Spoon glaze in center of torte and then arrange orange slices around the outside.

Glaze:

1/2 cup granulated sugar
1 tablespoon cornstarch

3/4 cup cranberries
2/3 cup water

Stir together the sugar and cornstarch; add the cranberries and water. Cook and stir until bubbly, just until the cranberry skins pop open. Cool to room temperature only. Do not chill before spooning on the torte.

This torte will serve around 10 people very well. Do not let the length of the recipe frighten you! This is easy and delicious.

CRUNCHY APPLES

1/2 cup corn flakes
1/3 cup all-purpose flour,
  sifted
3/4 cup light brown sugar,
  packed

1/3 cup butter
4 cups tart apples, pared and
  sliced

Measure corn flakes, flour and sugar into a large mixing bowl. Add butter and cut in with a pastry blender until mixture is crumbly. Place thinly sliced apple in a buttered casserole dish and sprinkle the sugar mixture over top. Bake around 30 minutes or until the top is brown and crunchy.

A good tart apple is the secret!

DOUBLE CHOCOLATE BROWNIES

3/4 cup all-purpose flour
1 cup granulated sugar
1/2 teaspoon baking powder
1/2 teaspoon salt
1/2 cup vegetable shortening
2 large eggs, unbeaten
1 teaspoon pure vanilla
  extract

2 squares unsweetened
  chocolate, melted and cooled
1 cup chopped pecans
3/4 cup semi-sweet chocolate
  chips

Sift together flour, sugar, baking powder and salt. Add shortening, eggs and the vanilla; beat 1 minute. Add melted chocolate and beat until batter is evenly blended; stir in pecans and chocolate chips. Spoon into a greased 8-inch square baking pan. Bake at 350 degrees for around 20 minutes or until done. Cool in the pan. Cut into squares or rectangles and then remove to serving plate.

Doubly delicious!

LEMON SQUARES

Crust:
1 cup butter, softened
1/2 cup confectioners sugar

2 cups all-purpose flour

Cream butter until soft and fluffy; add sugar and blend. Beat in flour well. Flour hands and pat stiff batter into a buttered 9 X 13-inch baking dish or pan. Bake at 350 degrees for 20 minutes or until brown.

Topping:
4 large eggs, beaten
2 cups granulated sugar
1/3 cup lemon juice, freshly
  squeezed

1/4 cup all-purpose flour
1/2 teaspoon baking powder
Confectioners sugar, for
  garnish

Beat eggs until light and smooth; gradually add sugar, beating well. Stir in juice. Sift flour and baking powder; blend in thoroughly. Spoon over baked crust. Return to 350 degree oven and bake for 30 additional minutes. Remove from oven and sprinkle with sifted confectioners sugar while hot. Cool completely and cut into squares to serve.

LEMON ICE CREAM

2 cups granulated sugar
2 tablespoons all-purpose flour
1/4 teaspoon salt
2 cups whole milk
2 cups half and half
2 cups whipping cream,
  unwhipped

4 teaspoons lemon rind, grated
1/2 cup lemon juice, freshly
  squeezed
3 drops yellow food coloring

Blend sugar, flour and salt in top of double boiler; gradually stir in milk. Place over boiling water and cook, stirring, until milk is hot and flour is cooked, around 10 minutes. Remove from heat and place in a pan of very cold water, stirring often until custard is cold. Now stir in remaining ingredients. Pour into freezer can and freeze according to directions.

LEMON PUDDING

3 large egg yolks, beaten
1 cup granulated sugar
5 tablespoons all-purpose flour
2 tablespoons butter, melted
1 cup whole milk
1/4 cup lemon juice, freshly
  squeezed

Grated lemon rind of 1/2
  lemon
3 large egg whites, beaten
Dash of salt

Butter a 9 X 9 X 2-inch casserole dish and set aside. Thoroughly blend egg yolks, sugar, flour, butter, milk, juice and rind in medium bowl. Beat egg whites and salt until stiff and shiny. Fold into first mixture gently. Pour into prepared dish. Place dish in shallow pan of hot water. Bake for 45 minutes at 350 degrees. Remove from oven when lightly browned and set. Let cool for 2 or 3 minutes; then turn out so pudding side will be up. Spoon into sherbet glasses to serve.

A dainty and delicious dessert!

MERINGUE KISSES

4 large egg whites
1-1/3 cups granulated sugar
1-1/2 teaspoons pure vanilla
  extract

1 cup pecans, chopped fine

Beat egg whites until frothy, gradually adding the sugar; beat until stiff but not dry. Stir in the vanilla and pecans. Drop by teaspoonfuls on an ungreased cookie sheet. Bake at 200 degrees for around 50 minutes. Do not open oven door while cooking! Makes 2 dozen kisses.

You will smack your lips when you taste these kisses!

PEACH COBBLER

2 cups ripe peaches, sliced
1/2 cup granulated sugar
1/2 cup butter
1 cup granulated sugar

3/4 cup all-purpose flour
2 teaspoons baking powder
1/4 teaspoon salt
3/4 cup whole milk

Combine peaches and 1/2 cup sugar; set aside. Preheat oven to 350 degrees. Place butter in deep baking dish and place in oven to melt. Combine the remaining ingredients and pour over melted butter; do not stir. Spoon sugared peaches on top of batter; do not stir. Bake for around 30 minutes until golden brown.

PEACH ICE CREAM

1-1/2 cups peach pureé
1-1/4 cups whipping cream,
   whipped

1 tablespoon lemon juice,
   freshly squeezed
1 cup confectioners sugar

Pare and slice very ripe peaches. Pureé in blender; measure and set aside. Whip cream until thickened; add lemon juice and continue beating until very stiff. Beat in the sugar and then fold in the pureé. Pour into refrigerator tray immediately and freeze for about 2 hours.

Easy to mix, so serve often during the summer peach season!

FROZEN LEMON SOUFFLÉ

8 large egg whites, stiffly
   beaten
1 cup, plus 2 tablespoons
   granulated sugar
Grated rind and juice of 8
   medium lemons, freshly
   squeezed

2 (8-ounce) cartons whipping
   cream, whipped
2 teaspoons pure lemon
   extract
2 drops yellow food coloring

Beat whites in large mixer bowl until stiff; gradually add sugar, beating until stiff and shiny; beat in the juice and rind. Beat cream until stiff; add flavoring and food coloring. Fold into the egg white mixture. Spoon into a large soufflé mold. Place in freezer for 6 hours before removing to serve.

FOUR LAYER DESSERT

3/4 cup butter
1 cup all-purpose flour
1 cup pecans, chopped
2 (8-ounce) packages cream
cheese, softened
1-1/2 cups confectioners sugar
1 (9-ounce) carton whipped
topping
2 (3-1/2-ounce) boxes instant
pudding mix (chocolate,
lemon, butterscotch or
vanilla)

3-1/2 cups whole milk
1 (10-ounce) carton whipped
topping for final layer
Pecans, chopped fine for
garnish
Chocolate curls, for garnish
(optional)

Melt butter; add flour and pecans; mix thoroughly. Spread over bottom of 13-1/2 X 9-inch glass dish. Bake at 325 degrees until lightly browned. Beat cream cheese until light and fluffy; add sugar and blend well; fold in whipped topping. Spread over first layer. Prepare pudding mix by directions on box but use 3-1/2 cups milk. Spread over second layer. Spread whipped topping over top and sprinkle with pecans. Add chocolate curls, if desired. Refrigerate for 6 to 8 hours or better still, overnight. Will serve 18.-

Rich and yummy!

FRIED APPLE AND BACON

12 slices bacon
4 cups apple, unpared and
sliced

4 tablespoons bacon drippings
1/2 cup granulated sugar

Cook bacon in large skillet until crisp. Drain and keep hot. Slice apple and lightly brown both sides in bacon drippings. Sprinkle with the sugar and cook slowly just until tender and browned. Place apple in center of platter with hot bacon around sides.

Interesting and good!

GINGERBREAD

1 cup vegetable shortening
1 cup granulated sugar
1 cup molasses
1 cup buttermilk
2 teaspoons baking soda
2-1/2 cups all-purpose flour

1/2 teaspon salt
1 teaspoon ground ginger
1 teaspoon ground cinnamon
1 teaspoon ground allspice
4 large eggs

Cream the shortening and sugar well; stir in molasses. Combine the buttermilk and soda; stir until soda is dissolved. Add alternately with the sifted dry ingredients; beat in eggs, one at a time, beating well after adding each egg. Pour into 2 greased and floured 9 X 12-inch pans. Bake at 325 degrees for around 50 to 60 minutes. Serve warm with or without a sauce.

Light and delicious flavor!

Fish

Fish tastes good and is good for you. Fish can be prepared any day of the year and cooks quickly. So, cook and serve fish often, and always buy the best and freshest fish!

BAKED FISH FILETS

2 pounds fish filets or steaks
2 tablespoons lemon juice,
  freshly squeezed
1 teaspoon onion juice
1/4 cup vegetable oil

1 teaspoon salt
1 teaspoon ground black
  pepper
1 teaspoon paprika

Place filets in large greased baking dish, skin side down. Mix other ingredients in small bowl and spoon over the fish filets. Bake at 325 degrees for around 20 minutes or until tender.

So easy and good for you! Delicious way to eat fish.

BAKED MULLET FILETS

2 pounds mullet filets
1/2 cup French dressing
1-1/2 cups cheese-flavored
  cracker crumbs

2 tablespoons hot vegetable oil
Paprika

Skin the filets and cut in serving pieces. Dip in dressing and roll in fine cracker crumbs. Arrange on a well greased baking sheet with sides, 15 X 12-inches. Drizzle hot oil over filets; sprinkle generously with paprika. Bake in 500 degree oven for 10 to 12 minutes or until filets flake when pricked with a fork. 6 servings.

BAKED RED SNAPPER

2 to 4 pounds red snapper
1 onion, thinly sliced
1/4 cup butter, melted
1 teaspoon salt
1/4 teaspoon ground black
  pepper

3 tablespoons orange juice
  concentrate
1 tablespoon soy sauce

Arrange fish in a greased baking pan. Make several slashes in skin; insert onion slices in slashes. Blend the remaining ingredients together. Spoon over fish. Bake for 20 to 30 minutes or until fish flakes easily. Baste often during baking time.

Easy to do and a satisfying fish dish!

FRIED FISH FILETS

2 large eggs, beaten
4 tablespoons whole milk
1 teaspoon salt
1/2 teaspoon paprika

Black and red pepper to taste
Corn meal
Vegetable oil

Beat eggs; add milk and blend well. Add salt, paprika, black and red pepper to taste. Dip filets in egg mixture and then roll in corn meal. Drop in deep hot oil in a heavy skillet and cook for around 5 minutes on each side. Fish should be nicely browned. Remove from pan and drain on paper toweling and serve on a hot platter.

TROUT ALMONDINE

2 to 3 trout
Salt and ground black pepper
1/4 cup fine soft bread crumbs
3 tablespoons almonds,
    chopped fine
3 tablespoons butter, melted

1 egg, slightly beaten
2 tablespoons lemon juice,
    freshly squeezed
1/4 teaspoon tarragon,
    crumbled
1/4 teaspoon salt

Clean and bone fish. Rinse in cold water and dry with paper towels. Flatten fish butterfly fashion and sprinkle with salt and pepper. Place flesh side down in a shallow pan. Combine the crumbs, almonds, butter, egg, juice, tarragon and salt, blending well. Spoon mixture over the fish. Bake at 400 degrees for 15 to 20 minutes or until fish flakes easily.

Different and delicious!

Crabmeat is sweet and delicious. Try the recipes for an extra special dinner!

CRABCAKES

2 (6-1/2-ounce) cans crabmeat, drained and flaked
1 cup breadcrumbs
1/3 cup melted butter
2 large eggs, slightly beaten
1 large carrot, scraped and grated
1-1/2 teaspoons chopped parsley
2 teaspoons mayonnaise
1 teaspoon Worcestershire sauce
1 teaspoon salt
1 teaspoon dry ground mustard
1/4 teaspoon ground black pepper
1 large egg, slightly beaten
2 tablespoons water
3/4 cup dry breadcrumbs
6 tablespoons melted butter

Combine first 11 ingredients, stirring well. Shape into 6 or 8 patties. Mixture will be slightly loose. Cover and chill in refrigerator for around 1 hour.

Combine egg and water, beating well. Dip patties in this mixture, then dredge in 3/4 cup dry breadcrumbs. Sauté crabcakes in melted butter in large saucepan over medium-to-hot heat, until golden brown, turning only once. Drain on paper towels.

A delicious dish that is easier to prepare than you might think!

CRAB-SHRIMP CASSEROLE

1 cup onion, chopped
1/2 cup green pepper, chopped
2 tablespoons vegetable oil
1/2 pound crabmeat, flaked
1 pound cooked shrimp, finely cut
1 cup mayonnaise
1 large egg, slightly beaten
1 tablespoon dry ground mustard
1 teaspoon salt
1/4 teaspoon ground black pepper
2 tablespoons Worcestershire sauce
1 tablespoon seafood seasoning
1 tablespoon parsley flakes
2 dashes Tabasco sauce
1 cup Cheddar cheese, grated
1/2 cup cracker crumbs
Paprika

Sauté onion and pepper in hot oil until tender. Combine with the crabmeat, shrimp, mayonnaise, egg and all seasonings. Spoon into a buttered casserole and top with cheese and crumbs. Sprinkle with paprika. Bake at 350 degrees for around 20 minutes or until cheese has melted and crumbs are golden brown.

CRABMEAT CASSEROLE

1-1/2 teaspoons dry ground
  mustard
1 cup green pepper, chopped
1 cup celery hearts, chopped
1 teaspoon salt
2-1/2 teaspoons
  Worcestershire sauce

Dash of hot sauce
1-1/2 cups mayonnaise
1 cup grated Cheddar cheese
5 large eggs, well beaten
1 pound crabmeat

Combine the mustard, pepper, celery, salt and sauces. Combine the mayonnaise, cheese and eggs; now add the crabmeat and then the first mixture. Spoon into a 2-quart greased casserole dish. Bake at 350 degrees for around 50 to 60 minutes or until firm and golden brown.

If you like crabmeat, you will love this casserole!

CRABMEAT DELIGHT

2 cups onion, chopped
1 cup green pepper, chopped
2 cloves garlic
1 cup olive oil
2 (6-ounce) cans tomato paste

1/2 teaspoon Tabasco sauce
1/2 teaspoon salt
2-1/4 cups water
1 pound crabmeat, flaked
Hot cooked rice

Combine the onion, pepper and garlic in olive oil; sauté until tender. Add the paste, sauce, salt and water; cook over low heat for 1-1/2 hours, stirring occasionally. Add the flaked crabmeat and continue to cook for 30 minutes longer. Spoon over hot cooked rice.

Try this!

Shrimp cooked any way will make an enjoyable meal!

FRIED SHRIMP

Shrimp, shelled and deveined
All-purpose flour
Beaten eggs

Whole milk
Cracker crumbs, fine
Vegetable shortening, or oil

Shell and devein shrimp. Wash, then roll in flour. Now dip in beaten eggs mixed with 2 tablespoons milk to each egg, then coat with cracker crumbs. Fry immediately in hot, deep fat. Remove and drain on paper towels. Serve while very hot.

You can't beat your very own fried shrimp for taste and quality!

SHRIMP CREOLE

1/2 cup margarine
5 tablespoons all-purpose flour
3 large onions, chopped
3 large green peppers, chopped
4 stalks celery, chopped
5 pods garlic, chopped
1-1/4 teaspoons salt
1 teaspoon ground red pepper
2 teaspoons parsley flakes

1/2 cup catsup
2 tablespoons Worcestershire
  sauce
2 (12-ounce) cans tomato paste
  with mushrooms
2 tablespoons granulated
  sugar
Water
4 pounds cooked shrimp

Melt margarine in large skillet; add flour and stir until brown over low heat. Add all ingredients, except shrimp, covering with water. Bring to a boil; reduce heat and cook slowly for 1 hour, stirring occasionally. Add shrimp last 15 minutes of cooking time.

So-o-o good!

SHRIMP FILLED PEPPERS

1 pound shrimp, cooked
1/2 cup onion, minced
2 tablespoons vegetable oil
1 teaspoon Worcestershire
  sauce
1 teaspoon salt
1/8 teaspoon ground black
  pepper

1-1/2 cups cooked rice
1 cup tomato juice
4 large green peppers
2 tablespoons butter, melted
3/4 cup soft bread crumbs

Cut cooked shrimp into 1/4-inch pieces and set aside. Sauté onion in hot oil until tender, stirring. Blend in next 5 ingredients; add shrimp and heat. Prepare peppers by cutting a thin slice from stem end, remove seeds and wash. Simmer in 2 cups boiling salted water for 5 minutes. Drain and lightly sprinkle salt inside each pepper; fill with shrimp mixture. Combine butter and crumbs; top peppers with crumb mixture. Place tightly in a casserole; cover and bake at 375 degrees for 30 minutes. Remove cover last 10 minutes to brown crumbs.

Takes time— but worth the effort!

SHRIMP-RICE CASSEROLE

4 tablespoons butter, melted
1 pound raw shrimp, shelled
  and deveined
1 cup onion, minced
1/2 cup fresh mushrooms,
  sliced
1 (16-ounce) can stewed
  tomatoes

1 teaspoon salt
1/2 teaspoon ground black
  pepper
1 tablespoon Worcestershire
  sauce
2 cups cooked rice

Melt butter in a large, heavy saucepan; sauté shrimp, onion and mushrooms. When shrimp turn pink, add tomatoes; stir in seasonings and rice. Bake at 350 degrees for 10 minutes. Remove and serve while hot.

Salmon and Tuna are great for meals in a hurry!

SALMON LOAF

2 cups canned salmon, drained
  and flaked (reserve liquid)
3 tablespoons butter
3 tablespoons all-purpose flour
1/2 cup evaporated milk
1/2 cup salmon liquid

Salt and ground black pepper
  to taste
2 tablespoons minced parsley
2 cups bread crumbs, coarse
  and dry
1 egg, beaten

Drain and flake salmon (remove bones); reserve liquid. Melt butter and blend in flour. Add milk and salmon liquid gradually, blending well. Cook and stir until sauce is thickened; add salt, pepper and parsley. Stir in flaked salmon, bread crumbs and beaten egg. Form mixture into loaf and turn into a greased loaf pan, uncovered. Bake at 350 degrees for around 30 minutes.

A main dish requiring no time at all!

SALMON PATTIES

1 (16-ounce) can red salmon,
    reserve liquid
2 eggs, slightly beaten
1 cup cooked potatoes, mashed
Salt and ground black pepper,
    to taste

1 tablespoon lemon juice,
    freshly squeezed
1/2 cup vegetable oil

Drain salmon and remove skin and bones. Mash salmon fine. Stir in the eggs, salmon liquid and the cooked mashed potatoes, blending well. Add salt and pepper to taste and then the lemon juice, mixing thoroughly. Shape in flat patties. Brown the patties slowly in hot oil on both sides; drain on paper towels quickly and remove to serving platter.

These can be made in a jiffy and are tasty!

TUNA CASSEROLE

1 (8-ounce) package fine egg
    noodles
1 (6-1/2-ounce) can white
    albacore tuna, drained and
    flaked

1 (10-3/4-ounce) can cream of
    chicken soup
1 (8-ounce) carton sour cream
Potato chips, crushed

Cook egg noodles by package directions; drain thoroughly and set aside. Combine tuna, soup, sour cream and noodles, stirring to blend well. Spoon mixture into a casserole dish; cover with crushed potato chips. Place in a 375 degree oven and bake for around 10 minutes or just until hot and bubbly.

You can serve this delicious casserole when you are in a hurry— takes no time at all!

Oysters are available throughout the year and can be eaten any-time. Try the quick and easy recipes for a special treat!

FRIED OYSTERS

Oysters, around 2 dozen
2 tablespoons lemon juice,
    freshly squeezed
Salt and pepper
Flour

1 large egg, beaten
Cracker crumbs
Cooking oil
Tartar sauce
Lemon wedges

Drain oysters and pat dry. Sprinkle with lemon juice, then with salt and pepper. Coat each oyster with flour, dip in beaten egg, then in crumbs. Place in refrigerator for about an hour to dry off. Pour oil into heavy saucepan and place oysters, one layer deep, into deep hot oil. Keep heat constant and fry until golden brown. Should only take around 2 minutes. Lift gently onto paper toweling to drain. Serve immediately on hot plates. Serve with Tartar Sauce and garnish with lemon wedges.

MINCED OYSTERS

1 small onion, chopped
1/3 cup butter, melted
1 quart oysters
1/2 cup oyster liquor
2/3 cup saltine crackers,
    rolled fine
1 large egg, beaten
2 hard boiled eggs, grated
1 cup celery, finely chopped

1 tablespoon pimiento, finely
    chopped
2 teaspoons salt
Dash ground black pepper
Dash of hot sauce
2 tablespoons Worcestershire
    sauce
2 teaspoons lemon juice,
    freshly squeezed

Sauté onion in butter until tender but not browned. Cut the oysters fine with kitchen shears. Combine all ingredients together in a large saucepan; cook and stir over low heat until mixture begins to thicken. Spoon into individual baking dishes; bake at 350 degrees for 20 minutes.

Meat

*Meat is the highlight for most family meals and is the item you will plan your menus around. Cook **meat** in a variety of ways by roasting, broiling, frying, braising or cooking in water and turn out an extraordinary meal!*

BEEF ROLLS CORDON BLEU

3 pounds ground beef
1 teaspoon salt
1 teaspoon dried vegetable
   flakes
1 (8-ounce) package sliced
   Swiss cheese, halved
   crosswise
1 (6-ounce) package sliced
   Canadian bacon

2 large eggs, beaten
1/4 cup water
1 cup fine, dry bread crumbs
1/3 cup butter, melted
1 (10-3/4-ounce) can condensed
   golden mushroom soup
1 cup whole milk
8 tomato wedges, optional

Combine the beef, salt and flakes. Shape into 8 patties. Top each pattie with a slice of cheese and bacon; roll up, jelly-roll fashion and set aside. Beat eggs and add water in a shallow bowl. Place crumbs in another shallow bowl. Dip meat rolls into egg mixture and then into crumbs to coat well. Melt the butter; now sauté the rolls until the beef is done. Remove to a hot platter and keep warm while making gravy. Stir soup and milk into the drippings. Heat slowly, stirring constantly; scrape bottom of pan. When mixture is boiling, remove from heat and pour into gravy dish. Place a tomato wedge between each meat roll and you are ready to serve.

A delicious main dish!

BEEF STROGANOFF

2 pounds round steak, cut in 1-
   inch strips
Flour
2 tablespoons vegetable oil
1 cup onion, chopped
1 (10-3/4 -ounce) can beef
   broth
4 tablespoons all-purpose flour

Water
1 tablespoon prepared mustard
1/3 cup sauterne wine
1 (6-ounce) can sliced
   mushrooms, drained
1/3 cup sour cream
Cooked rice or noodles

Dredge meat in flour and brown lightly in the oil. Lightly brown the onion, then add broth. Mix the flour and enough water to make a smooth paste; pour into meat mixture. Add mustard and wine; simmer for 1 hour or until meat is tender. Add mushrooms and sour cream just before serving. Serve hot over cooked rice or noodles.

An appealing taste!

BRAISED BEEF PATTIES

1-1/2 pounds ground beef
1 small onion, grated
1 egg, slightly beaten
1-1/4 teaspoons salt
1/8 teaspoon ground black
  pepper

1/2 teaspoon dry ground
  mustard
2 teaspoons prepared
  horseradish
2 tablespoons vegetable oil
1/2 cup water, about

Combine beef with grated onion, egg and seasonings. Shape into 8 patties and brown slowly in hot oil. Add 1/2 cup water, cover and simmer for 30 minutes. Add more water if needed during cooking time. Serve at once. Good with mushroom sauce or onion gravy. 8 servings.

Tasty and moist!

EASY CHILI

1 pound ground chuck
1 large onion, chopped
2 tablespoons chili powder

1 teaspoon paprika
1 clove garlic, minced

Brown meat and onion in a large skillet. Pour one half of the grease off. Add chili powder, paprika and the minced garlic, stirring until mixed very well. Now add enough water to give desired consistency. Cook and stir occasionally for at least one hour. If you can simmer for several hours the chili will taste even better.

Very good and freezes well!

GREAT CHILI

2 pounds ground beef
2 tablespoons butter
2 (14-1/2-ounce) cans whole
  tomatoes
1 cup celery, cut fine
1 cup onion, cut fine
2 medium green peppers, cut
  fine

2 teaspoons salt
1/2 teaspoon ground black
  pepper
2 cups tomato catsup
4 tablespoons chili powder

Cover beef with water; add butter and bring to a boil. Cook for 10 minutes, covered. While beef is cooking, mash tomatoes with a fork until fine. Combine tomatoes, celery, onion, peppers, salt and pepper. Cook until vegetables are tender, around 10 minutes. Add the vegetables to the meat; then add the catsup and chili powder. Cover and simmer for 45 minutes.

Great flavor!

BROILED SIRLOIN STEAKS

1/4 cup butter, melted
1 tablespoon Worcestershire
  sauce

1 teaspoon garlic powder
1 teaspoon salt
Sirloin steaks

Make a paste of all sauce ingredients. Spread on steaks. For rare steak, broil for 7 or 8 minutes. For well done steak, broil 9 or 10 minutes. Turn steaks once only.

CREAMED DRIED BEEF ON TOAST

1/4 pound dried beef
3 tablespoons margarine
3 tablespoons all-purpose flour

1-1/2 cups whole milk
Toasted bread slices

Separate beef slices and rinse in hot water. Drain and cut with scissors into fine pieces. Melt margarine; add beef and heat until beef curls. Remove from heat and blend in the flour, stirring constantly. Now add the milk and stir over heat until sauce boils and thickens. Serve hot over toast.

Quick and delicious!

CURRIED BEEF

2 pounds round steak, cut in
  small pieces
Flour
Vegetable oil
1 large onion, chopped

1/2 cup celery, chopped
1 (10-3/4-ounce) can
  mushroom soup
1/2 teaspoon curry powder
Cooked rice

Coat meat in flour and brown in oil. Sauté chopped onion and celery until tender. Add soup and curry, mixing well. Pour mixture into a casserole dish and bake at 350 degrees covered for 1 hour or until meat is tender. Serve hot over cooked rice.

A favorite dish!

HAMBURGER CASSEROLE

1 medium onion, chopped
1/4 cup green pepper, chopped
1 tablespoon vegetable oil
1 pound ground beef
2 cups cooked egg noodles

1 (10-3/4-ounce) can tomato
  soup, mixed with
  1/3 cup water
1-1/2 cups Cheddar cheese,
  grated

Brown onion and pepper in hot oil, stirring constantly; add meat and brown. Butter a casserole dish and layer the meat mixture, noodles, soup and water mixture and cheese, ending with the cheese on top. Bake at 350 degrees for 20 minutes.

Different and easy!

MEAT BALLS STROGANOFF

1-1/2 pounds ground chuck
3/4 cup whole milk
3/4 cup dry bread crumbs
1-1/2 teaspoons salt
1/4 teaspoon ground black
  pepper
3 tablespoons parsley, chopped
  fine
4 tablespoons butter, melted,
  divided
3/4 cup onion, minced
1/2 pound fresh mushrooms,
  sliced

3/4 teaspoon paprika
2 tablespoons all-purpose flour
1 (10-3/4-ounce) can beef
  bouillon, undiluted
3/4 teaspoon salt
1/8 teaspoon ground black
  pepper
1/2 cup sour cream
1/2 teaspoon Worcestershire
  sauce

Combine meat, milk, crumbs, 1-1/2 teaspoons salt, 1/4 teaspoon pepper and parsley. Shape into balls; sauté in 2 tablespoons melted butter until browned; remove and reserve. Now add 2 tablespoons butter to saucepan and sauté onion, mushrooms and add paprika, stirring until tender, about 5 minutes. Sprinkle flour over mixture and stir. Slowly add bouillon, 3/4 teaspoon salt and 1/8 teaspoon pepper. Return meatballs to sauce; cover and simmer 10 minutes. Just before serving, stir in sour cream and Worcestershire sauce; heat. Keep hot in chafing dish. Yields: 4 dozen small meatballs.

May be prepared early in the day!

ROLLED RUMP ROAST

Rolled rump roast, 4 to 6
  pounds (high quality)
Salt and pepper
1 tablespoon shortening

3 tablespoons Worcestershire
  sauce
2 cups water

Sprinkle roast with salt and pepper all over. Melt shortening; place roast in hot oil and brown quickly and evenly on all sides. Pour Worcestershire sauce over roast and add water. Cover and cook at 325 degrees; allow 40 minutes per pound cooking time. Drippings will make a delicious thin gravy or you may thicken with a roux made of flour and water to add to drippings.

MEAT LOAF

1-1/2 pounds ground round or
chuck
1 cup tomato catsup
1 cup cracker crumbs
1 cup celery, chopped fine
1 large onion, chopped fine
1 large egg, slightly beaten
1/2 cup cubed medium
Cheddar cheese

1/2 cup green pepper, chopped
fine
1-1/2 teaspoons salt
1/2 teaspoon black pepper
Grated medium Cheddar
cheese
1/2 cup water
1/2 cup tomato catsup

Combine first ten ingredients. Mix well and form into one large
or two small loaves. Freeze, if desired, and bake without thawing.
Cover top with grated cheese. Combine the water and 1/2 cup
catsup and pour over top. Bake in an uncovered baking pan for 45
minutes.

A favorite and easy to prepare!

SHORT RIBS

3 pounds short ribs
1-1/2 teaspoons salt

10 small onions
3 tablespoons water

Season ribs with salt. Place in roasting pan and bake at 350
degrees uncovered for 45 minutes or until ribs are browned. Add
onions and water. Cover and continue baking for 1-1/2 hours or
until tender. Serve with Yorkshire Pudding, if desired.

Yorkshire Pudding:

1-1/2 cups all-purpose flour,
sifted
1 teaspoon salt
4 large eggs, beaten

1-1/2 cups whole milk
1/2 cup roast beef drippings or
short ribs drippings

Sift together the flour and salt; stir in the beaten eggs gradually,
blending well. Add the milk and beat with electric beater until
thoroughly mixed. Cover and refrigerate for several hours. Have
drippings sizzling hot and pour the chilled and beaten batter into
the hot pan. Bake at 450 degrees for 15 minutes or until the
pudding puffs up. Reduce temperature to 300 degrees and bake for
another 15 minutes or until pudding is brown and crisp. Cut into
squares and place on serving platter around roast or ribs.

SPAGHETTI AND MEAT BALLS

Sauce:

1 (14-1/2-ounce) can tomatoes
1/2 teaspoon salt
1/4 teaspoon ground black
   pepper
2 teaspoons dry ground
   mustard
2 teaspoons chili powder

1/4 teaspoon ground allspice
1/2 teaspoon celery seed
1 teaspoon Worcestershire
   sauce
2 teaspoons light brown sugar,
   firmly packed

Mash tomatoes until fine or put them in blender. Combine tomatoes and all other ingredients; mix until well blended. Bring to a boil, stirring; reduce heat to simmer and cook for 20 minutes. While simmering, prepare the meatballs and then the spaghetti.

Meat Balls:

1 large egg, beaten
1 cup whole milk
1 cup dry bread crumbs
1 tablespoon onion, grated
1 teaspoon salt

1/4 teaspoon ground black
   pepper
1 pound ground beef
2 tablespoons vegetable oil
Cooked spaghetti

Mix together the first six ingredients, blending well. Add the beef and mix together thoroughly. Shape into 1-inch balls. Heat oil; add meat balls and cook until lightly browned. Add to the sauce and simmer for around 30 minutes. Pour over cooked spaghetti and serve while still hot.

Worth the effort and freezes well!

Lamb is appealing and tasty! Stop by the market and bring home some lamb to serve your family soon. Lamb is not served rare!

BRAISED LAMB CHOPS

4 small lamb steaks, 3/4-inch
   thick
2 to 3 tablespoons all-purpose
   flour
1-1/2 teaspoons salt

1/8 teaspoon ground black
   pepper
1-1/4 cups water
Hot vegetable oil

Dredge meat with the combined flour, salt and pepper and brown slowly in hot oil. Add 1/2 cup of the water, cover and simmer for around 1-1/2 hours, adding more water as needed. Serve with mint jelly.

LAMBURGERS

1 pound ground lamb
1-1/2 teaspoons salt
2 tablespoons water
1/8 teaspoon ground black
   pepper

2 teaspoons lemon juice,
   freshly squeezed
1/2 clove garlic, crushed
Mint, chopped

Combine lamb and next 5 ingredients. Blend thoroughly. Form into 4 uniform patties about 1/2-inch thick. Heat skillet until hot, sprinkle a little salt into skillet and lay in patties. Lift up and move around to prevent sticking. Cook until meat is golden brown on underside; turn over and brown on other side. Cover and cook around 10 minutes. Remove and drain off fat; add 1/2 cup water and scrape bottom of skillet. Heat to boiling and pour over patties. Garnish with the chopped mint.

LAMB CHOPS WITH RICH GRAVY

4 small lamb loin chops, 1 to 2   Mint Jelly
   inches thick (trim off all fat)

Place lamb chops in heavy skillet without any oil or seasonings. Quickly sear on both sides until delicately browned. Reduce heat to simmer, cover and cook for 1 hour, turning once or twice. The rich brown residue left sticking to the bottom of the skillet makes a flavorful gravy. Loosen residue when chops are turned. Pour gravy over chops or potatoes to be served with them. Mint jelly is a pleasing accompaniment for the lamb chops.

LAMB PILAFF

1 pound boneless lamb breast,
   cubed
1-1/2 teaspoons salt
1/8 teaspoon ground black
   pepper
2 tablespoons vegetable oil
1/2 cup onion, chopped

1/2 cup raw white rice
1 cup water
2-1/2 cups tomatoes, chopped
1/8 teaspoon ground cloves
1/8 teaspoon ground cinnamon
Parsley, for garnish

Season lamb with salt and pepper. Sauté in oil until browned. Add onion and cook until tender. Add rice, water, tomatoes, cloves and cinnamon. Cover and cook slowly for 1 to 1-1/2 hours. Add more water, if necessary. Sprinkle with chopped parsley.

BAKED HAM

1 smoked ham   Cloves, optional
Glaze, optional

Wipe ham clean with a clean, damp cloth. Wrap ham loosely with heavy duty aluminum foil and place, fat side up, on rack of a shallow pan. Do not cover pan and do not add water. For baking allow 15 minutes per pound for hams weighing 12 pounds or over; 18 minutes per pound for hams under 12 pounds. Allow 22 minutes per pound for half hams. Bake at 325 degrees until within 45 minutes of baking time; remove foil and cut rind from fat side of ham; then make several shallow cuts across fat and cut into diamonds. Spread with glaze and insert 1 clove in each square of fat. Return to oven and bake at same temperature, 325 degrees, for remaining 45 minutes, uncovered. (If you do not want to add a glaze or the cloves, just omit this procedure.)

Glaze:
1 cup light brown sugar,   3 tablespoons white vinegar
    packed   Pineapple slices, optional
1 teaspoon dry ground mustard   Maraschino cherries, optional

Combine the sugar, mustard and vinegar, blending well. Spread over ham 30 to 40 minutes before done. Place pineapple slices over ham with maraschino cherries inside slices when glaze is put over, if desired.

Baked ham is delicious alone, but with this glaze it becomes extra special!

DADDY'S FAT BACK AND MILK GRAVY

4 slices streak-of-lean salt   Shortening
    pork, thick slices

Cover meat with water; bring to a boil, drain off water. Fry in hot shortening until golden brown. Drain on paper toweling. Serve with milk gravy, if desired.

Delicious with any meal!

Milk Gravy:

2 tablespoons streak-of-lean
  drippings

2 tablespoons all-purpose flour
2 cups whole milk

Combine drippings and flour, stirring until brown. Slowly add milk; cook and stir until gravy has thickened. Good with biscuits, grits or rice.

FRANKFURTERS ON TOASTED BUNS

5 frankfurters
1/2 cup sharp cheese, grated
1/2 cup onion, grated
5 frankfurter buns

Butter, softened
Mustard, catsup
Dill pickles or sweet pickle
  relish

Cut frankfurters in half lengthwise, but not quite through, with a sharp knife. Mix together the cheese and onion; spoon 2 tablespoons of the mixture into each frankfurter. Place under broiler until cheese is brown and frankfurters are hot. Spread buns with butter and toast under broiler until lightly browned; place frankfurters inside. Serve while very hot with mustard, catsup, pickles or relish.

PORK ROAST

2-1/2 teaspoons salt
1-1/2 teaspoons black pepper
1/2 teaspoon ground nutmeg

1 teaspoon ground thyme
1 (5-6 pound) loin of pork

Combine seasonings and rub into meat thoroughly. Place in roaster, uncovered, for around 30 minutes in a 450 degree oven; remove and reduce temperature to 350 degrees. Add the following ingredients:

3 large carrots, cut in small
  pieces
2 large onions, chopped
2 cloves garlic, minced
  (optional)
2 whole cloves

1 stalk celery, chopped
1 teaspoon parsley
2 bay leaves
1 (10-1/2-ounce) can chicken
  consommé

Cover roaster and bake for around 3 hours longer or until very tender, basting often. Transfer roast to a serving platter. Skim fat from liquid in pan. Place vegetables in an electric blender (remove cloves and bay leaves). Serve gravy along with this delicious pork roast and if you have leftover roast, it will make tasty sandwiches. There will be generous portions for 10 people!

SWEET AND SOUR MEATBALLS

2 pounds ground round steak
  or chuck
1-1/2 cups soft bread crumbs
2 large eggs
1-1/2 teaspoons salt
1/4 cup finely chopped onion
1/2 cup whole milk

Combine all ingredients thoroughly; lightly mix. Make into one inch balls and place in a 15 X 19 X 1-inch baking pan or dish. Let brown in 375 degree oven for around 25 to 30 minutes. Remove and drain off the grease.

Sauce:

3 tablespoons cornstarch
3/4 cup white vinegar
1 cup light brown sugar,
  firmly packed
1 cup catsup
2 teaspoons Worcestershire
  sauce
1 (13-1/2-ounce) can pineapple
  chunks, drained
2 medium green peppers,
  finely chopped

Blend together the cornstarch and vinegar. Add the sugar, catsup and Worcestershire sauce. Pour mixture into a skillet and cook, stirring constantly until it thickens. Add to the meatballs; cover and simmer for around 20 minutes. Add the pineapple and peppers and continue cooking for 10 minutes longer. Good served over rice.

BARBECUED SPARERIBS

3 pounds spareribs, cut in
  serving-size pieces
1 large onion, chopped
1 tablespoon margarine
1 tablespoon white vinegar
1-1/2 tablespoons granulated
  sugar
4 tablespoons lemon juice,
  freshly squeezed
1/2 tablespoon prepared
  mustard
1/2 cup water
1 cup chopped celery
2 teaspoons salt
1/4 teaspoon ground red
  pepper
2 tablespoons Worcestershire
  sauce

Place spareribs in a shallow baking dish or pan and bake, uncovered, at 350 degrees for 30 minutes. While the ribs are baking, sauté onion in margarine for 4 or 5 minutes or until tender. Now add the remaining ingredients, mixing well. Simmer for 5 minutes. Pour mixture over the spareribs and continue baking for an hour longer, basting the ribs occasionally with the sauce. 5 servings.

You won't have any leftovers!

BRAISED PORK CHOPS

5 pork chops, cut at least
   1-inch thick
1-1/2 teaspoons salt

3 tablespoons all-purpose flour
1-1/2 cups whole milk

Lay chops down flat in a large, heavy skillet over medium heat. Increase heat slightly and brown on both sides. Sprinkle with salt and cover tightly, reducing heat to simmering. Cook for around 30 to 40 minutes or until meat is tender, turning once or twice during cooking. If chops seem tough, add 4 or 5 tablespoons water. When tender, remove chops to a hot platter and keep warm until ready to serve. To make gravy, drain off all but around 3 tablespoons fat; blend in the flour and stir until lightly browned. Add the milk and cook and stir constantly until smooth and thickened. Serve gravy hot with chops. (You may also dredge chops with flour before browning for variation.)

Easy and good any time!

PORK TENDERLOIN

1/4 cup margarine
1 large onion, finely chopped
2 tablespoons granulated
   sugar
1 tablespoon cornstarch (do
   not use flour)
2 teaspoons salt

1 teaspoon grated orange rind
1 bay leaf
1/2 cup freshly squeezed
   orange juice
1/3 cup cooking sherry
2 pork tenderloins, 1 pound
   each

Melt margarine; add onion and stir until tender. Combine sugar, conrstarch, salt, orange rind, bay leaf, orange juice and sherry; add onions. Place tenderloins in a roaster and pour over the orange mixture. Cover and cook at 325 degrees for around 1 hour or until tender. Remove tenderloins and serve on a platter. Pour the juices over the meat.

Deliciously different!

SAUSAGE-NOODLE CASSEROLE

1 pound sausage
1/2 cup onion, chopped
1 (8-ounce) package noodles,
   cooked
1 (10-3/4-ounce) can cream of
   mushroom soup

1 cup grated cheese
1 cup whole milk
Grated cheese, for top

Brown the sausage and onion, stirring constantly. Cook

noodles by package directions and drain well. Combine the sausage mixture, noodles, soup, 1 cup grated cheese and milk well. Spoon into a casserole dish and grate cheese over top. Place in a 350 degree oven until cheese melts and browns.

CHEESE STUFFED FRANKFURTERS

8 slices bacon   8 Cheddar cheese slices
8 frankfurters

Cook bacon slowly until half cooked; drain and let cool. Cut each frankfurter lengthwise to form a deep pocket. Cut a slice of cheese to fit pocket and then cut 7 more slices. Fit the slices into pockets and wrap bacon around frankfurters from end to end; secure with toothpicks, then place, cheese side down, in a shallow baking dish. Broil on all sides until bacon is crisp. Serve while hot.

SPANISH PORK CHOPS

5 thick pork chops   1/2 teaspoon ground black
1 tablespoon vegetable oil   pepper
1 medium onion, chopped   3 tablespoons all-purpose flour
2 cups canned tomatoes   1/4 cup cold water
1-1/2 teaspoons salt   4 cups hot cooked rice

Brown chops slowly on both sides in the oil. Remove them from pan and set aside. Now sauté onion in same pan; add chops, tomatoes and seasonings. Cover and simmer 45 minutes to an hour, or until tender. Remove chops. Make a smooth paste with the flour and cold water. Add this to the tomato mixture; boil 2 to 3 minutes, stirring constantly. Place cooked rice in center of meat platter. Arrange chops around rice and pour tomato sauce over the chops.

Wonderful taste!

BREADED VEAL CUTLETS

6 veal cutlets, 1/2-inch thick   1 cup fine bread crumbs
Salt   2 eggs, well beaten
Ground black pepper   Vegetable oil

Sprinkle salt and pepper on both sides of cutlets. Dip into bread crumbs, then into beaten eggs and again into the crumbs. Brown slowly in vegetable oil; allow 15 minutes for each side. Good with a tomato sauce.

SCRAPPLE

3 pounds fresh pork
1 pound fresh liver
8 cups water
4 teaspoons salt
1-1/3 cups plain corn meal
2 large onions, grated

1/2 teaspoon ground black
  pepper
1/4 teaspoon ground red
  pepper
2 tablespoons ground sage

Cook pork and liver, covered, in boiling, salted water until pork falls from bones. Remove meat from broth and grind into small pieces. Strain broth into a large saucepan; add cornmeal and cook, stirring constantly until mixture thickens, around 5 minutes or so. Add meats, onion and seasonings. Cook over boiling water for around 30 minutes. Pour into greased molds or loaf pans and cool. When ready to serve, slice and pan fry in small amount of shortening until lightly browned. Refrigerate any unused portion.

A delicious family recipe— you will like it!

VEAL CASSEROLE

1 pound veal, cubed
1 large onion, chopped fine
2 tablespoons vegetable oil
1 cup water
1 cup fresh mushrooms,
  chopped

1 (8-ounce) package noodles
  (fine), cooked and drained
1 teaspoon salt
1/2 teaspoon ground black
  pepper
1 (8-ounce) carton sour cream

Cook and stir veal and onion in hot oil until lightly browned. Add water; cover and simmer for 45 minutes to 1 hour. Add mushrooms, noodles, salt and pepper. Spoon mixture into a buttered casserole dish. Spoon sour cream over top. Bake at 350 degrees for around 40 to 45 minutes.

Unusually good!

VEAL PATTIES

1 pound ground veal
1 teaspoon salt
1/8 teaspoon ground black
  pepper
1 tablespoon onion, minced
1 large egg, beaten

2 tablespoons butter, melted
1 chicken bouillon cube
1 cup water
1 tablespoon butter, melted
Pineapple slices

Combine veal, salt, pepper, onion and egg, mixing well. Shape into 3/4-inch patties. Melt butter and brown patties slowly. Dissolve bouillon cube in hot water and pour around patties; cover and simmer for 30 to 45 minutes or until meat is done. Melt 1 tablespoon butter in saucepan and brown the pineapple slices. Serve while warm with the hot veal patties.

VEAL BIRDS

1-1/2 pounds boneless veal
  steaks or cutlets, thinly
  sliced
1/4 cup all-purpose flour
1 teaspoon salt
1/4 teaspoon ground black
  pepper
1 cup celery, finely cut

1/4 cup butter or margarine,
  divided
3 cups fine bread crumbs
1 chicken bouillon cube
1 cup water
1/2 teaspoon salt
Dash ground black pepper

Have veal cut into 5 or 6 pieces. Dredge one side only in flour, salt and pepper combined. Sauté celery in 2 tablespoons butter or margarine; add crumbs and lightly mix together. Set aside to cool. Dissolve the bouillon cube in water and add 1/2 cup to crumb mixture; add salt and pepper and mix well. Spoon a portion of the mixture on the unfloured side; roll up with stuffing inside. Fasten with toothpicks. Melt remaining butter or margarine; brown rolls slowly. Add rest of bouillon liquid and 1/4 cup water; cover and cook for around 1 hour or until veal is tender. Thicken gravy, if desired.

VEAL SCALLOPINI

1-1/2 pounds boneless veal
  steaks, 1/2-inch thick
1/2 teaspoon salt
1/3 cup all-purpose flour
1/3 cup butter, melted
1 cup sliced mushrooms
1 chicken bouillon cube

3 tablespoons water
1/8 teaspoon ground black
  pepper
2 tablespoons lemon juice,
  freshly squeezed
Buttered toast points

Have veal cut into 5 or 6 cutlets. Lightly salt cutlets. Pound flour in lightly on both sides until cutlets are about 1/4-inch thick. Melt butter and when hot, brown cutlets on both sides for 6 or 7 minutes. Remove cutlets and keep warm. Add mushrooms to saucepan, cover and cook for several minutes; shake or stir to prevent overbrowning. Dissolve bouillon cube in water and add to the mushrooms and gravy mixture. Stir in the pepper. Spoon the gravy and mushrooms around the veal cutlets and sprinkle the lemon juice over the veal. Serve while still hot with buttered toast points.

Pastry
and Pies

Pastry is a sometimes difficult task, but once you learn how you won't forget. There are so few ingredients that it seems impossible to make a mistake. The ingredients must be handled quickly and be mixed just so much and no more. Good pastry will be tender and flaky, golden brown and flavorful. Don't give up and you will succeed!

DOUBLE PIE CRUST

2 cups sifted all-purpose flour
1 teaspoon salt
3/4 cup vegetable shortening
1/4 cup cold water

Sift flour and then measure and sift together with the salt into a large mixing bowl. Cut in the shortening with a pastry blender until the mixture is blended. Sprinkle with the water and stir with a fork until mixture forms a ball. Divide dough in half and roll out each half on a floured surface to fit pie plate. Make edge of first half as high as possible. Fill pie shell and then roll out second half to cover filling. Fold edge under bottom crust and flute with fingers or fork. Prick or slit top crust to allow steam to escape. Bake according to time and temperature recommended in recipe to be used.

It takes a little practice to make a successful pie crust- but perseverance will reward you well!

SINGLE PIE CRUST

1-1/3 cups all-purpose flour, sifted
1/2 teaspoon salt
1/2 cup vegetable shortening
3 tablespoons cold water

Sift flour before measuring and then add the salt. Cut in the shortening with a pastry blender until blended. Sprinkle with the water and stir with a fork until the mixture forms a ball. On a lightly floured board, roll out dough to fit pie plate. Make edges a little higher than the plate; fold under and flute with fingers or fork. For unbaked pie shell, set aside for filling. For baked pie shell, bake at 425 degrees for 12 minutes, or until brown.

SWEET PIE CRUST

1-1/2 cups all-purpose flour
2 teaspoons granulated sugar
1 teaspoon salt
1/2 cup vegetable oil
2 tablespoons cold whole milk

Preheat oven to 425 degrees. Sift flour, sugar and salt into an 8-inch pie plate. Combine the oil and milk, blending well. Pour over the flour mixture and mix with a fork until flour is completely moistened. With spoon or fingers, press pastry evenly and firmly over bottom of plate. Now press sides and flute. Prick surface with a fork. Bake around 12 minutes or until golden brown. Cool and fill.

CRUMB PIE SHELL

1-1/2 cups vanilla wafer
  crumbs

1/2 cup granulated sugar
1/3 cup butter, melted

Combine all ingredients and blend well. Press firmly on bottom and sides of a 9-inch pie plate. Refrigerate until set.

GRAHAM CRACKER CRUMB PIE SHELL

1/4 cup butter, softened
1/4 cup granulated sugar

1-1/4 cups graham cracker
  crumbs

Blend together all ingredients and spoon into a 9-inch pie plate. Press crumb mixture firmly against bottom and sides of plate. Bake at 375 degrees for around 8 minutes. Cool and gently spoon in the filling.

Pie is the All-American dessert. Pies have been enjoyed for generations in homes everywhere. You can make a top-notch pie any day of the year...so, do it!

APPLE PIE

3/4 cup granulated sugar
1/4 cup light brown sugar,
  packed
1/4 teaspoon salt
3/4 teaspoon ground nutmeg
1/4 teaspoon ground cinnamon
2 tablespoons all-purpose flour

1 (21-ounce) can pie apples
1 teaspoon lemon juice, freshly
  squeezed
2 tablespoons butter
2 (9-inch) deep dish pie shells,
  unbaked

Combine sugars, salt, spices, flour and apple, blending well. Sprinkle lemon juice over the apple mixture. Spoon into one of the pie shells. Dot with butter. Carefully remove the other pie shell and place over the top. Seal with fingers or fork. Prick top in several places. Bake in 425 degree oven for around 40 to 45 minutes or until golden brown.

One taste calls for another!

APPLE CREAM PIE

Pie:

2 cups tart apples, finely
  chopped
1 teaspoon lemon juice, freshly
  squeezed
1 cup granulated sugar
3 tablespoons all-purpose
  flour, sifted

Pinch salt
2 large eggs, beaten
1 teaspoon pure vanilla extract
1 (8-ounce) carton sour cream
1 (9-inch) deep dish pie shell,
  unbaked

Pare and chop apples; sprinkle with juice and set aside. Combine the sugar, flour and salt; add eggs, vanilla and sour cream; beat until smooth. Fold in apples and mix well. Spoon mixture into pie shell and bake at 375 degrees for 15 minutes; reduce heat to 325 degrees and bake for 30 minutes longer. Remove from oven and add topping immediately.

Topping:

1/3 cup all-purpose flour
1/4 cup butter, melted

1/3 cup light brown sugar,
  packed

Combine all ingredients and blend well. Sprinkle over the baked pie and bake at 325 degrees for 20 minutes or until topping is brown.

Different and delicious!

APPLESAUCE PIE

1 cup granulated sugar
2 teaspoons all-purpose flour
1/2 teaspoon salt
3 large eggs
2 cups tart applesauce

3 tablespoons lemon juice
1 teaspoon grated lemon rind
3 tablespoons butter, melted
1 (9-inch) deep dish pie shell,
  unbaked

Combine sugar, flour and salt. Add eggs and beat with a rotary beater, or a portable electric beater, thoroughly; beat in applesauce. Gently stir in the juice and rind; then the butter. Spoon mixture into pie shell. Bake at 450 degrees for 15 minutes; reduce heat to 275 degrees and bake for 20 additional minutes. Remove and cool on cake rack for several hours before cutting.

BLACK BOTTOM PIE

Crust:

1 (8-1/2-ounce) box chocolate
  wafers, rolled fine (38 wafers)

1/2 cup butter, melted

Combine crumbs and butter, blending well. Press into a 9-inch pie plate and bake at 300 degrees for 10 minutes. Cool and then fill with pie filling.

Filling:

1 tablespoon unflavored gelatin
1/4 cup cold water
2 cups whole milk, scalded
4 large egg yolks, beaten
1/2 cup granulated sugar
4 teaspoons cornstarch
1-1/2-ounces unsweetened chocolate, melted
1 teaspoon pure vanilla extract
4 large egg whites, stiffly beaten
1/2 cup granulated sugar
1/4 teaspoon cream of tartar
1 (8-ounce) carton whipping cream, whipped
3 tablespoons granulated sugar
Shaved chocolate curls

Soften gelatin in water and set aside. Scald milk. Combine the beaten yolks gradually with the 1/2 cup sugar and cornstarch until blended. Gradually add the scalded milk in top of double boiler. Cook and stir over hot water until the custard coats a spoon. To 1 cup custard, add melted chocolate and vanilla. Pour this mixture into pie shell and refrigerate until chilled.

Add softened gelatin to remaining hot custard. Stir until gelatin is completely dissolved. Cool until slightly thickened. Beat egg whites until stiff, gradually add the sugar and cream of tartar, beat until shiny. Fold into the gelatin mixture and spoon over pie. Chill. When ready to serve, whip cream until stiff and gradually add the sugar, blending; spread over pie and shave curls of chocolate for top, if desired.

An attractive and delicious pie!

BANANA-PINEAPPLE PIE

1 (9-inch) pie shell, baked and cooled
1 (8-1/4-ounce) can crushed pineapple, with juice
1/2 cup granulated sugar
1 tablespoon cornstarch
1 large banana, sliced
1 cup chopped pecans
1 (8-ounce) carton whipping cream, whipped
2 tablespoons granulated sugar
Chopped pecans, for garnish, if desired

Bake pie shell and cool. Combine the pineapple, juice, sugar and cornstarch. Cook over low heat until thickened and glazed. Pour into pie shell. Place sliced banana over mixture and sprinkle with the pecans. Beat cream until thickened, gradually adding the sugar until well blended. Spoon over the pie and top with additional pecans, if desired.

APRICOT PIE

1/2 pound package dried
   apricots
2 cups cold water
1-1/4 cups granulated sugar,
   divided

1-1/2 tablespoons cornstarch
Dash salt
2 tablespoons butter
2 (9-inch) pie shells, unbaked

Rinse apricots in cold water. Place apricots and water in a large saucepan; cover and let soak for several hours. Now add one-half of the sugar; cover and boil mixture for around 20 minutes or until apricots are tender. Drain off juice and measure; add water to make 1 cup and add to apricots. Stir together the cornstarch, salt and rest of sugar. Blend in with the apricot mixture. Spoon into pie shell and dot with butter. Cut other pie shell into strips and make a lattice top by criss-crossing strips across top of pie. Bake at 425 degrees for around 30 minutes or until crust is golden brown and juice is bubbly. Cool for several hours before serving.

BANANA CHOCOLATE CREAM PIE

Crust:

2 cups cornflakes, rolled fine
1/2 cup butter, melted

1/4 cup granulated sugar

Combine all ingredients and mix well. Press on bottom and sides of a 9-inch buttered pie plate. Refrigerate while you prepare filling.

Filling:

4 large egg yolks
3/4 cup granulated sugar
2 cups whole milk, scalded
   (divided)
1 tablespoon unflavored
   gelatin
1/4 cup water

1-1/2 teaspoons pure vanilla
   extract
2 large bananas, sliced
1 (8-ounce) carton sour cream
1/2 cup semi-sweet chocolate
   chips

Beat yolks and sugar together until well mixed; add 3 table-spoons scalded milk, stirring constantly. Now add remainder of the milk and then cook, stirring constantly, until thickened. Soften gelatin in water and blend into custard. Stir in vanilla. Refrigerate until slightly congealed and then fold in the sliced bananas. Spoon into prepared crust. Spread sour cream over top; sprinkle chocolate chips over sour cream. Top with meringue.

Meringue:

4 large egg whites
Dash salt

1/4 teaspoon cream of tartar
1/4 cup granulated sugar

Beat egg whites until stiff; add salt and cream of tartar and blend. Now gradually add sugar, beating until shiny. Spread on pie. Brown at 450 degrees for several minutes. Cool and then refrigerate for several hours before serving.

A special pie!

BROWN SUGAR PIE

1 cup light brown sugar,
   firmly packed
1 tablespoon all-purpose flour
3 large eggs, separated
   (reserve whites for
   meringue)

1 cup whole milk
1/2 cup pecans, chopped
1 (9-inch) pie shell, baked

Combine the sugar and flour. Then add the egg yolks, blending well. Gradually add the milk, mixing thoroughly and then stir in the pecans. Pour ingredients into a medium saucepan and cook until it thickens. Pour into a 9-inch baked pie shell and top with meringue. Place in 350 degree oven until the meringue browns. Remove and cool before serving.

Meringue:
3 large egg whites (reserved)
4 tablespoons granulated
   sugar

Beat egg whites until stiff but not dry. Gradually add sugar and beat until stiff peaks form.

A delicious pie that you will want to serve again and again!

BUTTERMILK PIE

1/2 cup butter, softened
1-1/2 cups granulated sugar
2 tablespoons all-purpose flour
1/2 teaspoon baking powder
3 large eggs, beaten
1 cup buttermilk

1/2 teaspoon baking soda,
   dissolved in buttermilk
2 tablespoons pure vanilla
   extract
1 (9-inch) deep dish pie shell,
   unbaked

Cream butter and sugar. Sift together the flour and baking powder and blend in the creamed mixture. Add eggs, one at a time, beating well after each addition. Now add the buttermilk-soda combination and the vanilla, stirring to blend. Pour mixture into pie shell and bake at 350 degrees for around 45 minutes or until set.

Simple to make!

BUTTERSCOTCH PIE NO. 1

1 cup light brown sugar,
  packed
1/4 cup water
1/4 cup butter
1 tablespoon white corn syrup
1-3/4 cups whole milk, scalded
1/2 cup granulated sugar
2 tablespoons cornstarch
3 tablespoons all-purpose flour

1/4 teaspoon salt
2 large egg yolks, slightly
  beaten
1 (9-inch) deep dish pie shell,
  baked and cooled
1 (8-ounce) carton whipping
  cream, whipped
2 tablespoons granulated
  sugar

Combine sugar, water, butter and syrup; bring to a boil and cook until mixture forms a hard ball when dropped into cold water. Scald milk in top of double boiler. Combine granulated sugar, cornstarch, flour and salt and stir to mix well. Gradually add the scalded milk, stirring to mix thoroughly. Cook in top of double boiler for around 15 minutes, stirring constantly until thickened and smooth. Add butterscotch mixture and stir until smooth and shiny. Add beaten egg yolks and cook in double boiler for 2 additional minutes. Cool and pour into baked pie shell. Beat the cream until stiff, gradually adding the sugar until dissolved. Spoon on top of cooled pie. Refrigerate until ready to serve.

An extra-delicious pie!

BUTTERSCOTCH PIE NO. 2

1 cup granulated sugar
1/2 cup all-purpose flour
1/2 cup butter, melted
2 eggs, slightly beaten
1 (6-ounce) package
  butterscotch chips

1 cup pecans, chopped
1 teaspoon pure vanilla extract
1 (9-inch) pie shell, unbaked

Mix together the sugar and flour; add melted butter and blend well. Stir in the eggs, chips, pecans and vanilla. Pour the mixture into the pie shell. Bake at 325 degrees for around 1 hour or until golden brown and set.

Rich and yummy!

COCONUT PINEAPPLE PIE

3/4 stick butter or margarine
1-1/2 cups granulated sugar
3 large eggs
3 tablespoons all-purpose flour
1 cup crushed pineapple

1 (6-ounce) package frozen
  grated coconut
1 (9-inch) pie shell, deep-dish,
  unbaked

Melt butter and set aside to cool. Combine melted butter and sugar and beat to blend. Add eggs, one at a time, beating well after each addition. Add flour and mix well. Fold in the pineapple and coconut. Pour into unbaked pie shell. Bake for 1 hour at 350 degrees or until set.

CHESS PIE NO. 1

1 cup butter, softened
2 cups granulated sugar
2 teaspoons pure vanilla
   extract
1/2 cup all-purpose flour
1/4 teaspoon salt

4 large egg yolks, beaten
1 cup whipping cream,
   unwhipped
1 (9-inch) deep-dish, unbaked
   pie shell

Cream butter and add sugar gradually, beating well. Stir in vanilla, flour and salt. Beat in the egg yolks and then, gradually, the cream. Pour into pie shell and bake at 450 degrees for 10 minutes; reduce heat to 325 degrees and continue baking 25 to 30 additional minutes. Custard should be slightly soft in center when removed; it will become firm as it cools. Excellent served warm and equally as good cold. Refrigerate any uneaten portion.

CHESS PIE NO. 2

1 cup butter, softened
2 cups granulated sugar
5 large eggs, separated
   (divided)
Dash salt
1 teaspoon pure vanilla extract

1 cup pecans, chopped
1 cup raisins, chopped
1/3 cup granulated sugar
1 (9-inch) deep-dish pie shell,
   unbaked

Cream butter until soft and fluffy. Gradually add sugar, blending well. Add egg yolks, one at a time, beating well after each addition. Beat 2 egg whites until stiff and add to the creamed mixture along with the salt, vanilla, pecans and raisins; fold in thoroughly. Pour into pie shell. Bake at 450 degrees for 12 minutes; reduce heat to 300 degrees and bake for 20 additional minutes. While baking, beat 3 remaining egg whites until stiff, gradually adding the 1/3 cup sugar until stiff and shiny. Spread on top of pie and push meringue into sides. Return to oven and bake for 15 minutes, or until lightly browned. Cool on cake rack before serving.

CHOCOLATE CHIP PIE

2 large eggs, slightly beaten
1 cup granulated sugar
1/2 cup all-purpose flour
1/2 cup butter, melted
1 teaspoon pure vanilla extract
1 cup pecans, chopped
   (divided)
1 (6-ounce) package semi-sweet
   chocolate chips

1 (9-inch) deep dish pie shell,
   unbaked
1 (8-ounce) package whipping
   cream, whipped with 3
   tablespoons granulated
   sugar
1/4 cup pecans, finely chopped
Semi-sweet chocolate chips
   (few for garnish)

Beat eggs slightly; blend in sugar, flour, butter and vanilla. Stir in pecans and chocolate chips. Pour into pie shell. Bake in 325 degree oven for around 50 minutes or until set. Cool on a wire rack. Serve at room temperature. Just before serving, garnish with whipped and sweetened cream, pecans and chocolate chips, if desired.

You won't be able to forget the taste of this delicious pie!

CHOCOLATE FUDGE PIE

1-1/2 squares unsweetened
   chocolate
1/4 cup butter or margarine
1-1/2 cups granulated sugar
1/2 cup evaporated milk
2 large eggs, lightly beaten
1/2 teaspoon pure vanilla
   extract

1 (9-inch) frozen pie shell,
   unbaked
1 (8-ounce) carton whipping
   cream, whipped and
   sweetened to taste

Melt chocolate and butter over medium heat. Remove and add sugar, blending well. Now add the milk, a little at a time, until mixed; then slowly add the eggs and finally the vanilla, blending thoroughly. Pour mixture into a frozen pie shell. Bake at 350 degrees for around 45 to 55 minutes or until the pie is set. Serve while still warm and top with sweetened whipped cream, if desired.

This takes almost no effort and can be made on the spur of the moment yet tastes wonderful!

FRENCH STRAWBERRY GLAZED PIE

Crumb Pie Shell:

1/4 cup granulated sugar
1-1/2 cups vanilla wafer crumbs

1/3 cup melted butter or
   margarine

Combine all ingredients and blend well. Press firmly on bottom and sides of a 9-inch pie plate. Refrigerate until set.

Filling:

1 quart fresh strawberries
1 cup water, divided
2 tablespoons cornstarch (do
    not use flour)

1 cup granulated sugar

Wash, hull and drain fresh strawberries. Simmer 2/3 cup water and 1 cup strawberries for around 3 minutes. Then blend in the cornstarch, sugar and 1/3 cup water. Continue cooking until clear (or glazed). Cool. Set aside one half cup strawberries to garnish top. Place remaining strawberries in the pie shell and cover with the glazed mixture. Chill. Serve topped with whipped cream and strawberries.

Topping:

1 (8-ounce) carton whipping
    cream

2 tablespoons granulated
    sugar

Beat cream until slightly thickened. Add sugar gradually and beat until thickened.

Delightfully delicious!

CHOCOLATE MERINGUE PIE

1 (9-inch) pie shell, baked and
    cooled
3/4 cup granulated sugar
2 tablespoons cornstarch
1/4 teaspoon salt
4-1/2 tablespoons cocoa
1-1/4 cups evaporated milk

1 cup water
2 large egg yolks, beaten
1 teaspoon pure vanilla extract
2 large egg whites
2 tablespoons granulated
    sugar

Bake pie shell and set aside to cool. Combine the sugar, cornstarch, salt and cocoa in top of double boiler; add the milk and water gradually. Place over boiling water and cook for 20 minutes, stirring frequently. Remove from heat and stir in the beaten egg yolks. Return to heat and cook for 2 additional minutes, stirring. Add vanilla. Pour into pie shell. Beat egg whites until stiff. Gradually add the sugar until blended. Cover pie with meringue. Place in a 350 degree oven until meringue browns, around 5 minutes. Cool before serving.

Good news...this is easy and you will like the taste!

CRACKER PIE

22 butter-flavored crackers,
   crushed fine
1 cup granulated sugar, divided
1 teaspoon pure vanilla extract
1 cup pecans, chopped
3 large egg whites

1 (8-ounce) carton whipping
   cream, whipped
2 tablespoons granulated
   sugar
Sweet chocolate, grated

Combine crackers, 1/2 cup sugar, vanilla and pecans. Beat egg whites until stiff, add rest of sugar gradually until meringue is stiff and shiny. Now fold into cracker mixture. Pour into buttered pie plate. Bake in 350 degree oven for around 30 minutes. Cool completely. Whip cream until thickened and gradually add the 2 tablespoons sugar. Top pie with the cream and grate chocolate over it.

A conversation piece!

DAMSON CARAMEL PIE

2 cups light brown sugar,
   firmly packed
1 tablespoon all-purpose flour
3 large egg yolks, well beaten
1-1/2 cups damson preserves
1-1/2 cups sour cream

1/4 teaspoon salt
1 teaspoon pure vanilla extract
3 large egg whites, beaten
2 (9-inch) deep dish pie shells,
   unbaked

Mix together the sugar and flour; add the yolks, preserves, sour cream, salt and vanilla, beating until well mixed. Beat egg whites until stiff. Fold into the creamed mixture. Spoon into pie shells and bake at 450 degrees for 10 minutes; reduce heat to 350 degrees and bake for around 30 minutes or until top is browned.

Serve to your special company!

COCONUT PIE NO. 1

1 baked (9-inch) deep dish pie
   shell
3/4 cup granulated sugar
3 tablespoons white corn
   syrup
1/4 teaspoon salt

3 large eggs, slightly beaten
2 tablespoons butter or
   margarine
2 cups whole milk
1 teaspoon pure vanilla extract

Bake pie shell and set aside to cool. Combine all pie ingredients and cook together slowly for about 10 minutes or until slightly thickened. Pour into the baked and cooled pie shell. Let cool completely before slicing.

Wonderful taste!

COCONUT PIE NO. 2

1/2 cup butter, softened
1-1/2 cups granulated sugar
4 large eggs
1/4 cup buttermilk

1 teaspoon pure vanilla extract
1 cup flaked coconut
1 (9-inch) deep dish pie shell,
  unbaked

Beat butter until light and fluffy, gradually adding sugar until blended well. Add eggs, one at a time, beating well after each addition. Stir in milk and vanilla until blended, then add coconut. Pour into pie shell and bake at 350 degrees for 45 minutes or until set.

COCONUT PECAN PIE

3 large eggs, beaten
1-1/2 cups granulated sugar
1/2 cup butter, melted
1 teaspoon pure vanilla extract
2 teaspoons lemon juice,
  freshly squeezed

1 (3-1/2-ounce) can flaked
  coconut
1/2 cup pecans, coarsely
  broken
1 (9-inch) pie shell, unbaked

Beat eggs well; gradually add sugar until well blended. Add the butter, vanilla and juice and thoroughly combine. Stir in the coconut and pecans. Pour into the pie shell and bake at 350 degrees for around 45 to 50 minutes or until set.

FROZEN LEMON PIE

1 (9-inch) graham cracker
  crust, prepared
3 large eggs, separated
1/3 cup lemon juice, freshly
  squeezed
1 teaspoon lemon rind, grated
  fine

1 cup granulated sugar
1 tablespoon granulated sugar
1 (8-ounce) carton whipping
  cream, whipped

Prepare crust and place in refrigerator until ready for use. Combine egg yolks and lemon juice in top of a double boiler. Stir in the rind and 1 cup sugar. Cook, stirring constantly, until thickened. Cool mixture. Beat egg whites in small mixer bowl until stiff; add 1 tablespoon sugar and continue beating until shiny. Gently fold in egg yolk mixture. Now fold the whipped cream into the lemon mixture and pour into the crust. Freeze for several hours. Remove from freezer around 30 minutes before serving time.

Refreshing taste!

EGG CUSTARD PIE

1/4 cup butter, softened
1 cup granulated sugar
1/4 teaspoon salt
5 large eggs, beaten
2 cups whole milk

1-1/2 teaspoons pure vanilla
  extract
1/2 teaspoon ground nutmeg
1 (9-inch) deep dish pie shell,
  unbaked

Cream butter; add sugar and salt and mix well. Beat eggs and add to creamed mixture, blending well. Gradually add the milk and vanilla until thoroughly mixed. Pour custard into pie shell and sprinkle nutmeg over top. Bake at 450 degrees for 10 minutes; reduce heat to 325 degrees and continue baking for around 25 minutes or until custard is set and lightly browned.

Very rich and good!

GRAHAM CRACKER CREAM PIE

Crust:

1/4 cup granulated sugar
1 teaspoon ground cinnamon
1-1/4 cups graham cracker
  crumbs (reserve 3
  tablespoons for meringue)

1/3 cup butter, melted

Combine all ingredients, except <u>reserved</u> crumbs; press firmly on bottom and sides of a 9-inch pie plate. Bake at 375 degrees for around 8 minutes. Cool.

Pie Filling:

3 large egg yolks, lightly
  beaten
1 cup granulated sugar
4 tablespoons cornstarch

1 (12 fluid ounce) can
  evaporated milk
1 cup water
1 teaspoon pure vanilla extract

Combine egg yolks, sugar and cornstarch in top of double boiler; blend well. Gradually add milk, water and vanilla. Cook over boiling water, stirring occasionally until mixture begins to thicken. If lumps begin to form, just beat vigorously and they will disappear. Spoon into cooled crust, top with meringue and then sprinkle reserved crumbs over the meringue. Place in a 350 degree oven for around 5 minutes or until meringue is golden brown. Cool, then cut and serve.

Meringue:

3 large egg whites
Dash salt
1/8 teaspoon cream of tartar

4 tablespoons granulated
  sugar

Beat egg whites, salt and cream of tartar until whites are frothy; gradually add the sugar until stiff and shiny.

A family heirloom recipe...heavenly!

ELEGANT LEMON CHIFFON PIE

Shell:
1 (9 inch) deep dish pie shell,
baked and cooled

Filling:

1/2 teaspoon grated lemon	*1 cup granulated sugar*
rind	*1/4 teaspoon salt*
1/2 cup lemon juice, freshly	*1 tablespoon melted margarine*
squeezed	*4 egg whites*
2 teaspoons unflavored gelatin	*Dash of salt*
1/3 cup cold water, divided	*1/4 cup granulated sugar*
4 egg yolks	

Wash lemons and grate off 1/2 teaspoon lemon rind. Squeeze juice and remove seeds only. Sprinkle gelatin over 2 teaspoons of the cold water; let stand to soften. Beat egg yolks until thick, then beat in 1 cup sugar and 1/4 teaspoon salt. Add juice and rest of water; beat to mix well. Pour into top of double boiler. Place over boiling water; cook and stir until thickened. Add margarine and remove from heat. Stir in rind and gelatin. Set in a pan of iced water until mixture begins to thicken, stirring occasionally. Beat egg whites with dash of salt until almost stiff. Add sugar gradually beating until stiff and shiny. Fold lightly into lemon mixture until well blended. Spoon into pie shell and spread out evenly. Chill until set, 3 or 4 hours.

Topping:

1 (8-ounce) carton whipping	*1/2 cup grated coconut, fresh*
cream, whipped	*or frozen*
2 tablespoons granulated	
sugar	

Just before serving time, spread with sweetened whipped cream and sprinkle with coconut.

Well worth the time and effort!

GELATIN DESSERT PIE

Vanilla wafer pie shell,
  prepared
1-1/2 cups granulated sugar
1 (6-ounce) package
  strawberry gelatin dessert

1-1/2 cups pineapple juice
2 eggs, slightly beaten
1 (8-ounce) carton whipping
  cream, whipped

Prepare pie shell and set aside. Combine the sugar, gelatin, juice and eggs, mixing well. Bring to a hard boil over medium heat; remove from heat immediately and let cool. Beat cream until stiff. Fold gently into the gelatin mixture. Spoon into pie shell and refrigerate for several hours before serving.

A quick dessert and delightful to taste!

GRAPEFRUIT PIE

1 (9-inch) deep-dish pie shell,
  baked
2 cups granulated sugar
6 tablespoons cornstarch
1/2 cup water
2 cups grapefruit juice, freshly
  squeezed

3 large egg yolks, beaten
2 teaspoons grapefruit rind,
  grated (divided)
1-1/2 tablespoons butter

Bake pie shell and set aside to cool. Combine the sugar and cornstarch; add water and grapefruit juice. Cook and stir constantly over medium heat until mixture comes to a boil. Cook for around 5 minutes, stirring constantly. Remove from heat. Beat egg yolks and gradually stir into yolks a small amount of the hot mixture; now stir into remaining hot mixture and cook additional 2 minutes, stirring, then remove from heat. Add 1-1/2 teaspoons rind and butter. Cool and then spoon into pastry shell. Top with Meringue and sprinkle remaining 1/2 teaspoon rind over top. Bake at 350 degrees for 10-15 minutes or until meringue is lightly browned.

Meringue:

3 large egg whites (reserved)
Pinch salt
1/8 teaspoon cream of tartar

6 tablespoons granulated
  sugar

Beat egg whites, salt and cream of tartar until slightly stiff; gradually add the sugar and beat until very stiff and shiny. Spoon over filling.

INDIVIDUAL CHESS PIES

Pastry for 6 individual pie
  plates
1/2 cup butter, softened
1 cup granulated sugar
3 large egg yolks
1 large egg white

1 teaspoon pure vanilla extract
1 cup pecans, chopped
1 cup raisins, chopped
Sweetened whipped cream, for
  garnish

Prepare pastry and line 6 small individual pie plates. Cream butter until soft; gradually add sugar until well blended. Add egg yolks, one at a time, beating well after each addition. Beat egg white until stiff, then add to creamed mixture until well mixed. Stir in vanilla, pecans and raisins. Spoon into pie shells and bake at 400 degrees for 10 minutes; reduce heat to 350 degrees and bake until set and browned, around 20 minutes. Cool pies on cake rack and top with sweetened whipped cream just prior to serving.

LEMON MERINGUE PIE NO. 1

Shell:
1 (9-inch) deep dish pie shell,
  baked and cooled

Filling:

1/4 cup cornstarch
2 tablespoons all-purpose flour
1-1/2 cups granulated sugar
1/4 teaspoon salt
1 cup boiling water

4 large egg yolks
4 tablespoons butter
Grated rind of 1 lemon
1/3 cup lemon juice, freshly
  squeezed

Combine the cornstarch, flour, sugar and salt; stir in the boiling water and bring to a boil, stirring constantly until <u>thickened</u>, about 3 minutes. Beat egg yolks and quickly stir in around 1/3 cup of the hot mixture, then add remaining yolks and cook and stir in top of double boiler for 2 additional minutes. Remove from heat and stir in butter, rind and then juice in small portions, mixing well after each addition. Pour mixture into cooled pie shell. Top with meringue.

Meringue:
4 large egg whites

1/4 cup granulated sugar
  plus one teaspoon, for top

Beat egg whites until stiff; gradually add sugar until meringue is shiny and stands in peaks. Spread over pie and smooth into pie crust all around edges. Sprinkle with 1 teaspoon sugar. Bake at 350 degrees for around 5 minutes or until golden brown; watch carefully. Cool pie for several hours on a cake rack before serving. 8 servings.

LEMON MERINGUE PIE NO. 2

Shell:

1/4 cup butter, softened
1/4 cup granulated sugar

1-1/4 cups graham cracker
  crumbs

Blend together all ingredients and spoon into a 9-inch pie plate. Press crumb mixture firmly against bottom and sides of plate. Bake at 375 degrees for around 8 minutes. Cool and gently spoon in filling.

Filling:

1 cup granulated sugar
3 tablespoons all-purpose flour
1-1/2 cups whole milk

3 large egg yolks, beaten
Juice and grated rind of 2
  medium lemons

Combine sugar and flour in top of double boiler; add milk gradually and beat until smooth. Stir in the beaten yolks and cook, stirring until very thick. Add juice and rind and cook for 2 minutes. Pour mixture into cooled shell and top with meringue; sprinkle with crumbs.

Meringue and crumbs:

3 large egg whites
Dash salt
3 tablespoons granulated
  sugar

1 teaspoon pure vanilla extract
1 tablespoon graham cracker
  crumbs

Beat whites and salt until stiff. Gradually add sugar until shiny; blend in vanilla. Spread over top of pie and smooth into pie crust all around edges. Sprinkle with crumbs. Bake at 350 degrees for around 5 minutes or until golden brown; watch carefully. Cool pie several hours on a cake rack before cutting to serve. 8 servings.

Yummy and good!

LEMON CUSTARD PIE

1 teaspoon grated lemon rind
1/3 cup lemon juice, freshly
  squeezed
1 cup granulated sugar
  (divided)
2 tablespoons all-purpose flour

1/4 teaspoon salt
2 tablespoons butter, melted
3 large eggs, separated
1-1/4 cups whole milk
1 (9-inch) deep dish pie shell,
  unbaked

Grate and reserve lemon rind. Squeeze juice and remove seeds only; set aside. Blend 3/4 cup of sugar, the flour and salt in a large mixer bowl; stir in the butter. Beat in the egg yolks, then juice and milk. Beat the egg whites until stiff and gradually add remaining sugar until stiff and shiny. Fold whites and rind into the first mixture, blending well. Pour into pie shell. Bake for around 35 minutes or until crust and top are golden brown. Remove and cool for several hours before cutting. 8 servings.

Delicate and good!

LEMON CHESS PIE

1/4 cup butter, softened
2 cups granulated sugar
4 large eggs, unbeaten
1 tablespoon plain corn meal
1 tablespoon all-purpose flour
1/4 cup whole milk

1/4 cup lemon juice, freshly
  squeezed
4 teaspoons grated lemon rind
1 (9-inch) deep dish pie shell,
  unbaked

Cream butter and sugar well; add eggs and stir well but do not beat. Add corn meal and flour and blend. Now stir in the milk, juice and rind. Pour into pie shell and bake at 350 degrees for 35 to 45 minutes or until set and lightly browned.

Old time favorite!

MINIATURE PECAN PIES

Pie Shells:
1 (3-ounce) package cream
  cheese, softened

1/2 cup margarine, softened
1 cup all-purpose flour

Mix together as you would pie dough. Soften cream cheese and margarine and mix together with the flour until blended. Place in the refrigerator and chill.

Filling:
1-1/2 cups light brown sugar,
  firmly packed
2 large eggs
2 teaspoons softened butter

1 teaspoon pure vanilla extract
Crushed pecans (to be added
  separately)

Beat all ingredients together, except pecans, and set aside. Remove the dough from refrigerator and pat into sides of small muffin tins. Spoon 1 teaspoon of the brown sugar mixture into each one. Then 1/2 teaspoon crushed pecans. Now fill each cup to the top with the brown sugar mixture. Bake at 350 degrees for around 25 minutes. Allow to cool completely before removing from tins.

These little pies are so easy to make and will be a conversation piece at any get-together!

MINT CHIFFON PIE

1 (9-inch) deep dish pie shell
  (baked and cooled)
3 large egg yolks
1 cup granulated sugar
1 cup whole milk, scalded
1 tablespoon unflavored
  gelatin
2 tablespoons water

2 drops oil of peppermint
Green food coloring
3 large egg whites, stiffly
  beaten
1 (8-ounce) carton whipping
  cream, whipped (reserve
  part for garnish)
Chocolate curls, optional

Bake pie shell and set aside to cool. Combine the egg yolks and sugar; beat until well mixed. Add scalded milk gradually; cook in top of double boiler until mixture coats spoon, then remove from heat. Soak gelatin in water until dissolved. Add to milk mixture, then add oil of peppermint and just enough green food coloring to give a delicate green color. Fold in egg whites and whipped cream. Reserve enough cream to pipe around outside edges. Garnish with chocolate curls, if desired.

MINT CREAM PIE

Crust:

1 cup all-purpose flour
1/4 cup vanilla wafers, finely
  crushed

1/3 cup vegetable shortening
1/2 cup pecans, finely chopped
4 tablespoons cold water

Combine flour and wafers, tossing to mix. Cut in the shortening until mixture is in small pieces. Add the pecans and blend with a fork. Add 1 tablespoon water at a time to the mixture, tossing gently to moisten. Form dough into a ball and roll out in a round shape. Lift gently to a 9-inch pie plate allowing pastry to extend beyond edge. Prick bottom and sides with a fork and bake at 350 degrees for 10 to 12 minutes or until golden brown. Let cool as you prepare pie filling.

Filling:

1 cup granulated sugar
1/4 cup cornstarch
2-1/2 cups whole milk
2 (3-ounce) packages cream
  cheese, softened
3 large eggs, lightly beaten

2 tablespoons green creme de
  menthe
1 teaspoon pure vanilla extract
Sweetened whipped cream,
  optional

Combine the sugar and cornstarch; gradually add milk, then cream cheese. Cook and stir over medium heat until mixture is thickened, then continue to cook and stir for several minutes longer. Gradually stir small amount of hot mixture into beaten eggs, then return to saucepan. Cook, stirring for 2 additional minutes but do not boil mixture. Remove from heat and stir in creme de menthe and vanilla. Cool slightly and pour into prepared crust. Chill in refrigerator for several hours or overnight. Serve with sweetened whipped cream, if desired.

KEY LIME PIE NO. 1

Pie shell:

1-1/4 cups graham cracker crumbs

1/4 cup granulated sugar
1/3 cup butter, melted

Combine crumbs, sugar and butter until well blended. Press mixture into a 9-inch pie plate on bottom and sides with a spoon or by hand. Bake at 375 degrees for 8 minutes. Cool while you prepare filling.

Filling:

1 tablespoon (1 envelope) unflavored gelatin
1/4 cup boiling water
1/2 cup granulated sugar
1/4 teaspoon salt
4 large egg yolks
1/2 cup lime juice, freshly squeezed
1 teaspoon grated lime rind

2 drops green food coloring
4 large egg whites, stiffly beaten
1/2 cup granulated sugar
1 (8-ounce) carton whipping cream, whipped
Whipping cream, for garnish
Grated lime rind, for garnish

Mix gelatin and water; stir until completely dissolved. Add sugar and salt, blending well. Beat together the egg yolks and lime juice and stir into gelatin mixture. Cook over medium heat, stirring constantly, just until mixture comes to a boil. Remove from heat and stir in grated rind. Blend in the food coloring. Chill, stirring occasionally, until mixture mounds when dropped from spoon. Beat egg whites until slightly stiff, gradually adding 1/2 cup sugar until stiff and shiny. Fold gelatin mixture into whites and then fold in the whipped cream. Spoon into prepared crust. Spread additional sweetened whipped cream on top or spoon dollops of cream on top. Edge with grated rind.

A beautiful creation...rich and yet refreshing!

KEY LIME PIE NO. 2

Pie Shell:
*1 (9-inch) graham cracker pie
shell, baked and cooled*

Filling:
*4 large egg yolks, slightly
beaten*
*1 (14-ounce) can sweetened
condensed milk*

*1/2 cup lime juice, freshly
squeezed*
1 large egg white, beaten

Beat yolks; add milk and juice and beat until thick. Beat 1 egg white until stiff and fold into mixture. Pour into pie shell and top with meringue.

Meringue:
3 large egg whites, beaten
6 tablespoons granulated sugar

1/2 teaspoon cream of tartar

Beat egg whites until stiff, gradually add the sugar and cream of tartar; beat until stiff and shiny. Spoon over filling and bake at 350 degrees until golden brown, around 5 minutes. Cool and let set before serving.

KEY LIME BANANA CHEESE PIE

*1 (9-inch) graham cracker
crust, baked and cooled*
*1 (8-ounce) package cream
cheese, softened*
*1 (14-ounce) can sweetened
condensed milk*

*1 large egg yolk, slightly
beaten*
*1/3 cup lime juice, freshly
squeezed*
1 teaspoon pure vanilla extract
3 medium bananas, sliced

Bake pie crust and set aside to cool. Cream the cheese, then add milk and blend well. Beat in the egg yolk thoroughly. Now add the juice and vanilla, blending in well. Line the cooled pie shell with two sliced bananas. Spoon cheese mixture on top and then add the third banana sliced on top. Place in refrigerator to chill before serving.

Delectable and refreshing!

OATMEAL PIE

2/3 cup white corn syrup
2/3 cup granulated sugar
1/4 teaspoon salt
2/3 cup quick oats, uncooked

2/3 cup butter, melted
2 large eggs, beaten
1 teaspoon pure vanilla extract
1 (9-inch) pie shell, unbaked

Combine all pie ingredients; blend together until thoroughly combined. Pour into the unbaked pie shell and bake at 350 degrees for around 1 hour or until set and nicely browned.

LEMON MERINGUE PIE NO.3

Shell:
1 (9-inch) pie shell, baked and
  cooled

Filling:

1 cup granulated sugar
1/2 cup all-purpose flour
1/4 teaspoon salt
2 cups water
1/2 cup lemon juice, freshly
  squeezed

1 teaspoon lemon rind
3 large egg yolks, slightly
  beaten

Combine the sugar, flour, salt, water, juice and rind; stir until well blended. Beat in the egg yolks. Cook over medium heat until thickened, stirring constantly. Pour into baked pie shell and top with meringue.

Meringue:

3 large egg whites
1/8 teaspoon salt
6 tablespoons granulated
  sugar

1/2 teaspoon lemon juice,
  freshly squeezed

Beat egg whites until stiff; add salt and sugar gradually and beat until stiff and shiny. Stir in the juice well. Spoon over top of pie and bake at 350 degrees until top is golden brown, around 5 minutes.

LEMONADE PIE

2 (9-inch) pie shells, baked and
  cooled
1 (14-ounce) can sweetened
  condensed milk
1 (6-ounce) can lemonade
  concentrate

1 (8-ounce) carton whipping
  cream, whipped
2 tablespoons granulated
  sugar

Bake pie shells and set aside to cool. Combine the milk and lemonade. Beat cream until stiff; gradually add the sugar and beat until blended well. Fold into lemonade mixture. Pour into pie crusts. Refrigerate for several hours before serving.

Easy and delightfully good!

PEACH PIE NO. 1

2 (9-inch) frozen pie shells, cut
   in strips
2 cups ripe peaches, sliced
Water
1 cup granulated sugar
1 teaspoon ground cinnamon
1 teaspoon ground nutmeg
1/2 cup butter
Granulated sugar and ground
   nutmeg, for top

Thaw pie shells and cut in wide strips. Place wide strips in bottom of 8-inch square pan. Cover peaches with water; add sugar, cinnamon and nutmeg. Cook on low heat until peaches are tender; stir in butter and spoon mixture into pan. Criss-cross remaining strips of pastry on top of peaches. Sprinkle sugar and nutmeg over top. Bake at 350 degrees for around 30 minutes or until top is golden brown.

PEACH PIE NO. 2

3 cups peaches, pared and
   sliced
1 cup granulated sugar
6 tablespoons butter
3/4 cup granulated sugar
3/4 cup all-purpose flour
1 teaspoon baking powder
3/4 cup whole milk

Mix together the peaches and 1 cup sugar; cook until peaches are tender. Melt butter in a casserole dish. Mix together the remaining ingredients and spoon into the casserole evenly, without stirring. Pour cooked peaches on top of batter and do not stir. Bake at 375 degrees for around 30 minutes or until batter rises to the top and is golden brown.

Easy recipe and great way to serve fresh peaches!

PEACH PARFAIT PIE

1 (9-inch) deep dish pie shell,
   baked and cooled
3-1/2 cups fresh peaches,
   sliced
1/2 cup granulated sugar
Water
1 (3-ounce) box lemon gelatin
   dessert
1/2 cup cold water
1 pint vanilla ice cream
1 (8-ounce) carton whipping
   cream, whipped
3 teaspoons granulated sugar
Sliced peaches, for garnish

Bake pie shell and cool. Combine peaches and sugar and let stand for 15 minutes, then drain, reserving syrup. Add water to syrup to make 1 cup; heat to boiling point; add gelatin and stir until dissolved. Add cold water and stir well. Add ice cream by spoonfuls to hot liquid; stir until melted. Chill until mixture mounds slightly when dropped from spoon. Fold in peaches. Pour into cooled pie shell. Chill until firm. Whip cream until thickened; add sugar gradually until blended. Top pie with whipped cream and peaches, if desired.

You will receive nothing but compliments here!

PEANUT BUTTER PIE

1 (9-inch) graham cracker crumb crust, prepared
1 (8-ounce) package cream cheese, softened
2 cups confectioners sugar, sifted
1/2 cup smooth peanut butter
1 (8-ounce) carton whipping cream, whipped
1/4 cup peanuts, crushed fine

Prepare crust and set aside. Cream cheese and gradually beat in the sugar until light and fluffy. Add peanut butter and beat well. Whip cream and blend into mixture. Pour into crust and top with crushed peanuts. Chill thoroughly before serving.

Creamy and very good!

PEANUT BUTTER CHIFFON PIE

1 (9-inch) pie shell, deep dish, baked or 1 (9-inch) vanilla wafer crumb crust, prepared
1 tablespoon (1 envelope) unflavored gelatin
1/4 cup water
2 large egg yolks, beaten
1/2 cup granulated sugar
1 cup water, divided
1/2 teaspoon salt
1/2 cup peanut butter, creamy
1/2 teaspoon pure vanilla extract
2 large egg whites
1/2 cup white corn syrup

Bake pie shell and cool or prepare crumb crust and set aside. Soften gelatin in 1/4 cup water. Combine egg yolks, 1/2 cup sugar, 1/4 cup water and salt in top of double boiler. Stir in the gelatin and place over boiling water, beating constantly with a hand mixer until thick and fluffy; cool. Combine peanut butter and remaining water gradually; beat until smooth. Add cooled egg mixture and vanilla, blending with beater; refrigerate until slightly thickened. Beat egg whites until stiff; add corn syrup gradually, beating until shiny. Fold into peanut butter mixture. Spoon into baked pie shell or crumb crust. Chill until firm for several hours.

A delicate and appealing dessert!

MIRACLE PIE

1/4 cup **Genesis 18:8** (butter), softened
1 cup **Jeremiah 6:20** (sugar), granulated
4 **Deuteronomy 22:6** (eggs), large
1/2 cup **2 Kings 7:18** (flour), all-purpose
1/4 teaspoon **Matthew 5:13** (salt)

1/2 teaspoon **2 Kings 23:15** (baking powder)
2 cups **Hebrews 5:13** (milk)
1/2 teaspoon pure vanilla extract
1 cup **Genesis 43:11** (coconut), flaked or grated

Grease and flour a 10-inch pie plate and reserve. Measure all ingredients into a blender and blend thoroughly. Pour into the prepared pie plate. Bake at 350 degrees for 1 hour. Crust will form on bottom and coconut topping will appear over filling.

Be sure to try this easy pie recipe!

ORANGE CHIFFON PIE

Pie Shell:
1 (9-inch) deep dish pie shell, baked

Filling:
1/2 teaspoon orange rind, grated
1-1/4 cups orange juice, freshly squeezed
2-1/4 teaspoons unflavored gelatin
1 cup granulated sugar

1 tablespoon all-purpose flour
1/4 teaspoon salt
3 tablespoons lime juice, freshly squeezed
1 (8-ounce) package whipping cream, whipped

Topping:
2 teaspoons orange rind, grated, mixed with 2 teaspoons granulated sugar

Bake and cool pie shell. **Filling:** Grate rind of orange and reserve 1/2 teaspoon. Squeeze juice and remove seeds only. Soak gelatin in 1/2 cup of the orange juice for around 5 minutes to soften. Blend together the sugar, flour and salt in a large saucepan; stir in 1/2 cup of the orange juice. Place over heat and cook and stir until mixture is thickened. Remove from heat and stir in gelatin and rest of orange juice, lime juice and rind. Set in a pan of iced water until consistency of unbeaten egg white, stirring occasionally. Fold in whipped cream very lightly until blended in well. Spoon into shell evenly and refrigerate to set, around 3 or 4 hours. Just before serving time, sprinkle over the topping of orange rind and sugar combined.

Creamy and delicious!

PECAN PIE

1/2 cup butter, melted
1 cup white corn syrup
1 cup granulated sugar
3 large eggs, well beaten
1-1/2 teaspoons pure vanilla
   extract

1 cup pecans, chopped
1 (9-inch) deep dish pie shell,
   unbaked

Melt butter and brown slightly, stirring all the time. Let cool. Beat together the syrup, sugar, eggs and vanilla well. Remove beaters and stir in the pecans until well coated. Pour mixture into the unbaked pie shell and bake at 425 degrees for 10 minutes; reduce heat to 325 degrees and bake for around 40 additional minutes or until set.

A tasty pie!

PINEAPPLE PIE

4 tablespoons butter, melted
1-1/2 cups vanilla wafer
   crumbs
1/2 cup butter, melted
1 cup confectioners sugar,
   packed
2 large eggs, beaten

1 (8-ounce) carton whipping
   cream, whipped
3 tablespoons granulated
   sugar
1 (20-ounce) can crushed
   pineapple, well drained
1/2 cup pecans, chopped

Melt 4 tablespoons butter; add crumbs and mix well. Press the crumbs into a buttered pie plate and bake at 375 degrees for around 8 minutes. Set aside to cool. Melt 1/2 cup butter in top of double boiler; add confectioners sugar and eggs; blend well. Cook and stir constantly over boiling water until mixture thickens. Let cool. Spread cooled filling over crumbs. Beat cream until stiff, gradually adding the 3 tablespoons sugar until blended. Now spread 1/2 of the cream over the filling. Spoon pineapple over the cream; sprinkle pecans over pineapple. Spread remaining cream on top. Sprinkle a few pecans over top. Chill at least 6 hours before serving.

Sure to give a lot of eating pleasure!

PECAN PIE, HONEY!

1/2 cup granulated sugar
1 cup honey
3 large eggs
1/4 cup butter, melted and
cooled

2 teaspoons pure vanilla
extract
2 cups pecan halves
1 unbaked (9-inch) pie shell

Beat sugar and honey until mixed; then add the eggs, one at a time, beating well after each addition. Add butter and vanilla, blending well. Stir in the pecans. Pour mixture into pie shell and bake at 350 degrees for around 50 to 55 minutes. Filling should be firm around edges but soft in the center. Cool completely before serving.

Very tasty!

PRUNE CREAM PIE

Pie Shell:
1 (9-inch) pie shell, baked and
cooled

Filling:
1/2 pound dried prunes, pitted
1 cup boiling water
1 cup granulated sugar
2 tablespoons cornstarch
Dash salt
2 whole eggs and 3 egg yolks

1 (8-ounce) carton sour cream
1 teaspoon lemon juice, freshly
squeezed
Grated rind of 1 lemon
1 teaspoon pure vanilla extract

Bake and cool pie shell and set aside. **Filling:** Place prunes in top of double boiler; add boiling water. Cook over high heat until mixture is hot; reduce heat and simmer until prunes are softened. Remove and blend in sugar, cornstarch and salt. Return to heat and cook, stirring often for around 10 additional minutes. Beat eggs and egg yolks and stir in the sour cream. Slowly add to the prune mixture and cook, stirring, for around 5 more minutes. Stir in the lemon juice, rind and vanilla. Spoon into pie shell and set aside while you prepare the meringue.

Meringue:
3 egg whites
Dash of salt
1/8 teaspoon cream of tartar
1/2 cup granulated sugar

1 teaspoon granulated sugar
mixed with 1/2 teaspoon
ground cinnamon

Beat egg whites, salt and cream of tartar until stiff but not dry. Now gradually add the 1/2 cup sugar until stiff and shiny. Spread over prune mixture. Sprinkle with the sugar-cinnamon mixture. Bake at 350 degrees until top is golden brown, around 10 minutes. remove and cool for several hours before cutting.

RAISIN PIE

4 large egg yolks
2 tablespoons butter, melted
2 cups granulated sugar
1 teaspoon ground allspice
1 teaspoon ground cinnamon
4 tablespoons white vinegar

1 cup pecans, chopped
1 cup golden seedless raisins,
* cut up*
1 (9-inch) deep dish pie shell,
* unbaked*

Beat egg yolks well; add butter, sugar and spices; blend well. Now add the vinegar, nuts and raisins; stir until mixed thoroughly. Pour mixture into pie shell and bake at 300 degrees for around 1 hour and 20 minutes or until set.

Spicy and good!

RASPBERRY PIE

Crust:
1/2 cup butter, melted
1/4 cup light brown sugar,
* packed*

1 cup all-purpose flour
1/2 cup pecans, chopped

Combine all ingredients and spread evenly in a flat dish. Bake at 400 degrees for 12 to 15 minutes or until set. Let cool for 5 minutes. Crumble and press into a 9-inch pie plate.

Filling:
1 (10-ounce) package frozen
* raspberries, thawed*
1 cup granulated sugar

2 egg whites, unbeaten
1 (8-ounce) carton whipping
* cream, whipped*

Combine raspberries, sugar and egg whites; beat at high speed for 12 to 15 minutes. Fold in whipped cream and spoon into pie crust. Freeze overnight. Remove about 30 minutes before serving.

ROCKY ROAD PIE

1 (9-inch) pie shell, baked and
   cooled
2 (8-ounce) cartons whipping
   cream, divided
2 cups miniature
   marshmallows

2 teaspoons pure vanilla
   extract
1 cup semi-sweet chocolate
   pieces
1/2 cup pecans, chopped

Bake pie shell and set aside to cool. Combine 1 carton cream and marshmallows in a medium saucepan; cook and stir over medium heat until marshmallows are melted. Stir in the vanilla. Refrigerate until mixture begins to thicken. Melt chocolate pieces in top of double boiler and set aside to cool. Beat the other carton of cream until stiff peaks form. Fold into chilled marshmallow mixture thoroughly, but do not beat. Remove half of mixture to another bowl and fold in melted chocolate. Spoon fillings alternately into the prepared crust and swirl slightly. Sprinkle top all over with the pecans. Refrigerate until serving time; takes several hours to set.

Rich and delicious!

RUM PIE

1 (9-inch) graham cracker
   shell, prepared
6 large egg yolks
1 cup granulated sugar
1 tablespoon unflavored
   gelatin
1/2 cup cold water
1 (8-ounce) carton whipping
   cream, whipped

2 tablespoons rum flavoring
1 (8-ounce) carton whipping
   cream, whipped for garnish
3 tablespoons granulated
   sugar
Shaved chocolate curls, for
   garnish

Prepare pie shell and refrigerate until ready to fill. Beat egg yolks until light, gradually adding the sugar until blended well. Soften the gelatin in cold water and then heat to boiling point to dissolve. Blend in with the egg mixture, beating in well. Beat 1 carton whipping cream until stiff and fold into the egg mixture. Stir in the flavoring. Cool until mixture begins to thicken. Pour into prepared pie shell and refrigerate until thoroughly chilled and set. When ready to serve, whip other carton of cream until stiff, gradually adding the sugar until blended. Top each slice of pie with the cream and chocolate curls, if desired.

Rich and tasty!

STRAWBERRY GLAZE PIE

1 (9-inch) baked pie shell
1-1/2 quarts fresh strawberries
1/2 cup water
1 cup granulated sugar
3 tablespoons cornstarch (do
   not use flour)

2 tablespoons butter or
   margarine
Red food coloring, if desired

Bake pie shell and set aside to cool. Wash, hull and drain strawberries. Place 1 quart whole berries in baked pie shell. Crush remaining strawberries, then combine with water, sugar and cornstarch in a saucepan. Boil for 2 minutes, or longer, until mixture is clear. Add butter and enough red coloring to give a bright red color. Spoon glaze over whole strawberries, making sure all are covered. Cool and serve topped with sweetened whipped cream or plain.

Dee-licious!

VINEGAR PIE

1 cup seedless raisins, cut up
1/4 cup butter, softened
2 cups granulated sugar
1/2 teaspoon ground allspice
1/2 teaspoon ground cinnamon

4 eggs, separated
3 tablespoons 5% cider vinegar
1 (9-inch) deep dish pie shell,
   unbaked

Cut raisins with kitchen shears in 2 or 3 pieces. Cream butter and sugar thoroughly. Add spices and blend well. Beat in yolks until smooth and creamy. Add vinegar and again beat until smooth. Stir in raisins. Beat egg whites until stiff. Fold in the creamed mixture thoroughly. Spoon into pie shell and bake for 15 minutes at 425 degrees; reduce heat to 300 degrees and bake for 20 minutes longer or until top is browned and filling is set. Cool for several hours before serving.

A flavorful dessert!

SHERRY PIE

1-1/2 cups chocolate wafer
   crumbs
1/2 cup butter, melted
1 envelope unflavored gelatin
4 tablespoons cold water
2 large eggs, separated
3/4 cup whole milk

1/2 cup granulated sugar
Dash salt
1/4 teaspoon ground nutmeg
1/3 cup cooking sherry
1 (8-ounce) carton whipping
   cream, whipped
Chocolate, grated (if desired)

Combine crumbs and melted butter; press into a 9-inch pie plate and refrigerate. Sprinkle gelatin over cold water and stir to dissolve. Combine slightly beaten egg yolks, milk and sugar in top of double boiler; cook over boiling water until mixture thickens, stirring constantly. Now add the gelatin, salt and nutmeg; stir vigorously until all is dissolved. Stir in the sherry. Refrigerate until custard begins to thicken; fold in stiffly beaten egg whites and then whipped cream. Spoon into pie shell and refrigerate for several hours or overnight. Sprinkle grated chocolate over top just before serving, if desired.

SQUASH PIE

3 cups cooked, strained
   yellow squash (drain well)
2 large eggs, well beaten
1-1/2 cups granulated sugar
1/2 teaspoon salt

2 teaspoons ground nutmeg
1 teaspoon ground cinnamon
3 cups evaporated milk
1 (9-inch) unbaked pie shell
   (deep-dish)

Cut up squash and cook in small amount of water until tender. Strain to remove seeds and cool. Beat eggs, add to squash and gradually add the sugar, salt and spices; add the milk, blending well. Pour into the unbaked pie shell and bake at 425 degrees for 15 minutes. Then reduce heat to 350 degrees and bake for around 45 minutes or until the pie is set.

A different and surprisingly delicious pie!

SWEET CHOCOLATE PIE

Shell:

2 large egg whites
1/2 cup granulated sugar
1/8 teaspoon cream of tartar
1/8 teaspoon salt

1/2 teaspoon pure vanilla
   extract
1/2 cup pecans, finely chopped

Beat whites until slightly stiff; gradually add the sugar, cream of tartar and salt until very stiff and shiny. Beat in the flavoring and pecans until well blended. Spoon mixture into a greased 9-inch pie plate. Bake at 275 degrees for 1 hour. Cool completely and then spoon in filling.

Filling:

1/4 cup boiling water
1 (4-ounce) package German's
  sweet chocolate
1 (8-ounce) carton whipping
  cream, whipped

1 tablespoon granulated sugar
1 teaspoon pure vanilla extract

Boil water and melt chocolate, stirring until smooth; let cool. Beat cream until thickened; gradually add the sugar until blended. Stir in the vanilla; spoon mixture into cooled shell. Refrigerate until chilled before serving.

STRAWBERRY PIE

1 (9-inch) baked pie shell
1 (3-ounce) package strawberry
  gelatin dessert
1/2 cup granulated sugar
1 tablespoon cornstarch (do
  not use flour)
1 (10-ounce) package frozen
  strawberries, with syrup
  (thawed)

1 (8-ounce) carton whipping
  cream, whipped with
  2 tablespoons granulated
  sugar

Bake pie shell and set aside to cool. Combine gelatin, sugar and cornstarch over medium heat; stir until thickened. Remove from heat and add strawberries. Fill pie shell with mixture and place in refrigerator for two hours. When chilled, top with whipped and sweetened cream mixture.

So easy to prepare and yet perfectly delicious!

Poultry

Chicken *may* *be* *prepared* *in* *endless* *ways:* *baked,* *barbecued,* *braised,* *broiled,* *pan-fried,* *oven-fried,* *steamed,* *stewed,* *roasted.* *Prepare* *an* *elegant* *chicken* *dish* *soon!*

BUTTERMILK FRIED CHICKEN

1 (2-1/2 to 3 pound)
  fryer, cut up
Salt and pepper
Cold water

Buttermilk
All-purpose flour
Hot vegetable oil

Wash chicken, dry and then salt and pepper each piece. Place in a large pan and cover with cold water. Let stand for 30 minutes. Heat 2 inches oil. Dip chicken in buttermilk; then in flour, coating all sides. Fry in hot oil until golden brown and well done, around 30 to 40 minutes. Serve hot.

Stays moist and is delicious!

CHICKEN AND MUSHROOMS

4 chicken breast halves,
  boned
Salt and ground black pepper
  to taste
2 celery tops
1 small whole onion
1 bay leaf

Fresh mushrooms, sliced
1/2 cup butter
Paprika
1 (8-ounce) carton
  whipping cream,
  unwhipped

Combine chicken breasts, salt and pepper, celery, onion and bay leaf. Cover with water and bring to a boil; reduce heat and simmer until chicken is tender. Place chicken breasts in a shallow, buttered casserole. Cover with sliced mushrooms; dot with butter and add paprika. Gently pour over the whipping cream. Bake at 350 degrees for around 30 minutes.

Pleasing flavor!

CHICKEN BREASTS WITH ALMONDS

3 whole chicken breasts,
  halved and boned
Salt
Ground black pepper
6 tablespoons butter
2 tablespoons butter
1 tablespoon onion,
  chopped

1/3 cup slivered almonds
1 teaspoon tomato paste
1 tablespoon all-purpose
  flour
1-1/4 cups chicken broth
Pinch dried tarragon

Halve chicken breasts; remove skin and sprinkle with salt and pepper. Melt 6 tablespoons butter in a large, heavy skillet. Add chicken and brown, about 25 minutes. Remove chicken to platter. Add remaining 2 tablespons butter, onion and almonds; cook until almonds are browned. Blend in tomato paste and flour. Gradually add broth and cook until mixture thickens. Add cooked chicken and tarragon; cover and simmer for 20 minutes.

A delight for everybody!

CHICKEN CASSEROLE NO. 1

2 cups cooked chicken,
  cubed
1 (10-3/4-ounce) can
  cream of chicken soup
1 (8-ounce) carton
  sour cream

1 (8-ounce) package
  fine egg noodles,
  cooked and drained
1-1/2 cups potato chips,
  crushed fine

Combine the cooked chicken, soup, sour cream and cooked egg noodles, mixing well. Spoon mixture into a buttered casserole dish. Spread crushed potato chips evenly over top. Bake at 400 degrees for around 15 minutes or until very hot and bubbly.

Easy and delicious!

CHICKEN-RICE CASSEROLE

1 cup mixed wild rice
  and herbs, cooked
1/2 cup margarine,
  melted
1/2 cup onion, chopped
1/4 cup all-purpose
  flour
1 (6-ounce) can sliced
  mushrooms, reserve
  liquid
Chicken broth

1-1/2 cups light cream
3 cups cooked chicken,
  diced (around
  3 whole chicken
  breasts)
1/4 cup pimiento, diced
1-1/2 teaspoons salt
1/4 teaspoon ground
  black pepper
1/2 cup slivered,
  blanched almonds

Prepare rice by package directions and set aside. Melt butter and sauté onion until tender, but do not brown. Remove from heat and stir in flour, blending well. Drain mushrooms, reserving liquid. Add enough chicken broth to liquid to measure 1-1/2 cups. Gradually stir into the flour mixture. Add cream; cook and stir until mixture begins to thicken. Now add rice, mushrooms, chicken, pimiento, salt and pepper. Pour into a 2 quart buttered casserole. Sprinkle with almonds Bake at 350 degrees for around 30 minutes. Serves 8 to 12.

CHICKEN ASPARAGUS SUPREME

8 chicken breast halves,
  boned
1/2 cup celery leaves,
  chopped
1/2 cup onion, chopped
1 teaspoon salt
Water
2 (15-ounce) cans
  asparagus spears
1 cup mayonnaise
2 (10-3/4 ounce) cans
  cream of chicken
  soup

2 teaspoons lemon juice,
  freshly squeezed
1 teaspoon grated
  lemon rind
1/4 teaspoon curry
  powder
1/2 cup grated sharp
  Cheddar cheese
Parsley, optional
Pimiento, optional

Place chicken breasts in a large saucepan; add celery leaves, onion, salt and cover with water. Bring to a boil; cover and cook until tender. Remove from heat and cool. Bone and skin chicken. Place asparagus spears in a large flat buttered casserole dish; then the chicken breasts. Set aside and prepare the sauce: combine the mayonnaise, soup, juice, rind and curry; mix well. Spoon over the chicken and top with grated cheese. Bake at 350 degrees for 25 to 30 minutes or until sauce is bubbly. Garnish with parsley and pimiento, if desired.

CHICKEN TETRAZZINI

1 4-pound stewing
  chicken, cut up
2 teaspoons salt
1 teaspoon ground
  black pepper
2 bay leaves
4 cups cooked thin
  spaghetti
1/2 cup pimiento,
  chopped

2 (10-3/4-ounce) cans
  cream of mushroom
  soup, undiluted
1 cup reserved broth
1 tablespoon celery salt
1 large onion, chopped
3 cups Cheddar cheese,
  grated

Place chicken in a large saucepan and cover with water; add salt, pepper and bay leaves. Cook until chicken is tender. Remove from heat and let cool. Reserve broth and cut chicken into cubes or small pieces. Cook spaghetti by package directions; drain well. Now combine the cooked chicken pieces, cooked spaghetti, pimiento, soup, 1 cup of the reserved broth, celery salt, onion and cheese; mix well. Spoon into a buttered casserole dish and bake at 350 degrees for 1 hour.

CHICKEN CASSEROLE NO. 2

1 (2 to 2-1/2 pound)
frying chicken
1 tablespoon salt
1-1/2 cups water
1 tablespoon lemon
juice, freshly
squeezed
2 tablespoons onion,
chopped
1 cup celery, thinly
sliced

1 (10-3/4 ounce) can cream of
chicken soup,
undiluted
3/4 cup mayonnaise
3 hard boiled eggs,
chopped
1/2 cup pecans, chopped
2 cups corn flakes,
finely crushed

Combine chicken, salt and water; cook until chicken is tender. Cool; remove bones and cut into cubes or small pieces. Combine all ingredients, except crushed corn flakes; mix well. Spoon into a buttered casserole dish; top with crushed corn flakes. Bake at 350 degrees for 25 to 30 minutes.

CHICKEN CROQUETTES

Croquette sauce:
4 tablespoons butter
4 tablespoons all-
purpose flour
3/4 cup chicken broth
1/2 cup whipping cream,
unwhipped

1/8 teaspoon curry
powder
Salt and pepper

Melt butter and stir in flour, blending well over low heat. Slowly add the broth and cream, stirring constantly. Bring to boiling point and cook for 2 minutes. Season with curry, salt and pepper.

Croquettes:
2 cups cooked chicken,
chopped
1/2 teaspoon salt
1/8 teaspoon ground
red pepper
1-1/2 teaspoons lemon
juice, freshly
squeezed

1/4 teaspoon minced
onion
1 cup croquette sauce,
about
1 egg, beaten with
2 tablespoons water
Fine bread crumbs

Mix together the chicken, salt, pepper, juice and onion. Add enough sauce to hold the mixture together; chill thoroughly. Shape into croquettes; dip in egg mixture and then in crumbs. Fry in hot oil until nicely browned. Serve hot.

CHICKEN DIVAN

2 boneless chicken
   breasts, cooked
1 (10-ounce) package
   frozen broccoli,
   cooked and drained
1 (10-3/4-ounce) can
   cream of chicken
   soup

1/2 cup water
1/2 cup sharp cheese,
   shredded
1/4 cup fine bread
   crumbs

Cook chicken breasts until tender, cool and slice. Cook broccoli in a small amount of water until tender; drain well. Spoon broccoli into a buttered casserole dish and place chicken slices on top. Combine the soup and water and pour over the chicken. Sprinkle with cheese and bread crumbs. Bake at 350 degrees until hot and bubbly, around 15 minutes.

CHICKEN DUMPLINGS

1 (4-pound) stewing
   chicken, cut up
Water
2 teaspoons salt
1/2 teaspoon ground
   black pepper

1-1/2 cups all-purpose
   flour
1 teaspoon salt
3 tablespoons vegetable
   shortening
1/2 cup whole milk

Place chicken in a large saucepan and cover with water; add salt and pepper. Bring to a boil and cook, covered, until meat is tender. Remove chicken and cool. Combine the flour, salt and shortening and mix well with a pastry blender or fork. Gradually add the milk, blending to make a firm ball. Roll out on a lightly floured surface until very thin. (If dough sticks, add a small amount of flour to rolling pin and lightly sprinkle top of dough.) Cut in strips. Drop in boiling chicken broth. Cover and cook until tender; do not stir. Serve hot.

CHICKEN MUSHROOM CASSEROLE

6 chicken breast
   halves, boned
6 bacon slices
1 cup dried beef,
   cut up
1 (10 3/4 ounce) can
   cream of mushroom
   soup

1 (8-ounce) carton
   sour cream
No salt (dried beef
   is salty)
Hot cooked rice

Wrap breast halves with bacon slices and secure with toothpicks. Cut beef in small pieces and place in casserole dish. Arrange chicken on top of beef. Combine soup and sour cream, stirring to mix well. Pour over chicken. Bake at 325 degrees for around 1-1/2 hours. Add water or milk, if necessary, to prevent dryness. Serve with hot cooked rice.

CREAMED CHICKEN NO. 1

2 tablespoons butter
2 tablespoons all-
  purpose flour
1-3/4 cups whole milk
1/2 teaspoon salt

1/8 teaspoon ground
  red pepper
1 cup chicken breasts,
  cooked and cubed
Toasted bread slices

Melt butter in top of double boiler and blend in the flour; add milk, salt and pepper. Cook until slightly thickened. Add chicken and cook until meat is heated. Serve on slices of toast.

Wonderful leftover chicken dish!

CREAMED CHICKEN NO. 2

1 (4 to 5 pound)
  chicken, cut up
2 large onions, chopped
2 cloves
1-1/2 cups celery,
  chopped
2-1/2 quarts boiling
  water
1 quart chicken broth,
  divided
3/4 cup all-purpose
  flour
1 small onion, chopped

1 teaspoon
  Worcestershire
  sauce
3 tablespoons pimiento,
  minced
1 tablespoon salt
Juice of 1 lemon
1 quart celery, cut in
  1/2-inch sticks
  and parboiled
3 large eggs, well
  beaten
1-1/2 teaspoons paprika

Combine chicken, 2 onions, cloves, celery and water; cover and simmer slowly until tender; let cool in stock. Remove skin and cut chicken in cubes or small pieces, about 1/2 inch. Combine 1 cup broth and flour and blend until smooth, then add rest of broth; blend thoroughly and bring to a boil, stirring until thickened. Now add the remaining ingredients and spoon into a large casserole dish. Bake at 350 degrees for 30 to 35 minutes. Serve on toast points or in timbale molds.

CHICKEN PIE NO. 1

1 (3-pound) chicken,
  cut up
1 cup celery, chopped
1/2 cup onion, chopped
1 teaspoon salt
1/2 teaspoon ground
  black pepper
Water
2 cups hot chicken broth

1 (10-3/4 ounce) can
  cream of celery
  soup
2 large hard boiled
  eggs, chopped
1/2 cup butter, melted
1 cup whole milk
1 cup self-rising flour

Combine chicken, celery, onion, salt and pepper; cover with water. Bring to a boil; reduce heat, cover and cook until chicken is tender. Remove chicken; cool, remove bones and cut chicken into very small pieces. Measure 2 cups broth and add chicken pieces and soup; place over heat and stir until mixture boils. Remove from heat. Place chicken pieces in a buttered casserole dish; spread chopped eggs over top of chicken. Spoon broth mixture over eggs. Blend together the butter, milk, and flour until smooth. Pour over the top and <u>do not stir.</u> Bake at 425 degrees for around 30 minutes or until golden brown.

CHICKEN PIE NO. 2

2 cups cooked chicken,
  cubed
1 cup cooked rice
1/2 cup celery,
  chopped fine
1/2 cup onion,
  chopped fine
1 tablespoon lemon
  juice, freshly
  squeezed
1/2 cup mayonnaise

3 hard boiled eggs,
  chopped
1 cup cream of chicken
  soup
1 teaspoon salt
1/2 teaspoon ground
  black pepper
20 butter flavored
  crackers, crumbled
1/2 cup butter or
  margarine, melted

Combine the chicken, rice, celery, onion, juice, mayonnaise, eggs, soup, salt and pepper; stir until well blended. Spoon into a buttered casserole dish. Sprinkle cracker crumbs over top and pour the melted butter over the crumbs. Bake at 350 degrees for 30 to 40 minutes.

CURRIED CHICKEN NO. 1

1 (2-1/2 to 3-pound)
  fryer, cut up
1 (10-3/4-ounce) can
  cream of chicken
  soup
1/3 cup mayonnaise

1/2 cup celery, finely
  chopped
1 teaspoon curry powder
1 teaspoon salt
1/4 teaspoon ground
  black pepper

Place chicken pieces in a 13 x 9 x 2-inch baking dish. Bake at 350 degrees for 30 minutes. Combine remaining ingredients; stir to blend well. Spoon evenly over chicken; cover with aluminum foil and continue baking 30 to 40 minutes or until chicken is tender.

COUNTRY CAPTAIN

8 chicken breast halves,
  boned and skinned
1-1/2 cups shortening
All-purpose flour
Salt and pepper to
  taste
2 large onions, finely
  chopped
1/2 teaspoon ground
  white pepper
2 green peppers, chopped
1 teaspoon curry powder
2 (14-1/2 ounce) cans
  whole tomatoes,
  pureéd

1 teaspoon chopped
  parsley
1/2 teaspoon ground
  thyme
2 cups hot cooked rice
1/2 pound almonds,
  slivered and
  toasted
3 tablespoons currants
  or raisins
Parsley for garnish

Remove skin from chicken breasts. Melt around 1-1/2 cups shortening in large, heavy skillet. Roll breasts in a mixture of flour, salt and pepper. Brown in melted shortening. Remove from pan and keep hot. Add the onion, white pepper and green pepper to pan; cook very slowly, stirring constantly. Add the curry and salt and pepper to taste. Pureé the tomatoes and add them along with the parsley and thyme. Place chicken breasts in a roaster and pour over the mixture. Rinse the pan with water and add enough water to cover the chicken. Bake at 375 degrees for around 45 minutes or until tender. Place the chicken breasts in the center of a large platter. Spoon the rice all around the chicken breasts. Add the currants or raisins to the sauce and stir; pour over the rice. Scatter the toasted almonds on top and garnish with parsley.

A wonderful dish for special company!

CURRIED CHICKEN NO. 2

4 chicken breast halves,
  boned
1/2 cup butter, melted
1 teaspoon salt
1/2 teaspoon curry
  powder
1/8 teaspoon ground
  thyme

1/4 cup prepared
  mustard
1/3 cup honey
1/4 cup slivered
  almonds
1/4 cup currants
2 cups hot cooked rice

Arrange chicken in a buttered casserole dish. Combine butter, salt, curry powder, thyme, mustard and honey. Pour mixture over chicken; sprinkle the almonds and currants over top. Bake at 350 degrees for 1 hour. Serve over hot rice.

FRIED CHICKEN LEE

1 (2 to 3 pound)
  broiler-fryer
  chicken, cut up
2 cups all-purpose flour
1 teaspoon salt

1/4 teaspoon ground
  black pepper
1 egg, slightly beaten
1/2 cup whole milk, plus
Hot vegetable oil

Place chicken pieces in a large saucepan and cover with water. Boil for 10 minutes; remove from water and set aside to cool. Combine the flour, salt and pepper and set aside. Blend together the egg and milk and add the flour mixture gradually; add additional milk if necessary to make a thin to medium batter. Heat 1 inch oil in a heavy skillet; dip chicken in batter and place in skillet. Cover and cook over medium heat until one side is golden brown; carefully turn to other side and brown, covered. Keep covered and cook over medium heat for around 30 minutes or until all sides are golden brown. Drain on paper towels. 4 servings.

You will want to serve this fried chicken again and again!

FRIED CHICKEN LIVERS

Chicken livers
Salt and pepper
Buttermilk

Flour
Butter or bacon
  drippings

Wash and pat livers dry. Sprinkle with salt and pepper. Place livers in buttermilk for several minutes. Dip in flour until well coated. Cover bottom of heavy skillet with butter or bacon drippings; place livers in pan over medium heat. Cover pan and cook until livers are lightly browned, turning often. Remove cover last 3 or 4 minutes of cooking time. Do not overcook livers; entire cooking time should last around 10 to 12 minutes.

MARINATED FRIED CHICKEN

1 small (2 to 3 pound)
  chicken, cut up
1 cup vegetable oil
1 large egg, beaten
1/2 teaspoon oregano
1/2 teaspoon rosemary
1/2 teaspoon tarragon

1 teaspoon paprika
1 clove garlic, crushed
1 cup all-purpose flour
Salt and ground black
  pepper, to taste
Vegetable oil for
  frying

Arrange chicken in a marinating container or large, flat pan. Combine the 1 cup oil, egg, oregano, rosemary, tarragon, paprika and garlic; pour over the chicken, turning to coat on all sides. Place in refrigerator for several hours, then remove chicken from marinade. Sift together the flour, salt and pepper. Roll chicken in flour mixture until coated. Heat at least 1-inch oil in heavy saucepan and add chicken; cover and fry over medium heat, turning occasionally, until done, around 30 to 40 minutes. Chicken should be golden brown.

Great flavor!

SOUTHERN FRIED CHICKEN

1 small (2 to 3 pound)
  chicken, cut up
Salt and ground black
  pepper
2 cups all-purpose flour
1 teaspoon ground red
  pepper

1 large egg, slightly
  beaten
1/2 cup whole milk
Vegetable oil

Season chicken with salt and pepper. Sift together the flour and red pepper on waxed paper and set aside. Combine beaten egg and milk; dip chicken in egg mixture then roll in flour until coated. Heat at least 1-inch oil in large heavy saucepan; place chicken in hot oil; cover and cook over medium heat until golden brown, turning occasionally until done. Cooking time should take around 30 to 40 minutes. Drain on paper toweling.

Chicken will be moist and delicious!

WILD RICE AND CHICKEN

2 cups chicken broth
1 cup wild and white
  rice mixed,
  uncooked
Butter
1 teaspoon salt
1/8 teaspoon ground
  black pepper
1 (3-ounce) can
  mushrooms, drained

6 chicken breast
  halves, boned and
  skinned
1/2 (2.7 ounce) package
  onion soup mix
1 (10-3/4-ounce) can
  cream of mushroom
  soup, plus
1 cup water
Paprika

Pour chicken broth over rice in a large, flat buttered casserole. Dot with butter and add salt and pepper. Add drained mushrooms and place chicken breasts on top of the mixture. Sprinkle onion soup mix over all. Dilute the mushroom soup with water and spoon over chicken. Finally, sprinkle with paprika. Cook at 350 degrees for 1 hour uncovered; cover with foil and continue cooking for 30 additional minutes.

Turkey, once served mainly for holidays, now is enjoyed year-round. Roast turkey can't be beat for flavor and taste and turkey gravy is unique in flavor. Use leftover turkey for sandwiches and in recipes calling for cooked turkey.

TURKEY WITH SWEET POTATOES AND TURNIPS

3 cups chicken broth
1 bay leaf
1 large sweet potato,
  pared and cubed
1/2 pound turnips,
  pared and quartered
2 tablespoons margarine
2 large onions, chopped
2 cups cooked turkey or
  chicken, cubed

1/2 cup whipping cream,
  unwhipped
1 large egg yolk,
  slightly beaten
1/2 teaspoon dried
  tarragon
Salt and pepper to taste
Minced tarragon, for
  garnish

Combine broth and bay leaf in a large saucepan. Bring to a boil and then add the potato and turnips; lower heat, cover and simmer for around 10 to 12 minutes. Remove vegetables and strain broth. Melt margarine on low heat. Add onion; cook and stir until golden brown. Add turnips and potato and cook until vegetables are brown. Add broth and boil for around 5 minutes; mixture should be slightly syrupy. Add turkey or chicken and remove from heat. Combine whipping cream and egg yolk, then add to the turkey, stir in the 1/2 teaspoon tarragon. Place over low heat and thicken. Sprinkle with salt and pepper to taste and then the minced tarragon. Serve while still hot.

A delicious dish and easy to prepare!

TURKEY DIVAN

2 (10-ounce) packages
  frozen, chopped
  broccoli, cooked
  and drained
3/4 pound sliced,
  cooked turkey
1/4 cup butter, melted
1/4 cup all-purpose
  flour

2 cups chicken or
  turkey broth
1/2 cup grated cheese
1/2 cup whipping cream,
  unwhipped
2 tablespoons cooking
  sherry
1/4 cup grated Parmesan
  cheese

Arrange equal amounts of broccoli and turkey in 6 individual baking dishes; set aside. Melt butter and stir in flour, blending well. Gradually add broth and cook, stirring for 1 minute; add remaining ingredients, except Parmesan cheese. Spoon equal amounts over broccoli-turkey; sprinkle with Parmesan cheese. Broil for around 4 or 5 minutes or until lightly browned.

Dressing and Gravy *served at least once a year at Christmas is a real treat!*

GIBLET GRAVY

2 large hard boiled
  eggs, finely
  chopped
Cooked giblets, finely
  cut and broth from
  giblets, plus
  1 cup broth from
  boiled hen or baked
  turkey or
  3 tablespoons
  margarine, melted

Salt and ground black
  pepper
Self-rising corn meal

Boil eggs; cool, chop and combine with giblets, broth, salt and pepper to taste and gradually add enough corn meal to thicken broth. Bring to a boil gently and cook and stir for around 3 minutes. Serve hot.

CORN BREAD DRESSING

Corn bread:

1-1/2 cups self-rising corn
   meal
1 cup buttermilk
1 large egg, slightly
   beaten

2 tablespoons
   margarine,
   melted

Combine the corn meal and milk; add the beaten egg and stir to mix well. Blend in the margarine. Pour mixture into a greased, 9-inch baking pan. Bake at 425 degrees for around 20 minutes or until golden brown. Cool and crumble coarsely.

Biscuits:

2 cups self-rising
   flour

1/4 cup shortening
1 cup buttermilk

Sift flour and cut in shortening with a pastry blender. Stir in buttermilk. Knead dough lightly on a well floured surface until dough pulls away from your hands. Cut biscuits with a biscuit cutter or form with your hands. Place in a greased 9-inch baking pan. Bake at 450 degrees for around 12 to 15 minutes or until golden brown. Cool and coarsely crumble.

Dressing:

1 recipe corn bread
1 recipe biscuits
6 cups broth from
   boiled hen or
   baked turkey
1 cup onion, finely
   chopped

1 teaspoon salt
1/2 teaspoon ground
   black pepper
5 large eggs slightly
   beaten

Bake corn bread and biscuits day before you plan to prepare dressing. Crumble, cover and reserve. Boil 1/2 hen and use broth or bake a turkey and reserve broth.

Combine the crumbled corn bread and biscuits. Add the reserved broth, onion, salt, and pepper; blend well. Add the eggs and beat in well. The mixture should be thick but not dry; add additional broth or water, if necessary. Spoon into lightly greased baking dishes. Bake at 400 degrees for around 45 minutes or until golden brown. Serve hot with Giblet Gravy, if desired.

Salads and
Salad Dressings

Salads are popular and are enjoyed all over the world. Start by using fresh vegetables and fruits and consider color to create a beautiful and appetizing salad!

APRICOT CONGEALED SALAD

1 (12-ounce) package
   dried apricots
1 cup water
1/2 cup granulated sugar
1 (6-ounce) package
   lemon gelatin
   dessert
1 (3-ounce) package
   lemon gelatin
   dessert

5 cups boiling water
1 (20-ounce) can
   crushed pineapple,
   drained
1 cup slivered almonds
Crisp salad greens

Combine the apricots and water; bring to a boil and simmer until apricots are tender. Remove from heat and stir in the sugar until it dissolves. Beat mixture until smooth. Reserve 1/2 cup of this mixture for use in the topping. Now dissolve the gelatins in 5 cups boiling water, stirring for several minutes until gelatin is completely dissolved. Stir in the apricot mixture and then the pineapple and almonds. Pour into a 13 x 9 x 2-inch glass dish and chill in refrigerator until firm. To serve, spread topping and cut into squares. Serve on crisp salad greens. Will serve around 16 salad plates.

Topping:

1 (8-ounce) package
   cream cheese,
   softened
1/2 cup reserved
   apricot mixture
2 tablespoons
   cooking sherry

1 (8-ounce) carton
   whipping cream, whipped
1/4 cup confectioners
   sugar
1 teaspoon pure
   vanilla extract

Beat cream cheese until smooth; blend in the reserved apricot mixture and sherry. Beat the cream until thickened; gradually add the sugar and vanilla. Fold into the cream cheese mixture, beating until smooth.

Your guests will enjoy this congealed salad!

BING CHERRY SALAD

1 (6-ounce) package
  cherry or black
  cherry gelatin
  dessert
2 cups boiling water
1 cup _cold_ water
2 teaspoons lemon juice,
  freshly squeezed
2 tablespoons cooking
  sherry

1 (8-ounce) carton
  sour cream
2 cups pitted bing
  cherries, halved
1/2 cup pecans, chopped
Lettuce leaves
Sour cream, for garnish
Chopped pecans, for
  garnish

Combine gelatin and boiling water; stir for several minutes until completely dissolved. Measure 1 cup of this mixture into another bowl; add 1 cup cold water, juice and sherry, stirring to combine well. Pour into a 2-quart mold and chill until set. Chill remaining gelatin until partially set, then beat until fluffy; fold in sour cream, cherries and pecans. Pour on top of the chilled mixture in the mold. Refrigerate until chilled and firm. Cut and serve on lettuce leaves. Top with a spoon of sour cream and a few nuts, if desired.

CRANBERRY SALAD

1 (6-ounce) package
  lemon gelatin
  dessert
1 cup granulated sugar
1 cup boiling water
2 large unpared apples,
  ground
4 cups fresh
  cranberries, ground

1 large unpared orange,
  ground (remove
  seeds)
1 cup pecans, chopped
Lettuce leaves
Mayonnaise
Orange slices, unpared

Dissolve gelatin and sugar in boiling water. Add apples, cranberries, orange, and pecans; stir until mixture is well blended. Pour into a lightly oiled 6-cup ring mold; place in refrigerator until set. Arrange lettuce leaves on serving plate and unmold ring on leaves. Fill center of ring with mayonnaise and garnish with thin slices of unpared oranges.

DIVINITY SALAD

1 (6-ounce) jar red
  maraschino
  cherries, drained
1 (6-ounce) jar green
  maraschino cherries,
  drained
1 (8-1/4-ounce) can
  crushed pineapple,
  drained
1 (8-ounce) carton
  whipping cream,
  whipped

1 tablespoon
  granulated sugar
1 teaspoon pure
  vanilla extract
1 cup chopped pecans
1 (10-1/2-ounce) package
  miniature
  marshmallows
Lettuce leaves

Cut cherries with kitchen shears in very small pieces. Drain cherries and pineapple and set aside. Beat the cream until stiff; add the sugar and vanilla; blend well. Fold in pineapple, pecans and marshmallows. Now fold in the cherries. Place in a covered dish and refrigerate overnight, if possible. Spoon mixture into arranged lettuce cups when ready to serve.

Serve this for special guests!

LEMON LIME DREAM CONGEALED SALAD

2 cups boiling water
1 (3-ounce) package
  lemon gelatin dessert
1 (3-ounce) package
  lime gelatin
  dessert
1 (8-ounce) package
  creamed cottage
  cheese

1 (8-1/4-ounce) can
  crushed pineapple,
  plus syrup
1 (7-ounce) jar
  marshmallow creme
4 cups whipped topping
1/2 cup chopped pecans
Lettuce leaves

Bring two cups water to a boil. Combine gelatins and water; stir until completely dissolved. Place this mixture in the refrigerator and let slightly congeal only. Then add cottage cheese, crushed pineapple, plus syrup, marshmallow creme and whipped topping. Beat in mixer until well blended. Remove from mixer and stir in the pecans. Pour mixture into a 13-1/2 x 8 3/4 x 1 3/4-inch glass dish. Refrigerate until completely congealed. Cut in squares and serve on lettuce beds, if desired.

A very special congealed salad that you and your guests will remember forever!

ORANGE LAYERED CONGEALED SALAD

1 (6-ounce) package
lemon gelatin
dessert
1 (6-ounce) package
orange gelatin
dessert
1-1/2 cups boiling
water
2 cups cold water

3 bananas, mashed
2 (8-1/4-ounce) cans
crushed pineapple
(reserve juice)
1 (10-1/2-ounce)
package miniature
marshmallows

Dissolve gelatins in boiling water, then add cold water. Add the mashed banana and pineapple; stir and pour into a 3 quart rectangular bowl. Spread the marshmallows on top. Refrigerate until firm.

Custard Sauce:

1/2 cup granulated
sugar
2 tablespoons all-
purpose flour
Reserved pineapple
juice (around
1 cup)
1 large egg yolk,
slightly beaten

2 tablespoons butter
or margarine,
melted
1 (8-ounce) carton
whipping cream,
whipped
Grated Cheddar cheese
for top (around
1-1/2 to 2 cups)

Combine sugar and flour in a little pineapple juice; gradually add rest of juice and egg yolk. Cook gently until thickened. Add butter and cool in pan of cold water. Stir in the whipped cream then spread on top of gelatin mixture. Top with grated cheese. Return to refrigerator until ready to serve. Cut in squares and serve on salad greens.

Different and a wonderful addition to your table!

PEACH SALAD

1 (3-ounce) package
peach gelatin
dessert
1 (8-1/4-ounce) can
crushed pineapple,
undrained

1-1/2 cups buttermilk
1 (10-ounce) envelope
whipped topping mix

Combine the gelatin and pineapple; stir over low heat until gelatin is completely dissolved; cool. Add buttermilk and whipped topping mix; stir to blend. Refrigerate until chilled and set before serving.

FROZEN FRUIT SALAD

1 (3-ounce) package
cream cheese,
softened
2 tablespoons whipping
cream, unwhipped
1/3 cup mayonnaise
2 tablespoons lemon
juice, freshly
squeezed
1 cup crushed pineapple,
drained

1 cup orange sections,
sliced
1/2 cup cherries,
pitted and
quartered
1/2 cup pecans, chopped
1 (8-ounce) carton
whipping cream,
whipped
2 tablespoons granulated
sugar

Cream cheese; then add the 2 tablespoons whipping cream and mayonnaise and blend well. Stir in the lemon juice. Combine the fruit and pecans. Fold into the creamed mixture. Whip the cream and gradually add the sugar until well blended. Fold into the salad. Spoon mixture into a refrigerator tray or dish and freeze without stirring. Cut into squares and serve on lettuce leaves, if desired.

A great favorite!

ORANGE DELIGHT CONGEALED SALAD

2 cups boiling water
1 (6-ounce) package
orange gelatin
dessert
1 (8-ounce) package
cream cheese,
softened
1 (8-1/4-ounce) can
crushed pineapple,
undrained

2 tablespoons granulated
sugar
2 tablespoons mayonnaise
1 (8-ounce) carton
whipped topping
1/2 cup chopped pecans
Crisp lettuce leaves

Bring water to a boil and stir in gelatin until completely dissolved. Let cool. Beat cream cheese until smooth; stir in the pineapple and juice. Now add the sugar and mayonnaise; blend well. Fold in the whipped topping and then the pecans. Combine this mixture with the gelatin mixture. Pour into a square dish and chill in refrigerator until congealed. Cut in squares and serve on crisp lettuce leaves.

A congealed salad treat!

FRUIT SLAW

6 cups green cabbage,
  finely shredded
1 cup pimientos, finely
  chopped and drained
1 cup pineapple chunks
2 cups green seedless
  grapes, halved
1 cup celery, finely
  chopped
1 cup pecans, chopped

1 cup mayonnaise
1/4 cup sour cream
2 tablespoons lemon
  juice, freshly
  squeezed
1/4 teaspoon grated
  lemon rind
1/2 teaspoon salt
1 teaspoon granulated
  sugar

Combine the cabbage, pimientos, pineapple, grapes, celery and pecans; toss to mix well. Combine the mayonnaise, sour cream, lemon juice and rind, blending until smooth. Add the salt and sugar and blend well. Pour dressing over slaw and toss to coat well. Cover and chill until ready to serve.

LIME PINEAPPLE SALAD

1 (8-ounce) package
  cream cheese,
  softened
1 (3-ounce) package
  lime gelatin
  dessert

1-1/2 cups boiling water
1 large apple, cut up
1 (8-1/4-ounce) can
  crushed pineapple,
  undrained
1/2 cup pecans, chopped

Cream cheese until smooth. Dissolve gelatin in boiling water, stirring until completely dissolved. Gradually add to cream cheese and beat until smooth. Pare and cube apple; stir into cheese mixture. Add pineapple and pecans. Pour into gelatin mold and refrigerate until congealed. Cut into squares and serve on crisp lettuce leaves, if desired.

GREEN PEA SALAD

1 (8-ounce) can green
  peas, well drained
1/2 cup sharp Cheddar
  cheese, cut in
  1/4-inch cubes
2 tablespoons
  scallions, thinly
  sliced

2 tablespoons sweet
  pickle relish
2 tablespoons
  mayonnaise
Lettuce leaves

Combine all ingredients, except lettuce leaves. Toss to mix well. Spoon on lettuce when ready to serve.

MANDARIN ORANGE CONGEALED SALAD

1 cup boiling water
1/3 cup granulated
 sugar
1 (3-ounce) package
 orange gelatin
 dessert
1 (8 ounce) package
 sour cream
1/4 teaspoon pure
 vanilla extract

1 (8-1/4-ounce) can
 crushed pineapple,
 drained
1 (11-ounce) can
 mandarin orange
 sections
1/2 cup chopped pecans

Bring 1 cup water to a boil. Dissolve sugar and gelatin in boiling water. Chill in refrigerator until partially set. Add sour cream and vanilla. Whip with electric mixer until fluffy. Fold in drained pineapple, orange sections and pecans. Pour into mold. Refrigerate until firm. Serve on lettuce, if desired.

A most delicious congealed salad that you will want to serve again and again!

CAULIFLOWER SALAD

1 head cauliflower
2/3 cup mayonnaise
1 tablespoon crushed
 pineapple
1 tablespoon pineapple
 juice
1/2 teaspoon lemon
 juice, freshly
 squeezed
1 tablespoon whipping
 cream, unwhipped
1 tablespoon cider
 vinegar

1 tablespoon
 granulated sugar
1/2 teaspoon prepared
 mustard
1/8 teaspoon celery
 seed
1/8 teaspoon ground white
 pepper
4 tablespoons bacon
 bits
1/2 cup grated
 Cheddar cheese

Wash and trim cauliflower; separate into small flowerets and soak in iced water for several hours. Mix together mayonnaise, pineapple and juices, cream, vinegar, sugar, mustard, celery seed and white pepper. Place in refrigerator to chill well. Now drain the cauliflower and combine with the mayonnaise mixture, bacon bits and cheese, tossing to mix well.

Especially good!

CARROT SALAD

4 carrots, grated fine
1/2 cup seedless
raisins
1/2 cup pecans, chopped
3 tablespoons
mayonnaise
2 tablespoons whipping
cream, whipped
lightly

2 tablespoons lemon
juice, freshly
squeezed
2 teaspoons granulated
sugar

Combine the carrots, raisins and pecans; toss. Combine the mayonnaise, cream, juice and sugar; blend and add to the salad; mix well.

Good and good for you!

CARROT AND CELERY SALAD

1-1/2 cups carrots,
coarsely shredded
1-1/2 cups celery,
finely cut
1/2 cup green pepper,
finely cut
2 teaspoons onion,
grated
1 teaspoon salt

1/2 teaspoon ground
black pepper
1/4 teaspoon dry
ground mustard
1 cup sharp Cheddar
cheese, grated
1/4 cup mayonnaise
Crisp lettuce leaves

Combine all of the ingredients except lettuce leaves. When ready to serve, place lettuce leaves on salad plates and add the carrot-celery mixture.

COLESLAW

3 tablespoons
granulated sugar
1/2 teaspoon salt
Gound black pepper,
to taste
1 tablespoon minced
onion

1/3 cup vegetable oil
4 tablespoons white
vinegar
1 large head green
cabbage, finely
cut
Paprika, for garnish

Combine sugar, salt, black pepper, onion, oil and vinegar. Toss with the cabbage and lightly stir until well combined. Garnish with paprika.

Delicious and stores well in the refrigerator for future use!

CABBAGE AND NOODLES SALAD

1 head green cabbage,
  chopped fine
1/2 cup onion, chopped
  fine
1/2 green pepper,
  chopped fine
2 tablespoons
  granulated sugar
2 tablespoons white
  vinegar
1/2 cup vegetable oil

1 teaspoon salt
1 chicken-flavor packet
  (in 3-ounce
  package Ramen
  noodles)
1/2 teaspoon ground
  black pepper
1/2 cup sliced almonds
1 (3-ounce) package
  Ramen noodles,
  crumbled

Combine the cabbage, onion and green pepper; toss together. Combine sugar, vinegar, oil, salt, chicken-flavor packet and black pepper. Add dressing to cabbage mixture and blend well. Place in refrigerator for at least 2 hours or overnight. Just before serving, stir in the almonds and noodles.

Crunchy and good!

CABBAGE SLAW

1 head green cabbage, chopped
1 green pepper, chopped
4 branches celery,
  chopped
1 onion, chopped
1/8 teaspoon salt
1/8 teaspoon ground
  black pepper

1 cup granulated sugar
1 teaspoon mustard
  seed
1 tablespoon turmeric
1 cup apple cider
  vinegar

Combine chopped vegetables and toss together; sprinkle with salt and pepper and set aside. Combine the sugar, seed and turmeric; blend in the vinegar and bring to a boil. Spoon over the vegetable mixture and refrigerate for 24 hours before serving.

CREAMED CUCUMBER

1/2 cup white vinegar
1/2 cup water
1 teaspoon salt
1/4 teaspoon ground
  black pepper

1 large cucumber,
  thinly sliced
1 onion, thinly sliced
1 (8-ounce) package
  sour cream

Combine vinegar, water, salt and pepper; add cucumber slices and place in refrigerator covered for around 2 hours. Remove and drain well. Now combine the cucumber slices with onion and sour cream. Serve immediately.

Good anytime!

CUCUMBER AND DRESSING

2 cucumbers, pared
  and sliced
1 cup onion, grated
1/2 cup white vinegar
1/2 cup cooking sherry

2 tablespoons
  granulated sugar
Fresh parsley, for
  garnish

Pare cucumbers and slice. Combine the onion, vinegar, sherry and sugar; stir to combine. Pour over cucumber and chill. Garnish with parsley, if desired, just before serving.

DELICIOUS CABBAGE SLAW

Cabbage:
1 head green cabbage,
  6 cups or more,
  shredded fine

Grate or shred cabbage and place in refrigerator.

Dressing:
2 tablespoons butter,
  melted
2 tablespoons all-
  purpose flour
2 tablespoons
  granulated sugar
1 teaspoon salt

1 teaspoon dry ground
  mustard
1 cup whole milk
3 large egg yolks,
  slightly beaten
1/4 cup white vinegar

Melt the butter; stir in flour and blend well. Now add the sugar, salt and mustard until well blended. Slowly stir in the milk until smooth; cook and stir until mixture is thickened. Remove from heat and beat small amount of cooked mixture into beaten egg yolks. Return mixture to saucepan and cook, stirring constantly, without boiling, for 1 or 2 minutes. Remove from heat and slowly stir in the vinegar. Pour mixture into a bowl; cover and chill. When thoroughly chilled, add dressing to cabbage and mix well. You may serve at once or cover and chill until ready to serve.

An extra delicious slaw!

FIESTA VEGETABLE MOLD

1 cup water
1 (3-ounce) package
  lime gelatin
  dessert
1/2 teaspoon salt
1 (6-ounce) can
  evaporated milk
  (2/3 cup)
1 cup mayonnaise
1 tablespoon cream-
  style horseradish

1/3 cup oil and vinegar
  dressing
1/2 cup chopped celery
1/2 cup shredded green
  cabbage
2 tablespoons pimiento,
  chopped
2 tablespoons green
  pepper, chopped

Bring water to a boil. Add gelatin and salt; stir until dissolved. Gradually add evaporated milk to mayonnaise and mix until well blended. Stir in the horseradish, dressing and gelatin mixture. Chill until just slightly thickened. Fold in remaining ingredients. Pour into a 1 quart mold. Chill until firm; unmold on serving dish or cut and serve on lettuce leaves. Around 6 servings.

Good!

CUCUMBER SALAD

1 (3-ounce) package
  lemon gelatin
  dessert
2/3 cup boiling water
2/3 cup partially pared
  cucumber, shredded
2 tablespoons onion,
  grated

1 cup creamed cottage
  cheese
1 cup mayonnaise
2/3 cup almonds or
  pecans, sliced

Dissolve gelatin in boiling water, stirring for 2 minutes. Place in refrigerator and allow to partially set. Remove and stir in remaining ingredients until well blended. Pour in mold and chill in refrigerator until congealed before serving.

LETTUCE SALAD

1 medium onion, chopped
1 large head lettuce,
  shredded
1/2 teaspoon salt
1/4 teaspoon ground
  black pepper

1 tablespoon granulated
  sugar
4 tablespoons
  mayonnaise

Combine all ingredients well. Chill and serve immediately.

OKRA SALAD

8 slices bacon, fried
   crisp and crumbled
1-1/2 pounds fresh okra,
   cut in slices
1 cup plain cornmeal
1 tablespoon all-
   purpose flour

1/2 teaspoon salt
1 fresh tomato, chopped
1 medium onion,
   finely chopped
1/2 teaspoon salt
1/4 teaspoon ground
   black pepper

Fry bacon in a heavy skillet until crisp; drain on paper toweling and reserve drippings. Crumble bacon and set aside. Wash okra and dry off with paper towels. Cut off tip and stem ends, then cut okra crosswise into 1/2-inch slices. Sift together the cornmeal, flour and salt. Roll okra in this mixture and sauté in reserved drippings until a golden brown; drain on paper toweling. In a large salad bowl, combine the okra, chopped tomato and onion; then add crumbled bacon, salt and pepper; toss lightly and serve.

OVERNIGHT SLAW

Slaw:

1 large head green
   cabbage, shredded
1 medium onion, chopped

3/4 cup granulated
   sugar

Combine the ingredients and reserve.

Dressing:

1 cup white vinegar
1 tablespoon granulated
   sugar

1-1/2 teaspoons salt
1 teaspoon celery seed
1/4 cup vegetable oil

Bring all ingredients to a boil. Let cool and then pour over the reserved cabbage mixture. Cover and refrigerate overnight.

POTATO SALAD

4 cups cooked red
   potatoes, cubed
   (and warm)
1 teaspoon salt
1/2 teaspoon ground
   black pepper

1/2 cup onion, chopped
   fine
1/2 cup mayonnaise,
   plus

Pare and cube potatoes; cover with water and cook until tender. Watch closely and do not overcook. Drain well. Combine with salt, pepper and onion; toss to mix. Add enough mayonnaise to give the consistency you like.

POTATO SALAD SUPREME

8 medium-size red
  potatoes, boiled
  in jackets
1-1/2 cups mayonnaise
1 (8-ounce) carton
  sour cream
1-1/2 teaspoons prepared
  horseradish

1 teaspoon celery seed
1 teaspoon salt
1/2 teaspoon ground
  black pepper
2 medium onions,
  finely minced
1 cup parsley,
  freshly chopped

Peel boiled potatoes and cut in thin slices. Combine mayonnaise, sour cream, horseradish, celery seed, salt and pepper and set aside. In another bowl, mix onion and parsley and set aside. Arrange layers of potatoes; salt each layer very lightly, then cover with a layer of the first mixture, then the second mixture, layering and ending with the onion-parsley mixture. Do not stir. Cover and store in refrigerator for at least 8 hours before serving.

Interesting and different ... also very tasty!

SWEET AND SOUR CUCUMBER AND ONION

1 large cucumber, pared
  and sliced
1 large onion, sliced
1 (8-ounce) glass of
  cold water
1/2 cup white vinegar

1/4 cup granulated
  sugar
1/4 teaspoon salt
1/8 teaspoon ground
  black pepper

Place cucumber and onion in a bowl; combine the remaining ingredients and stir to mix well. Pour over cucumber and onion; cover and refrigerate until chilled before serving.

PERFECTION SALAD

4 tablespoons
  unflavored gelatin
  (4 envelopes)
1 cup cold water
2 cups boiling water
3 cups granulated sugar
1 cup white vinegar
1 tablespoon salt

1-1/2 cups cabbage,
  finely cut
1 (2-ounce) jar
  pimientos, chopped
1 cup green pepper,
  chopped
1 cup pecans, chopped
Individual salad molds

Soak gelatin in cold water; when softened, add hot water, sugar, vinegar and salt. Stir until mixture begins to thicken, then add cabbage, pimientos, pepper, and pecans. Rinse salad molds in cold water before filling with mixture so salad will come out easily. Refrigerate until ready to serve.

Delightful taste!

CHICKEN SALAD

3 cooked chicken breast
   halves, boned and
   cubed
1 cup celery, chopped
   fine
1 cup canned pineapple,
   cut into small
   pieces
1 cup toasted, chopped
   pecans

3/4 cup mayonnaise
1/4 cup sour cream
1 teaspoon curry
   powder
1 teaspoon freshly
   squeezed lemon
   juice
1/2 teaspoon salt
Lettuce leaves

Combine chicken, celery, pineapple pieces and pecans; blend well. Stir in the mayonnaise and sour cream. Then blend in the curry powder, lemon juice and salt. Chill in refrigerator until ready to serve. Arrange on salad plates on top of lettuce leaves.

Very tasty indeed!

ELEGANT CHICKEN SALAD

2 cups cooked chicken
   breasts, chopped
   fine
3/4 cup celery, chopped
   fine
1/4 cup cucumber,
   chopped
1/4 cup vegetable oil
1/4 cup white vinegar
1 (11-ounce) can
   mandarin oranges,
   well drained

1 cup green grapes,
   seedless (halved)
2 tablespoons green
   onion tops, minced
1/2 cup slivered
   almonds, toasted
1/2 cup mayonnaise
Lettuce leaves

Place chicken, celery and cucumber in a medium bowl; combine oil and vinegar and pour over chicken mixture. Cover and refrigerate for at least 1 hour. Drain well and then add the remaining ingredients. Serve on beds of lettuce.

A wonderful luncheon salad!

WALDORF SALAD NO. 2

3 large unpared apples,
  diced
1/2 cup chopped pecans
  or walnuts
1 cup celery, sliced
1 (3-ounce) package
  cream cheese,
  softened

2 to 4 tablespoons
  orange juice
2 tablespoons almonds,
  chopped
1/4 cup raisins,
  seedless
Lettuce leaves

Combine the apple, nuts and celery; toss. Cream the cheese and blend in the juice to right consistency for dressing. Stir in the almonds and raisins. Arrange lettuce leaves on salad plates; spoon in the apple mixture and then the dressing on top.

Easy!

HOT CHICKEN SALAD

1-1/2 cups chicken
  breasts, cooked
  and diced
1/2 cup celery,
  finely cut
1/2 teaspoon salt
1/8 teaspoon ground
  black pepper
1 teaspoon onion,
  grated

2 hard boiled eggs,
  grated
1 (10-3/4-ounce) can
  cream of chicken
  soup, undiluted
1/2 cup mayonnaise
1-1/2 cups butter-
  flavored cracker
  crumbs, divided

Combine all ingredients except 1/2 cup crumbs. Blend together well. Spoon into a large buttered casserole dish. Top with reserved crumbs. Bake at 350 degrees for 30 to 35 minutes.

JELLIED CHICKEN SALAD

2 cups cooked chicken,
  diced (reserve broth)
2 tablespoons
  unflavored gelatin
1/2 cup cold water
1-1/2 cups hot chicken
  broth (reserved)
1-1/2 cups celery,
  finely chopped

1-1/2 tablespoons green
  pepper, minced
1-1/2 tablespoons
  pimiento, minced
2 tablespoons lemon
  juice, freshly
  squeezed
2 hard boiled eggs,
  grated

Cook chicken and reserve broth. When chicken is cool, cut in cubes and set aside. Soak gelatin in cold water; stir in hot broth and cool. Combine rest of the ingredients with the chicken and spoon in with the gelatin mixture, stirring to blend. Pour into 6 individual molds and chill until set before serving.

Delightful!

SHRIMP SALAD NO. 1

1 pound medium shrimp,
  steamed
2 teaspoons lemon juice,
  freshly squeezed
3 cups celery, finely
  chopped
2 cups sweet pickle,
  finely chopped
1 cup green pepper,
  finely chopped

1/2 teaspoon celery salt
Salt and pepper to taste
1/4 cup mayonnaise,
  about
Lettuce leaves
Tomatoes, quartered,
  for garnish
Lemon wedges, for
  garnish
Capers, for garnish

Steam shrimp; cool and devein. Combine the juice, celery, pickle, pepper and shrimp, tossing to combine. Sprinkle over the celery salt and salt and pepper to taste. Add enough mayonnaise to blend together. Serve on lettuce leaves with tomatoes, lemon wedges and capers for garnish. Serve with assorted crackers.

Excellent salad!

SHRIMP SALAD NO. 2

1 pound small shrimp,
  steamed
1 cup celery, chopped
1/4 cup mayonnaise
1 tablespoon
  Worcestershire
  sauce
1 tablespoon lemon
  juice, freshly
  squeezed

1/2 teaspoon salt
1/4 teaspoon ground
  white pepper
Lettuce leaves
Fresh parsley, for
  garnish
Tomatoes, quartered,
  for garnish
Lemon wedges, for garnish

Steam shrimp, cool and devein. Combine the shrimp and celery; set aside. Mix together the mayonnaise, Worcestershire sauce and juice well. Add to the shrimp and celery; toss lightly Add the salt and pepper and taste; add additional salt and pepper, if needed. Serve on lettuce leaves and garnish with parsley, quartered tomatoes and lemon wedges.

Makes an attractive dish!

ASPARAGUS SALAD

1 (15-1/2-ounce) can
  asparagus, drained
  (reserve liquid)
3 tablespoons butter,
  melted
2 tablespoons all-
  purpose flour
Juice of 1 lemon,
  freshly squeezed
1/2 teaspoon salt

4 large eggs, well
  beaten
1 tablespoon unflavored
  gelatin
1/2 cup water
1 (8-ounce) carton
  whipping cream,
  whipped
Lettuce leaves
Mayonnaise

Drain asparagus and reserve liquid. Melt butter; blend in flour until smooth. Slowly stir in the asparagus liquid, lemon juice and salt. Cook and stir until thickened. Remove from heat and add a small amount of the cooked mixture to the well beaten eggs. Now place all in a double boiler and stir until the eggs are cooked and the mixture is thickened and creamy. Dissolve the gelatin in water and add to the cooked mixture. Beat the cream until thickened and when the first mixture has cooled, fold in the cream. Arrange layers of asparagus and creamed mixture in a large shallow dish. Refrigerate until well chilled. Serve on lettuce leaves; garnish with mayonnaise.

A real taste treat!

BEET SALAD NO. 1

1 cup beets, cooked and
  chopped (reserve
  3/4 cup liquid)
1 cup boiling water
1 (3-ounce) package
  lemon gelatin
  dessert
3 tablespoons white
  vinegar

1/2 teaspoon salt
1/2 teaspoon onion,
  grated
2 teaspoons prepared
  horseradish
1/2 cup celery,
  finely cut

Cook beets; drain and reserve 3/4 cup beet liquid. Cool beets and then chop and set aside. Boil the water and dissolve the gelatin, stirring for several minutes. Add the liquid, vinegar, salt, onion and horseradish. Place in refrigerator and chill until mixture is slightly thickened. Fold in the celery and chopped beets; pour into a lightly oiled mold.

Refreshing taste!

BEET SALAD NO. 2

1 (16-ounce) can diced
  beets
3/4 cup beet liquid
1 (3-ounce) package
  lemon gelatin
  dessert
1/4 teaspoon salt
1 cup boiling water

2 tablespoons white
  vinegar
1-1/2 cups cabbage,
  finely shredded
1-1/2 teaspoons
  prepared
  horseradish
Endive leaves

Drain beets and reserve liquid. Dissolve gelatin and salt in boiling water, stirring for several minutes. Add liquid and vinegar. Chill in refrigerator until slightly thickened, then stir in beets, cabbage and horseradish. Pour into mold and refrigerate for several hours until set. Cut and serve on endive leaves, if desired.

BROCCOLI SALAD

2 cups cooked broccoli,
  chopped fine
1 tablespoon unflavored
  gelatin
1/4 cup cold water
1 cup hot beef consomme'
  or chicken
  consomme'
1/2 teaspoon salt

2 teaspoons lemon
  juice, freshly
  squeezed
2 hard boiled large eggs,
  cooked and mashed
1/2 cup mayonnaise
1/4 cup half and half
Lettuce leaves
Mayonnaise

Cook broccoli, drain, cool and chop. Soak gelatin in cold water, then dissolve in the hot consomme'. Combine with the salt, juice, eggs, mayonnaise and half and half. Fold in the broccoli. Pour into a lightly oiled mold. Refrigerate until well chilled before serving. Cut in squares and serve on lettuce leaves; top with a spoonful of mayonnaise, if desired.

An easy do-ahead dish!

WALDORF SALAD NO. 1

4 cups apple, diced
1 cup seedless raisins
1 cup celery, chopped
1 cup pecans or walnuts,
  chopped

Mayonnaise
Lettuce leaves

Combine the apple, raisins, celery and nuts. Blend in enough mayonnaise to moisten. Chill and serve on lettuce beds.

Tasty!

PEAR SALAD

5 fresh pears, chilled
and halved or 10
canned pear halves

Crisp lettuce leaves

If fresh pears are used, dip in lemon juice to prevent discoloration. Place pears on lettuce leaves and fill hollows with desired dressing.

Dressing No. 1

1/2 pound creamed
cottage cheese
1/4 pound American
cheese, grated

Mayonnaise

Beat the cheese until mixed. Add enough mayonnaise to hold the mixture together. Spoon lightly into hollows of pears and top with mayonnaise.

Dressing No. 2

2 (3-ounce) packages
cream cheese, softened
Mayonnaise
1/4 cup celery, chopped
fine

1/4 cup pecans, chopped
fine
Mayonnaise or French
dressing

Beat the cream cheese until smooth. Add enough mayonnaise to soften, then add the celery and nuts. Spoon into pear hollows and add a little mayonnaise or French dressing over top.

Dressing No. 3

Mayonnaise
Medium Cheddar
cheese, grated

Spoon mayonnaise into pear hollows. Top with grated cheese and then with a little additional mayonnaise on top.

Dressing No. 4

1 (8-ounce) carton sour
cream
1-1/2 tablespoons honey
1/4 teaspoon lemon
rind, grated

1 tablespoon sesame
seed, toasted
1 tablespoon poppy seed

Blend together the sour cream, honey and rind well. Top pear hollows with the creamed mixture. Combine seed and sprinkle over each salad.

Any way you decide to serve the pears, you will find the dressings are a delicious addition!

STRAWBERRY CONGEALED SALAD

2 cups boiling water
1 (3-ounce) package
  strawberry gelatin
  dessert
1 (3-ounce) package
  cherry gelatin
  dessert
1 (10-ounce) package
  frozen
  strawberries, with
  syrup (thawed)

1 (8-1/4-ounce) can
  crushed pineapple,
  in heavy syrup
1/2 cup chopped pecans
2 large ripe bananas,
  mashed
1 (8-ounce) package
  sour cream
Lettuce leaves

Dissolve gelatins in boiling water. Add strawberries and pineapple including the syrup; stir in pecans. Pour one half of the mixture into an 8 x 8 x 2-inch square glass dish. Place in the refrigerator until congealed. Mash bananas and combine thoroughly with the sour cream. Spoon this mixture over the congealed portion and then add the rest of the first mixture slowly. Refrigerate until firm, several hours or overnight. Cut in squares and serve on lettuce, if desired.

You will receive raves when you serve this congealed salad!

STRAWBERRY RING MOLD

1 (8-ounce) package
  cream cheese,
  softened
2 tablespoons granulated
  sugar
2 tablespoons mayonnaise
1 (8-1/4-ounce) can
  crushed pineapple,
  in heavy syrup
2 cups frozen
  strawberries,
  thawed

1/2 cup pecans, chopped
1 (8-ounce) carton
  whipping cream,
  whipped
1 pint fresh
  strawberries,
  sliced and sugared
  for center of ring
Whole strawberries for
  garnish

Beat the cream cheese until smooth. Add the sugar, mayonnaise, pineapple and syrup, strawberries and nuts. Fold in the whipped cream with a large spoon. Pour into a 10-inch ring mold. Refrigerate until firm. Unmold on an attractive serving plate or cake plate on a pedestal. Place in the refrigerator for 1-1/2 hours. Now place the sugared strawberries in the center of ring. Garnish sides with whole strawberries with the leaves still on, if desired.

POPPY SEED DRESSING

2/3 cup granulated
  sugar
1/2 teaspoon salt
1-1/2 teaspoons dry
  ground mustard
1/2 cup white vinegar

1-1/2 cups vegetable
  oil
2 tablespoons onion,
  grated
1/4 cup poppy seed

Mix together the sugar, salt and mustard. Add vinegar and then beat in the oil. Stir in onion and poppy seed. Good with any fruit salad.

Tasty fruit dressing!

BLUE CHEESE DRESSING

1/4 pound blue cheese
1 (8-ounce) carton
  sour cream
1/4 cup mayonnaise
1/4 teaspoon salt
1 tablespoon white
  vinegar

1/8 teaspoon ground
  black pepper
1/4 teaspoon celery
  salt

Crumble cheese and mix with sour cream. Add rest of ingredients and blend well.

Especially good!

ROQUEFORT CHEESE DRESSING NO. 1

1 cup mayonnaise
1 (8-ounce) carton
  sour cream

1/2 cup buttermilk
1 cup Roquefort cheese
1 teaspoon celery salt

Beat mayonnaise until smooth. Blend in cream and buttermilk. Now mix in the cheese and salt until thoroughly blended, but do not beat out the lumps.

Delicious on green salad!

ROQUEFORT CHEESE DRESSING NO. 2

1 cup vegetable oil
1/4 cup wine vinegar
1 teaspoon salt
1/4 teaspoon ground
  white pepper
1/2 teaspoon paprika

1-1/2 teaspoons
  granulated sugar
1/2 teaspoon dry
  ground mustard
1 cup Roquefort cheese

Combine and beat all ingredients with the exception of cheese, until smoothly blended. Crumble the cheese into the bowl and blend but do not beat out the lumps.

VEGETABLE SALAD NO. 1

1 (16-ounce) can cut
  green beans
1 (16-ounce) can
  green peas
1 (2-ounce) jar
  pimientos, chopped
4 stalks celery, cut up

1 medium green pepper,
  cut up
1 medium onion, cut up
1 teaspoon salt
1 cup granulated sugar
1/2 cup vegetable oil
3/4 cup white vinegar

Toss the vegetables in a large bowl. Combine the salt, sugar, oil and vinegar. Add this mixture to the vegetables. Cover and place in refrigerator for 24 hours. Drain and serve. Keeps well for around 3 weeks in refrigerator.

Nice vegetable salad to have on hand anytime!

VEGETABLE SALAD NO. 2

1 tablespoon unflavored
  gelatin
1/4 cup water
1 (10-3/4-ounce) can
  old fashioned
  vegetable soup
  with beef stock

1 cup mayonnaise
1/2 cup celery,
  finely chopped

Soak gelatin in water. Place soup in small saucepan and bring to boiling point. Remove from heat and stir in gelatin mixture; dissolve completely. When cool, add mayonnaise and celery. Mold in 8 large muffin rings; place in refrigerator until chilled and set before serving.

FRENCH DRESSING

2 cups vegetable oil
1/3 cup wine vinegar
1/2 cup onion, chopped
1 garlic clove, chopped
1 tablespoon dry
  ground mustard

1 teaspoon salt
1/4 teaspoon ground
  white pepper

Combine ingredients and place in blender on low speed; gradually increase to high speed and blend until smooth. Serve over green salads.

Sandwiches
and Soups

Sandwiches—*Perhaps you know the story of how John Montague, Earl of Sandwich, 4th lord of the British admiralty, wanted to continue playing at a gaming table and called for a piece of meat between 2 slices of bread. He called it a* **sandwich.** *Today* **sandwiches** *are made in more ways than one can count and play and important role in our lives. The Earl of Sandwich lived from 1718 to 1792 which means the first* **sandwich** *was made over 200 years ago. Remember the story as you prepare the* **sandwich** *recipes.*

BANANA SANDWICH SPREAD

1/2 cup pecans, ground
1/2 cup raisins, ground

1 large banana, mashed
Mayonnaise

Combine ground pecans and raisins; fold in mashed banana, then stir in enough mayonnaise to moisten for sandwiches.

Hearty spread for sandwiches!

CARROT-RAISIN SANDWICHES

1/2 cup butter,
  softened
2 large carrots, finely
  grated

1/2 cup seedless
  raisins
Dash salt
Mayonnaise

Cream butter until smooth. Blend in carrots, raisins and salt. Add enough mayonnaise to give right spreading consistency. Refrigerate and spread on slices of bread just before serving. Cut sandwiches in half.

CHEESE SANDWICH SPREAD

1 (8-ounce) package
  cream cheese,
  softened
1/2 cup butter,
  softened

1/4 cup prepared
  horseradish
1/4 cup mayonnaise

Cream the cheese and butter until blended; add horseradish and mayonnaise and blend until smooth. Delicious spread for roast beef sandwiches and party rolls.

CUCUMBER SANDWICHES

1 (8-ounce) package
  cream cheese,
  softened

1 large cucumber, pared
  and cubed
1 small onion, chopped

Place all ingredients in blender or food processor. Blend until smooth. Tint a delicate green, if desired. Chill in covered container in refrigerator for several hours before serving. Serve between bread rounds or on lengthwise cut bread.

Irresistible!

DATE-NUT SANDWICHES

3/4 cup pitted dates,
  finely cut
1/2 cup pecans, finely
  chopped
1 teaspoon lemon juice,
  freshly squeezed
1/8 teaspoon salt
Mayonnaise
Bread slices

Combine the dates, pecans, lemon juice and salt. Add enough mayonnaise to make right spreading consistency. Spread on bread slices just before serving. Cut sandwiches in half.

EGG-BACON SANDWICHES

3 hard boiled eggs,
  finely chopped
3 slices crisp-cooked
  bacon, chopped
1 tablespoon mayonnaise
6 slices bread,
  buttered
Lettuce

Combine the egg, bacon and enough mayonnaise to give good spreading consistency. Spread on three slices of bread, cover with a leaf of lettuce and top with remaining bread slices. Cut into quarters or halves.

EGG SALAD SANDWICHES

3 hard-boiled eggs,
  finely chopped
Salt and pepper to
  taste
1 tablespoon chopped
  pickles (sweet or
  dill)
1/2 teaspoon prepared
  mustard
Mayonnaise
6 slices bread,
  buttered

Combine the eggs, salt and pepper, pickles and mustard. Add enough mayonnaise to give good spreading consistency. Spread mixture on three slices of bread and top with remaining slices. Cut each sandwich in thirds to make finger shaped sandwiches.

HAM AND CHEESE SANDWICHES

1 cup baked ham, ground
1 cup American cheese,
   grated

1/4 cup sweet pickles,
   finely chopped
Mayonnaise

Combine ham and cheese, stir in pickle and add enough mayonnaise to give good spreading consistency. Spread on bread slices just before serving. Top with bread slices and cut sandwiches in half.

OLIVE-CREAM CHEESE SANDWICHES

1 (3-ounce) package
   cream cheese,
   softened
1 cup pecans, finely
   chopped

3/4 cup pimiento-
   stuffed olives,
   finely chopped
Mayonnaise

Cream cheese until smooth. Add pecans and olives and blend well. Add enough mayonnaise to make right spreading consistency. Spread on bread slices and cut sandwiches in half.

PERFECT CHICKEN SALAD SANDWICHES

4 chicken breast
   halves, boned,
   cooked and cubed
1-1/2 cups celery,
   finely cut
Juice of 4 lemons,
   strained

1-1/2 tablespoons
   celery seed
Salt to taste
1 cup mayonnaise,
   or more

Boil chicken breasts until very tender. Cool and then skin and cut into small pieces. Add celery, lemon juice, celery seed and salt to taste. Then blend in the mayonnaise, enough to give good spreading consistency.

PIMIENTO-CHEESE SANDWICHES NO. 1

1 (16-ounce) package
   Cheddar cheese,
   grated
1 (2-ounce) jar
   pimientos, mashed
   fine

1/2 cup onion, grated
1 tablespoon lemon
   juice, freshly
   squeezed
Mayonnaise

Beat cheese until smooth; blend in pimiento, onion and juice.

Add enough mayonnaise to give right spreading consistency. Spread on bread or crackers.

PIMIENTO-CHEESE SANDWICHES NO. 2

1 (8-ounce) package
  medium Cheddar
  cheese, grated
1 (2-ounce) jar
  pimientos, finely
  chopped

1/8 teaspoon ground
  red pepper
Mayonnaise
10 slices buttered
  bread

Blend together the cheese, pimiento and pepper. Add enough mayonnaise to give right spreading consistency. Spread on half the bread slices and top with remaining slices. Cut sandwiches in thirds to obtain finger shapes.

STRAWBERRY-CREAM CHEESE SANDWICHES

1 (3-ounce) package
  cream cheese,
  softened

2 tablespoons
  strawberry jam

Cream the cheese until smooth; add the jam and blend well. Spread on toast, crackers or use as a sandwich filling.

TURKEY SANDWICHES

1-1/2 cups cooked
  turkey, cubed
1 cup celery, finely
  chopped
1 teaspoon onion,
  grated

2 tablespoons minced
  chutney
Mayonnaise

Combine all sandwich ingredients and mix with enough mayonnaise to give good spreading consistency. Spread on slices of bread and top with bread slices. Cut in quarters and serve on lettuce, if desired.

*Soups—A small bowl of **soup** served as an appetizer can whet the appetite; however, a hearty soup or chowder can serve as a main dish. The warm flavor and nutritional value are exciting qualities. Serve **soup** often!*

BEAN SOUP

1 pound package dried
  Great Northern
  beans
6 slices streak-of-lean
  meat
1 large onion, chopped
  fine

1/2 cup celery, diced
1 teaspoon granulated
  sugar
Salt to taste

Place beans in a large saucepan and cover with water; cover and soak overnight. Next morning, cook meat in boiling water until almost done; then add onion, celery, sugar, salt and beans. Bring to a boil and cook, stirring for 15 minutes; reduce heat and simmer around 3 hours or until tender, stirring often. If you have any leftover beans, use them for baked beans.

Tasty and filling!

BLACK BEAN SOUP

3 cups dried black
  beans
3-1/2 quarts bouillon
  (14 cups)
1/4 pound salt pork,
  diced
1/4 pound ham, chopped
1-1/2 cups onion,
  chopped
1/2 ounce garlic,
  chopped
Salt
Ground black pepper, to taste

1/8 teaspoon ground
  red pepper
Hot oil
2 teaspoons white
  vinegar
2 ounces cooking sherry
Hot cooked rice
Onion, chopped, for
  garnish
Ham, chopped, for
  garnish
Lime slices, for
  garnish

Wash beans and cover with water; soak overnight. Next morning, drain and add bouillon. Sauté the pork, ham, onion, garlic, salt, black and red pepper in the oil. Combine with the beans; cover and cook slowly for around 4 hours. Add vinegar and sherry. Serve with cooked rice, chopped onion, chopped ham and lime slices. Serves 12.

A German soup but served all over the world; wonderful flavor!

BRUNSWICK STEW

1 (3 to 4-pound)
   stewing chicken,
   cut up or 2 (1-1/2
   to 2-pound) fryer
   chickens, cut up
4 large potatoes,
   diced
1 pint green
   butterbeans or
   green lima beans
2 large onions, chopped
2 teaspoons salt
1 teaspoon ground black
   pepper

Water
1 (16-ounce) can
   creamed corn or
   6 ears fresh corn,
   grated
1 (16-ounce) can
   tomatoes or
   8 fresh tomatoes,
   cut up
2 tablespoons butter
1 cup biscuit crumbs or
   white bread crumbs
   (not fine)

Combine chicken, potatoes, beans, onion, salt and pepper. Cover with water and cook, covered until tender. Remove chicken bones and then add the corn and tomatoes. Return to heat and cook until vegetables are tender, around 15 minutes. Add butter and crumbs to thicken. Serve to a large crowd very hot. Everyone will want seconds!

Wonderful dish!

CREAM OF BROCCOLI SOUP

1/2 cup butter, melted
6 tablespoons all-
   purpose flour
1 quart chicken broth
1 (10-ounce) package
   frozen chopped
   broccoli
1 small onion, chopped
1 tablespoon butter
1/2 teaspoon salt

Dash garlic powder
1 teaspoon ground white
   pepper
2 cups whole milk
1 cup whipping cream,
   unwhipped
1/2 cup buttermilk
2 tablespoons sour
   cream
1/2 cup butter, melted

Melt 1/2 cup butter; blend in flour to make a pourable roux. Thin with a little water if too thick. Bring the chicken broth to a boil. Add broccoli and simmer until done. Sauté onion in 1 tablespoon butter; add to broccoli, then the seasonings and roux, stirring constantly until thickened. Heat the milk, cream and buttermilk, but do not boil; add to the broccoli mixture, stirring constantly. Do not boil again. Remove from heat and stir in sour cream and melted butter. Serve while hot.

So delicious!

CABBAGE SOUP

4 cups cabbage, shredded
2 cups carrots, sliced
3 cups red potatoes,
    cubed
1 tablespoon salt
1/2 teaspoon ground
    black pepper

1 tablespoon granulated
    sugar
3 cups water, about
1 quart whole milk,
    scalded
3 tablespoons butter

Combine the cabbage, carrots, potatoes, salt, pepper, sugar and water to just barely cover. Bring to a boil and cook until vegetables are tender; around 15 minutes. Add the hot milk and butter. Serve hot.

A great soup that can be served any time of the year!

CAULIFLOWER SOUP

1 head cauliflower
4 cups chicken broth, about
1 cup half and half
1 teaspoon salt

1/2 teaspoon ground white
    pepper
1/4 cup parsley, freshly
    chopped

Wash and trim cauliflower; separate flowerets leaving stems attached. Drop into boiling chicken broth (to 1/2-inch above cauliflower). Cover and simmer until tender, around 8 minutes. Cool and then purée cauliflower in food processor or blender until smooth. Return to broth; add half and half, salt and pepper and bring to boiling point. Sprinkle each serving with the parsley.

Tempting flavor!

CHICKEN STEW

Hot vegetable oil
1 (3 to 4 pound)
    stewing chicken,
    cut up
1 cup all-purpose flour
1 teaspoon salt
3 cups water
4 tomatoes, peeled and
    cut up
2 large onions,
    chopped

2-1/2 teaspoons salt
1 teaspoon ground
    black pepper
2 cups okra, cut in
    slices
1 tablespoon all-
    purpose flour
1/4 cup water

Heat oil in large, heavy skillet. Dredge chicken in the 1 cup flour and salt. Brown slowly in hot oil, on all sides. Add 3 cups water, cover and reduce heat. Simmer gently for 1 hour. Add tomatoes, onion, salt and pepper. Continue to simmer and just before chicken is done, add the okra and cook uncovered until okra and chicken are tender. Combine the 1 tablespoon flour and water until smooth. Blend gently into stew, stirring constantly. Cook until stew thickens slightly. Serve while still very hot.

Excellent flavor!

HAM BEAN SOUP

1 (16-ounce) package	1-1/4 cups potatoes,
Navy beans	cubed
3 pound meaty ham bone	1/2 teaspoon salt
1 cup celery, chopped	1/4 teaspoon ground
1-1/2 cups carrots,	black pepper
chopped	

Rinse beans and place in large dutch oven with ham bone and water to cover. Bring to a boil; reduce heat and simmer 3 to 3-1/2 hours. Remove ham bone; cool and cut ham in small pieces. Add ham pieces, vegetables, salt and pepper. Simmer until vegetables are tender, stirring occasionally.

JIMMY WALKER'S NEW ENGLAND CLAM CHOWDER

1 large onion, chopped	2 cups half-and-half
2 cloves garlic, minced	Salt and ground white pepper
6 tablespoons butter or	to taste
margarine (divided)	Chopped parsley,
3 (8-ounce) cans minced	optional
clams, drained	Chopped chives,
2 cups clam juice	optional
3/4 cup diced salt pork	
2 medium potatoes,	
cubed	

Sauté onion and garlic in two tablespoons butter for five minutes. Add clams and clam juice; cover and cook over low heat for 10 to 15 minutes. Fry salt pork until golden brown; drain on paper toweling. Cook potatoes in boiling salted water until barely done; drain. Add salt pork and potatoes to clams. Gradually stir in half-and-half; heat thoroughly, but do not boil. Add salt and pepper to taste. Thickly slice four tablespoons butter or margarine and float on top of chowder. Sprinkle each serving with parsley and chives, if desired.

Yield: about 6 to 8 servings.

CREAM OF SPINACH SOUP

2 (10-ounce) packages
  chopped spinach,
  frozen
1/2 cup onion, chopped
3 cups chicken broth
4 tablespoons butter
5 tablespoons all-
  purpose flour

1 quart half and half
1 teaspoon tarragon
1 teaspoon salt
1/4 teaspoon ground
  white pepper
Bacon bits
Croutons

Cook spinach and onion in broth until tender. Pureé in blender until smooth. Mix together the butter and flour until blended, then add this to the spinach mixture until blended throughout. Add half and half and then the tarragon, salt and pepper. When serving, garnish each bowl with bacon bits and croutons, if desired.

A most satisfying dish!

OYSTER STEW

1 quart oysters, with
  liquor
1/2 cup butter, melted
2 tablespoons all-
  purpose flour
3 cups whole milk
1 pint whipping cream,
  unwhipped

1/4 teaspoon celery
  salt
1/2 teaspoon salt
1/8 teaspoon ground
  black pepper

Drain oysters and reserve liquid; remove shell pieces and set oysters aside. Melt butter in top of double boiler; stir in flour gradually, mixing until smooth. Gradually add oyster liquor, milk and cream, stirring until blended well. Cook over boiling water until slightly thickened, stirring occasionally. Add seasonings and stir to blend. Add oysters and cook until oysters begin to curl at edges, around 5 minutes. Serve immediately while hot.

POTATO SOUP

6 large red potatoes,
  diced
1 large onion, chopped
  fine
1 cup celery, chopped
  fine
2 quarts whole milk,
  scalded

1 cup bread crumbs
1 teaspoon salt
1/4 teaspoon ground
  black pepper
3 tablespoons butter

Cook potatoes, onion and celery in hot water until tender. Drain off any water left. Now add the milk, bread crumbs, salt, pepper and butter. Bring to a boil; cook and stir constantly for several minutes until well blended.

You will want to serve this often!

SHE-CRAB SOUP

1 cup white crab meat
2 tablespoons butter
1 small onion, grated
1/2 teaspoon salt
1/8 teaspoon ground
  black pepper
1/2 cup celery,
  finely cut
2 cups whole milk,
  scalded
1/2 cup whipping cream,
  unwhipped

2 tablespoons
  Worcestershire
  sauce
2 teaspoons all-
  purpose flour
1 tablespoon water
3 tablespoons cooking
  sherry
Boiled egg yolks,
  optional

Place crab meat in top of double boiler. Add butter, onion, salt, pepper and celery; let simmer for 5 minutes. Heat milk and add to crab mixture, stirring. Add cream and Worcestershire sauce. Make a paste of the flour and water until smooth. Add to the crab mixture and stir to thicken. Add the sherry and cook over low heat for 30 minutes. If desired, crumble boiled egg yolks in bottom of each bowl before filling.

SHRIMP GUMBO

1/4 cup vegetable oil
1/2 cup all-purpose
  flour
3 large onions, chopped
2 large green peppers,
  chopped
4 stalks celery,
  chopped

5 pods garlic, chopped
4 quarts boiling water
1-1/2 teaspoons salt
1/2 teaspoon ground
  black pepper
4 pounds cooked shrimp
Hot cooked rice

Heat oil in a large skillet; add flour, stirring until browned. Add onion, pepper, celery, garlic, boiling water and then salt and pepper to taste; simmer for around 2 hours. Add shrimp and simmer 15 additional minutes. Serve over hot rice.

MRS. BLAIR'S CLAM CHOWDER

1 pound bacon
10 (8-ounce) cans
  minced clams,
  drain, reserve
  juice
3 large onions
1 stalk celery
2 pounds carrots

2 large green peppers
Salt and ground pepper to
  taste
Dash ground red pepper
5 large white or red
  potatoes, cubed
2 (12-ounce) cans
  evaporated milk

Cook bacon until crisp and drain on paper towels. Crumble and set aside. Drain clams and save juice. Grind onions, celery, carrots and green peppers; add to bacon drippings. Add salt and pepper to taste and a dash of red pepper. Pour into a large saucepan and add the cubed potatoes and clam juice. Cook until done; around 30 minutes. Add bacon and clams; bring to a boil. Add evaporated milk and bring to a boil again. Serve piping hot with saltine crackers.

Most delicious!

TOMATO SOUP

1 quart whole milk
1 (14-1/2-ounce) can
  whole tomatoes,
  puréed

4 tablespoons butter
Saltine crackers
Salt and ground black pepper,
  to taste

Bring milk to boiling point. Add puréed tomatoes and butter. Stir and bring to boiling point once again. Add enough crumbled crackers to give desired consistency. Add salt and pepper to your taste. (You may want to serve the soup and let each guest add crackers and seasonings.)

A delicious soup when served very hot!

WILD RICE CHICKEN SOUP

4 cups water or chicken
  broth
1/2 cup Wild rice
1/2 cup celery,
  finely cut
1/2 cup carrots,
  finely cut
1/2 cup onion, chopped
2 chicken bouillon
  cubes

2 tablespoons butter,
  melted
2 tablespoons all-
  purpose flour
1 cup whole milk
1/2 cup almonds, sliced
1 cup cooked chicken,
  cubed
Lemon pepper, to taste

Combine water or broth, rice, celery, carrots and onion. Cook until vegetables are tender; add bouillon cubes. Make a white sauce by melting butter, blending in flour and gradually adding milk until smooth. Now add white sauce to vegetable broth along with almonds, chicken and lemon pepper. Stir until creamy. Makes 8 servings.

PEANUT SOUP

2 tablespoons butter, melted
1/2 cup onion, chopped fine
1/2 cup celery, chopped fine
2 tablespoons all-purpose flour
2 cups hot chicken broth

1/2 cup creamy peanut butter
Dash celery salt
1/4 teaspoon salt
1 teaspoon lemon juice, freshly squeezed
3 tablespoons peanuts, chopped

Melt butter; add onion and celery. Sauté for around five minutes, stirring to prevent any browning. Add flour and stir until flour is well blended. Heat chicken broth in a separate saucepan and then add to the onion mixture. Cook for around 30 minutes. Remove from heat and strain broth; stir in the peanut butter, celery salt, salt and lemon juice. Sprinkle peanuts on soup just before serving.

Nutritious and good!

Sauces, Pickles
and Relishes

Sauces are flavorful and should enhance the foods they accompany. Plan ahead and try a new sauce recipe soon!

BARBECUE CHICKEN SAUCE

3/4 pound butter or margarine, melted
1 cup vegetable oil
1/2 cup lemon juice, freshly squeezed and strained
1/2 cup water
1/2 cup white vinegar

3 teaspoons salt
3 tablespoons granulated sugar
1/3 teaspoon ground black pepper
1-1/2 teaspoons paprika
2 tablespoons grated onion

Melt butter; add rest of ingredients and stir until combined. The sauce is ready when you are! Baste the chicken often and cook chicken slowly.

The sauce gives chicken a wonderful flavor and keeps the meat moist!

BARBECUE MEAT SAUCE

1 tablespoon salt
1 tablespoon ground black pepper
1-1/2 tablespoons granulated sugar
1 tablespoon dry ground mustard
1/4 tablespoon ground red pepper

5 tablespoons white vinegar
3 tablespoons Worcestershire sauce
1/2 cup butter or margarine

Combine the dry ingredients well; add just enough water to make a paste. Add the vinegar, Worcestershire sauce and butter. Heat over low heat until butter is melted. Baste on chicken, beef, pork or fish.

Excellent sauce and good flavor!

BARBECUE SAUCE FOR BARBECUE PIG

1 (gallon) jug white vinegar
1 (32-ounce) jar catsup
1 (16-ounce) jar prepared mustard
1 (2-ounce) can ground black pepper

1 (1.12-ounce) can ground red pepper
1 (6-1/4-ounce) bottle hot sauce

Warm vinegar short of boiling; slowly stir in all ingredients, one at a time, making sure each ingredient is fully dissolved (especially black pepper). When pig is almost done, baste heavily with sauce, making sure sauce gets in between joints.

This is Ray Hodge's famous and secret (until now) barbecue sauce recipe; hot but ... wonderful!

BÉARNAISE SAUCE

4 large egg yolks
1 cup butter, melted and
   divided
1 tablespoon lemon
   juice, freshly
   squeezed
1 tablespoon tarragon
   vinegar

1/4 teaspoon salt
1 teaspoon parsley,
   chopped fine
1 teaspoon onion,
   minced
Dash ground red pepper

Beat egg yolks well and blend with about 1/3 of the melted butter; stir to blend. Add remaining butter and cook in top of double boiler over boiling water until sauce thickens, stirring constantly. Remove from heat and add the remaining ingredients. Serve with broiled meats.

CHEESE SAUCE

1/2 cup butter or
   margarine, melted
3 green onions, finely
   chopped
1 tablespoon green
   pepper, chopped

4 tablespoons all-
   purpose flour
Ground black pepper,
   to taste
2 cups extra sharp
   cheese, grated

Melt butter; add onion and pepper; cook until tender, stirring occasionally. Add flour and blend well; stir in pepper and cheese. Cook, stirring until thickened. Good with asparagus, broccoli and cauliflower.

DIANE'S SEAFOOD COCKTAIL SAUCE

3/4 cup mayonnaise
1/2 cup catsup

1 tablespoon prepared
   horseradish

Beat mayonnaise until smooth. Slowly blend in the catsup and then the horseradish until well blended. Great on shrimp!

A "must" sauce for boiled shrimp!

BUTTERSCOTCH SAUCE NO. 1

1-1/2 cups light brown
  sugar, packed
2/3 cup white corn
  syrup
1/3 cup water

1/4 cup butter
2/3 cup evaporated
  milk
1 teaspoon pure
  vanilla extract

Combine sugar, syrup, water and butter until well blended. Cook and stir over medium heat until mixture reaches soft ball stage. Remove from heat and cool; stir in milk gradually and then the vanilla. Store in a covered jar in refrigerator. Serve warm or cold over ice cream, pudding or cake.

An elegant sauce!

BUTTERSCOTCH SAUCE NO. 2

1 egg yolk, slightly
  beaten
1/4 cup butter
1/3 cup water
1-1/2 cups light brown
  sugar, packed
2/3 cup white corn
  syrup

2/3 cup thin cream or
  evaporated milk
Dash of salt
1/2 teaspoon pure
  vanilla extract

Combine egg and next 4 ingredients; cook, stirring frequently until thickened. Stir in the cream gradually, then salt and vanilla. Serve warm or cold.

CHOCOLATE SAUCE

3/4 cup granulated
  sugar
3 tablespoons cocoa
  powder
Dash salt
2 tablespoons cold
  water

1 (6-ounce) can
  evaporated milk
2 tablespoons butter
1 teaspoon pure
  vanilla extract

Combine sugar, cocoa, salt and water, blending well until dissolved. Add the milk and bring to a boil; cook gently for 3 or 4 minutes, stirring constantly to prevent burning. Remove from heat and stir in the butter and vanilla. Spoon over ice cream or cake while the sauce is still hot. You may want to double the recipe and keep a portion in a covered jar in the refrigerator as it lasts well.

Dee-licious!

CHILI SAUCE

2 cups canned tomatoes,
  mashed fine
1 cup onion, finely
  chopped
1/2 teaspoon salt
1/8 teaspoon ground
  red pepper
1/8 teaspoon ground
  cinnamon
1/8 teaspoon ground
  cloves
4 tablespoons
  granulated sugar
1/2 cup white vinegar
2 tablespoons green
  pepper, finely
  chopped

Combine all ingredients and bring to boiling point; reduce heat and simmer for around 1-1/2 hours, stirring occasionally.

CRANBERRY SAUCE

4 cups cranberries
1-1/2 cups water
2 cups granulated sugar

Wash cranberries and place in a large saucepan with the water. Cover and cook until skins pop open; add the sugar and blend well. Cook slowly until the sugar completely dissolves. Cool before serving.

Easy and good with turkey and dressing!

MUSHROOM SAUCE

1 cup mushrooms, sliced
1/3 cup butter, melted
1/4 cup all-purpose
  flour
2-1/4 cups broth
  (chicken or beef)
1/2 cup whole milk
1/2 teaspoon salt
Dash ground black
  pepper

Sauté mushrooms in butter; blend in flour. Gradually add broth and then milk. Stir in the salt and pepper. Cook, stirring constantly, until thickened.

LEMON SAUCE

1 cup granulated sugar
1/2 cup boiling water
2 tablespoons butter
2 large eggs, beaten
1/3 cup lemon juice,
  freshly squeezed
Grated lemon rind
  of 2 lemons

Combine all ingredients in top of double boiler; cook over boiling water for around 8 to 10 minutes; sauce will thicken as it cools.

Great with gingerbread, bread pudding or plain cake.

HOLLANDAISE SAUCE

1/2 cup butter, melted
1/2 cup whipping cream,
    unwhipped
4 large egg yolks, well beaten
2 tablespoons lemon juice,
    freshly squeezed

1/4 teaspoon salt
1/8 teaspoon ground
    red pepper

Place butter in top of a double boiler and melt over boiling water; add cream and stir to blend. Gradually add the egg yolks, stirring well. Stir in the juice and salt; cook until thickened and very smooth, around 2 or 3 minutes. Remove from heat and vigorously beat until light. Stir in red pepper. Serve while hot over vegetables.

HORSERADISH SAUCE

1/2 cup sour cream or
1/2 cup whipping cream,
    unwhipped

1/2 teaspoon salt
3 tablespoons prepared
    horseradish

Whip cream until fluffy; fold in salt and horseradish until well blended. Very good with ham and beef dishes.

SEAFOOD COCKTAIL SAUCE

3 cups catsup
2-1/2 tablespoons
    Worcestershire
    sauce
4-1/2 tablespoons
    prepared
    horseradish

3-1/2 teaspoons
    granulated sugar
2 tablespoons lemon
    juice, freshly
    squeezed
Salt and ground black pepper
    to taste

Combine all ingredients and blend well. Chill until ready for use.

Delicious served with shrimp or any seafood!

TARTAR SAUCE NO. 1

3/4 cup mayonnaise
1 teaspoon onion,
    finely grated
1 teaspoon chives,
    chopped
2 teaspoons sweet
    pickle, chopped
    fine

1 teaspoon capers,
    minced
1 tablespoon parsley,
    minced
1 teaspoon celery,
    finely chopped
2 drops Tabasco sauce,
    optional

Combine all ingredients and mix lightly. Refrigerate until ready to serve. Great on fish.

TARTAR SAUCE NO. 2

1 cup mayonnaise
1 teaspoon onion,
  grated
1 tablespoon dill,
  minced

1 teaspoon parsley,
  minced
1 teaspoon pimiento,
  chopped

Blend together all ingredients, beating well, until thoroughly mixed.

Pickles and Relishes—Homemade pickles and relishes are delicious, easy to prepare, inexpensive and as good as the most expensive store-bought variety. Try some of the recipes and you will agree.

SQUASH PICKLE

8 cups squash, sliced
2 cups onion, sliced
1 tablespoon salt
1/2 cup green pepper,
  chopped
1/4 cup red pepper,
  chopped

1 cup cider vinegar
1-3/4 cups granulated
  sugar
1/2 teaspoon celery
  seed
1/2 teaspoon mustard
  seed

Combine the squash and onion. Sprinkle with salt and let stand 1 hour. Combine green and red pepper, vinegar, sugar and seed; bring to a boil. Add squash-onion mixture and return to boil. Pack squash pickles into hot sterilized jars; cover with vinegar mixture and seal. Yields: 4 pints.

Very good!

SWEET DILL PICKLES

1 quart sliced Kosher
  dill pickles
2-1/2 cups granulated
  sugar

4 pods garlic, crushed

Drain juice from pickles. Combine juice, sugar and garlic. Let stand at room temperature until clear. Pour over pickles in jar and refrigerate until chilled.

BEET RELISH

1 cup canned beets,
   finely chopped
3 tablespoons prepared
   horseradish, well
   drained

2 tablespoons lemon juice,
   freshly squeezed
2 teaspoons granulated
   sugar
1 teaspoon salt

Combine all ingredients and mix thoroughly.

CELERY RELISH

1-1/2 cups celery
   hearts and leaves,
   finely chopped
1-1/2 tablespoons
   granulated sugar

1 teaspoon salt
1/2 teaspoon prepared
   mustard
1/4 cup white vinegar

Combine all ingredients and mix thoroughly. Cover and place in refrigerator to chill. Drain and serve.

CRANBERRY RELISH

1 pound fresh
   cranberries
2 large oranges

Juice of 1 orange
2 cups granulated
   sugar

Wash cranberries and oranges; cut oranges to remove seeds and white pulp. Grind berries and 2 oranges in food chopper. Now add juice of one orange and the sugar, blending. Refrigerate in covered container until ready to serve. Delicious served with meats.

PEAR CHUTNEY

4 cups pears, pared
   and diced
1 cup seedless raisins,
   cut up
1/4 cup onion, finely
   chopped
1-1/2 cups white
   vinegar

1-1/2 cups granulated
   sugar
1-1/2 teaspoons celery
   seed
1 tablespoon salt
1/4 teaspoon ground
   red pepper

Combine all ingredients. Bring to a boil and cook and stir over medium heat for around 1 hour. Spoon into 3 half pint sterilized jars and seal. Delicious served with meat dishes.

Make this often!

Timbales

Timbales are perfect for luncheon entrées and make a rich and wonderful main dish!

ASPARAGUS TIMBALES

3 tablespoons butter,
  melted
3 tablespoons all-
  purpose flour
1 cup milk
2 cups asparagus,
  finely chopped
  (fresh or canned)

1/2 teaspoon salt
Dash ground black
  pepper
3 large eggs, well beaten

Melt butter and gradually blend in flour until smooth. Slowly add milk, stirring until thickened and smooth. Add asparagus, salt, pepper and eggs, gently blending together. Pour mixture into buttered timbale molds and place in a pan of hot water to reach almost to top of molds. Bake at 350 degrees for around 40 minutes or until set. Cool for several minutes before unmolding onto warm serving dishes.

Wonderful luncheon dish!

CHICKEN TIMBALES NO. 1

2 slices day old bread,
  crumbled
1 cup half and half
2 large eggs, beaten
1-1/2 cups cooked
  chicken breasts,
  finely cut up

1/2 teaspoon salt
Dash ground black
  pepper
2 teaspoons celery
  leaves, finely
  chopped

Place crumbled bread in the half and half and let soak for several minutes. Add beaten eggs and beat well; stir in the chicken, salt, pepper and celery. Pour mixture into buttered custard cups and place in a pan of hot water to reach almost to top of cups. Bake at 350 degrees for around 40 minutes or until custard is set. Cool for several minutes before unmolding onto warm serving dishes. Good with chicken broth.

Chicken Broth:

3 cups chicken broth
1 teaspoon salt
Dash ground black
  pepper

1/4 cup celery, chopped
1/2 cup onion, chopped
2 teaspoons parsley,
  chopped

Combine all ingredients; cover and bring to boiling point. Reduce heat and cook until onion and celery are tender. Strain and serve broth while very hot.

CHICKEN TIMBALES NO. 2

1 cup day old bread,
   crumbled
2 cups whole milk
2 large eggs, slightly
   beaten
1/2 teaspoon salt
1/4 teaspoon paprika
1/4 teaspoon ground
   thyme
1 teaspoon
   Worcestershire
   sauce

3 cups cooked chicken,
   cut up
1/2 cup celery,
   finely chopped
1/2 cup green pepper,
   finely chopped
1/4 cup lemon juice,
   freshly squeezed

Mix thoroughly all ingredients. Pack into 8 timbale molds. Place in a pan of hot water to reach almost to top of molds. Bake at 350 degrees for around 40 minutes or until set. Cool for several minutes before unmolding onto warm serving dishes.

HAM TIMBALES

1-1/2 cups baked ham,
   chopped fine
1-1/2 cups white bread
   crumbs
1 cup half and half
2 large egg yolks
1/2 teaspoon salt
1/8 teaspoon ground
   black pepper

1/4 teaspoon dry
   ground mustard
2 teaspoons parsley,
   finely chopped
2 large egg whites,
   stiffly beaten

Chop baked ham fine and set aside. Place crumbs in half and half to soak for several minutes. Then add the beaten yolks and beat well to blend. Stir in the ham, salt, pepper, mustard and parsley. Beat whites until stiff. Lightly fold into the ham mixture. Spoon into buttered custard cups and place in pan of hot water to almost reach top of cups. Bake at 350 degrees for around 40 minutes or until set. Let cool for several minutes before unmolding onto warm serving plates.

An easy main dish!

CHEESE TIMBALES

1 cup whole milk,
scalded
1/2 cup sharp Cheddar
cheese, grated
1/4 teaspoon salt

Dash ground black
pepper
1/4 teaspoon onion,
grated
3 eggs, well beaten

Scald milk in top of double boiler; add cheese, salt, pepper and onion; stir until cheese is melted. Beat eggs and then add cheese mixture, blending thoroughly. Pour into buttered custard cups Place cups in pan of water to almost reach top of cups. Bake at 350 degrees for around 40 minutes, or until set. Cool for several minutes before unmolding onto warm serving dishes. Serve with tomato sauce, if desired.

Tomato Sauce:

3 tablespoons vegetable
oil
1 small clove garlic
1/2 cup green pepper,
chopped fine
1/2 cup carrot, grated
fine
1 cup onion, chopped
4 cups canned tomatoes,
with juice

1 bay leaf
1/2 cup celery leaves,
cut up
1/2 teaspoon salt
1/4 teaspoon ground
black pepper
2 teaspoons granulated
sugar

Heat oil in a large saucepan; add the garlic, pepper, carrot and onion; sauté until vegetables are tender, stirring constantly. Now add the tomatoes, bay leaf, celery, salt, pepper and sugar. Cover and cook until sauce thickens, stirring occasionally; around 30 minutes. Remove bay leaf and rub through a fine sieve before serving. Reheat if necessary, but serve hot.

Sauce is delicious over the Cheese Timbales and also on spaghetti!

CARROT TIMBALES

1 tablespoon all-
purpose flour
1 cup whole milk
2 eggs, well beaten
1/2 cup dry bread
crumbs
2 tablespoons butter,
melted

1 teaspoon salt
1/8 teaspoon ground
black pepper
2 cups raw carrots,
grated
4 teaspoons onion,
grated

Combine the flour and milk; beat until smooth. Add eggs,

crumbs, butter, salt, pepper, carrots and onion; mix thoroughly. Spoon into buttered custard cups and place in a pan of hot water to reach almost to top of cups. Bake at 350 degrees for around 40 minutes or until set. Cool for several minutes before unmolding onto warm serving dishes.

Ideal for a luncheon entrée!

CORN TIMBALES

3/4 cup whole milk,
  scalded
2 large eggs, well
  beaten
1-1/2 cups whole
  kernel corn, fresh
  or canned

1 tablespoon butter,
  melted
1 tablespoon onion,
  grated
4 teaspoons parsley,
  chopped
1/2 cup bread crumbs

Scald milk and gradually add to beaten eggs; now blend in rest of ingredients thoroughly. Pour into buttered custard cups and place in pan of hot water to reach almost to top of cups. Bake at 350 degrees for around 40 minutes or until set. Cool for several minutes before unmolding onto warm serving plates.

Delicious!

NOODLE TIMBALES

4 ounces fine egg
  noodles (1/2 of
  8-ounce package)
3 large eggs, well
  beaten
1 cup whole milk

1/2 cup medium Cheddar
  cheese, grated
1/2 teaspoon salt
1/8 teaspoon ground
  black pepper

Cook noodles in boiling water until tender and drain well. Beat eggs; add milk and beat until smooth. Stir in the cheese, salt, pepper and well drained noodles, mixing thoroughly. Spoon into buttered custard cups and place in a pan of water to reach almost to top of custard cups. Bake at 350 degrees for around 40 minutes or until set. Cool for several minutes before unmolding onto warm serving dishes.

Um-m-m good!

LOBSTER TIMBALES

1 cup cooked lobster
  meat, chopped
1 tablespoon butter,
  melted
1 tablespoon all-
  purpose flour
1 teaspoon salt
1/4 teaspoon paprika

2 drops onion juice
2 large egg yolks,
  slightly beaten
1/3 cup whole milk
1/3 cup whipping
  cream, unwhipped
1 large egg white,
  stiffly beaten

Combine lobster and butter; cook and stir for around 5 minutes. Stir in flour, salt, paprika, onion juice, egg yolks and milk. Fold in cream and stiffly beaten egg white. Spoon into buttered custard cups and place in pan of hot water to almost reach top of cups. Bake at 350 degrees for around 40 minutes or until set. Let cool for several minutes before unmolding onto warm serving plates. Serve with sauce.

Sauce:

2 tablespoons butter,
  melted
2 tablespoons all-
  purpose flour
1/2 cup whole milk
1/2 cup whipping cream,
  unwhipped

1 teaspoon meat
  extract
1/2 cup diced canned
  lobster
Salt and ground
  black pepper, to taste

Melt butter and stir in flour until smooth. Slowly add the milk and cream, stirring constantly; bring to boiling point and cook for 2 minutes. Add meat extract, lobster and salt and pepper to taste.

SALMON TIMBALES

1 cup red salmon,
  flaked
1 cup salmon juice-
  whole milk
1/2 cup dry bread
  crumbs
2 eggs, well beaten

2 teaspoons lemon juice,
  freshly squeezed
1 teaspoon onion, grated
1/2 teaspoon salt
1/8 teaspoon ground
  red pepper

Drain juice from salmon and reserve. Flake salmon with fork and set aside. Add enough milk to juice to make 1 cup; add crumbs and let soak for a few minutes. Now blend in the beaten eggs and stir in the salmon. Beat well until thoroughly blended. Stir in the lemon juice, onion, salt and pepper. Spoon into buttered custard cups and place in a pan of hot water to almost reach top of custard cups. Bake at 350 degrees for around 40 minutes or until set. Cool for 2 or 3 minutes before unmolding onto warm serving dishes. Good with Tartar Sauce.

Tartar Sauce:

1 cup mayonnaise
1 teaspoon onion, grated fine
1 tablespoon celery,
  finely chopped
1 teaspoon chives, chopped
1 teaspoon parsley,
  finely chopped

1 teaspoon sweet pickle,
  chopped
3 drops hot sauce
1 teaspoon capers

Combine all ingredients and gently stir to blend. Keep refrigerated until ready to serve.

SPINACH TIMBALES

2 cups spinach, cooked,
  chopped and drained
2 large eggs, well beaten
1 cup bread crumbs
1 teaspoon onion,
  grated

1 teaspoon salt
Dash ground black pepper
1-1/2 cups half and
  half

Cook spinach, chop and drain well. Combine with rest of ingredients, mixing thoroughly. Spoon into buttered custard cups and place in pan of hot water to reach almost to top of cups. Bake at 350 degrees for around 40 minutes or until set. Leave in cups for several minutes before unmolding onto warm serving dishes. Serve plain or with Egg Sauce.

Egg Sauce:

3 tablespoons butter, melted
3 tablespoons all-
  purpose flour
2 cups whole milk
1/2 teaspoon salt
Dash ground black pepper

1/8 teaspoon
  Worcestershire sauce
1 teaspoon lemon juice
  freshly squeezed
4 eggs, hard boiled
  and diced

Melt butter and blend in flour until smooth. Gradually add milk, stirring constantly until sauce begins to boil and thicken. Add salt, pepper, Worcestershire sauce and juice, blending well. Remove from heat and fold in the eggs.

Worth the effort!

Vegetables

Vegetables — The nutritional value of vegetables can't be over emphasized. Select fresh vegetables and learn to be a good vegetable cooker!

ASPARAGUS CASSEROLE NO. 1

3 (15-ounce) cans asparagus
2 (10-3/4-ounce) cans cream of
mushroom soup
1 (8-ounce) can water chestnuts
4 hard boiled eggs, sliced
6 tablespoons pimientos,
chopped

1/2 pound sharp Cheddar
cheese
1 cup buttered bread crumbs
Paprika

Butter a large casserole dish and layer the asparagus, soup, chestnuts, eggs, pimientos and cheese. Top with crumbs and sprinkle paprika all over top. Bake in a 350 degree oven until mixture bubbles, around 30 minutes.

ASPARAGUS CASSEROLE NO. 2

2 tablespoons butter, melted
1 tablespoon all-purpose flour
1/4 teaspoon dry ground
mustard
1 (10-3/4-ounce) can cream of
mushroom soup
1 (15-1/2-ounce) can
asparagus, drained well

1/2 cup toasted, slivered
almonds
4 large hard-boiled eggs, sliced
1 cup bread crumbs
1 teaspoon butter, melted
1/2 cup American cheese,
grated

Melt butter; add flour, mustard and soup. Cook until thickened and set aside. Butter a casserole dish and layer the asparagus, almonds and sliced eggs until all is used. Spoon over the sauce. Place crumbs in saucepan and add the melted butter, stirring until lightly browned. Spread over top and sprinkle with the cheese. Bake at 300 degrees for around 30 minutes.

An ideal buffet dish!

ASPARAGUS SOUFFLÉ

2 tablespoons butter, melted
1 (10-3/4 -ounce) can cream of
mushroom soup
1 teaspoon onion, grated
1-1/2 cups grated American
cheese

3 large eggs, separated
1-1/2 cups asparagus, cut in
1-inch pieces
1/4 teaspoon salt

Combine the butter, soup, onion and cheese, stirring over low heat until the cheese is melted. Remove from heat and beat the egg yolks; add to the cheese mixture and blend well. Stir in the asparagus and salt. Beat the egg whites until stiff and then fold in with the asparagus mixture. Spoon into a buttered casserole dish and bake at 350 degrees for around 45 minutes.

Delightfully good!

BAKED BEANS

5 slices bacon, cooked and
  crumbled
1 onion, chopped
2 (16-ounce) cans pork and
  beans
1/4 cup light brown sugar,
  firmly packed

2 tablespoons molasses or
  dark corn syrup
3/4 cup catsup
6 slices bacon, uncooked

Cook bacon until crisp; crumble and set aside. Sauté onion in bacon drippings; then add the beans, sugar, molasses, catsup and crumbled bacon. Stir until well blended. Pour into a large casserole dish. Place 6 slices uncooked bacon on top and bake at 350 degrees for around 1 hour.

Great taste!

BROCCOLI DIANE

1 bunch fresh broccoli, cooked
  and chopped or
1 (10-ounce) package frozen
  broccoli, cooked and
  chopped
1 (10-3/4-ounce) can cream of
  mushroom soup, or cream of
  chicken soup

1 large egg, slightly beaten
1 tablespoon mayonnaise
1 (12-ounce) package medium
  Cheddar cheese, grated
  (divided)
Cracker crumbs

Steam broccoli for 7 minutes. Cut in small pieces and set aside to cool. If you use frozen broccoli, cook according to package instructions and drain well. Beat egg slightly, add mayonnaise and soup, mixing well. Blend with broccoli in a large bowl. Grate the cheese and add one half to the broccoli mixture. Spoon into a buttered casserole dish. Bake at 350 degrees for 20 minutes. Remove from oven and cover top with grated cheese. Cover the cheese with very fine cracker crumbs. Bake for 10 more minutes at 350 degrees. Do not overcook at this point.

A most delicious casserole that you can serve at any time of the year!

BEETS IN ORANGE SAUCE

2 tablespoons cornstarch
3 tablespoons granulated
  sugar
1/4 teaspoon salt
2/3 cup orange juice,
  freshly squeezed
1/8 teaspoon orange rind,
  grated

1/8 teaspoon lemon rind,
  grated
1 tablespoon butter
3 cups cooked fresh beets,
  coarsely grated or canned
  beets, well drained

Blend together the cornstarch, sugar and salt. Add the juice and cook, stirring constantly, until mixture thickens. Stir in the rind, butter and drained beets; mix together lightly. Reheat and stir until thoroughly blended.

Great way to serve beets!

BEETS IN SWEET-SOUR SAUCE

3 cups cooked beets, sliced
2 tablespoons all-purpose flour
2 tablespoons butter or
  margarine
3/4 cup whole milk

2 tablespoons white vinegar
1/4 cup light brown sugar,
  packed
1/4 teaspoon salt
Ground black pepper, optional

Prepare and cook beets and set aside. Blend together the flour, butter and milk until smooth. Cook and stir until thickened. Add vinegar, sugar, salt and pepper. Serve over drained beets.

A tasty dish!

BOILED RUTABAGA

Rutabaga, cut up
Water
Salt

Granulated sugar
Salt and ground black pepper
Butter

Pare and cut rutabaga into 1/4 inch pieces. Barely cover with water; add salt. Cook until tender. Drain and mash. Season with sugar, salt, pepper and butter to taste.

BOILED TURNIPS

Turnips
Water
Salt

Granulated sugar
Salt and ground black pepper
Butter

Pare and cut turnips into 1/2 inch pieces. Cover with water; add salt and boil, uncovered, until tender. Drain and mash. Add sugar, salt, pepper and butter to taste. Serve hot.

BROCCOLI CASSEROLE

2 (10-ounce) packages frozen,
  chopped broccoli
2 (10-3/4-ounce) cans cream of
  mushroom soup
1 cup celery, chopped

1 cup medium Cheddar cheese,
  grated
1 (8-ounce) carton sour cream
Buttered bread crumbs

Thaw broccoli and cook lightly before mixing; drain well. Combine the soup, celery, cheese and sour cream. Add to the broccoli and stir to mix well. Top with buttered bread crumbs. Bake at 350 degrees for 30 minutes.

BUTTERED CAULIFLOWER

1 head cauliflower
Salt

Melted butter
Paprika

Place cauliflower in a large saucepan and cover with cold salted water. Cover and soak for 30 minutes. Drain and wash head and then cut off base of stalk; discard large leaves. Leave the tiny leaves that cling to the flowerets. Break flowerets apart, removing main stem. Now add water and salt (1 teaspoon salt to each quart of water used), and cook rapidly in an uncovered saucepan until tender, around 6 to 8 minutes. Do not overcook. The cauliflower should be snow white and crisp. Drain well and place in serving dish. Drizzle with melted butter. Sprinkle with paprika. Serve while still hot.

CABBAGE CASSEROLE

1 small head green cabbage,
  cut in eighths
2 tablespoons butter, melted
2 tablespoons all-purpose flour
1 cup whole milk
1/4 cup green pepper, chopped
  fine, divided

1 cup sharp cheese, grated,
  divided
Cracker crumbs, rolled fine
Grated cheese
3 slices half-cooked bacon, cut
  in small pieces

Trim cabbage; wash and cut into eighths; remove core and cook, uncovered, for 8 minutes in boiling salted water. Remove from heat and drain. Place a layer of cabbage in a buttered casserole dish; layer with a sauce made by combining the butter, flour and milk, half the green pepper, and half the cheese. Repeat and then sprinkle top with cracker crumbs, cheese and chopped bacon. Bake at 375 degrees until top is toasted, around 15 minutes. Serve hot.

A good way to serve cabbage!

BUTTERED CARROTS

12 tiny, young carrots, whole
 or 6 medium carrots, whole
2 teaspoons granulated sugar

3 tablespoons butter
1/2 teaspoon salt
Chopped parsley

Scrub carrots and scrape lightly; barely cover with water. Cover and cook gently tiny carrots for around 15 minutes and medium carrots for around 45 minutes. Remove cover and evaporate remaining liquid; remove from heat and add sugar, butter and salt. Cover and let stand for around 15 minutes. Remove carefully to serving plate and sprinkle with parsley. Serve hot.

CARROT SOUFFLÉ

1 large (2 pound) package
 carrots
1 tablespoon all-purpose flour
1 cup whole milk
2 tablespoons melted butter or
 margarine

2 tablespoons granulated
 sugar
2 large eggs, separated

Scrape and cook carrots in a medium saucepan until tender. Combine the flour, milk and melted butter and beat until no lumps appear. Set aside. Beat cooked and drained carrots until smooth; add the sugar and sauce, blending until mixed. Add egg yolks and beat again. Beat egg whites until stiff. Fold into carrot mixture. Spoon into a greased casserole dish and bake at 350 degrees for about 20 minutes.

Good and good for you!

COMPANY GREEN BEANS

3 slices bacon, cooked crisp
 and crumbled
2 tablespoons bacon drippings
1/2 cup onion, finely chopped
1/4 cup green pepper, finely
 chopped
1 tomato, chopped

1-1/2 cups green beans, cooked
1 teaspoon salt
1/4 teaspoon ground black
 pepper
2 slices day old bread, toasted
 and cubed

Cook bacon until crisp; crumble and set aside. Reserve 2 tablespoons drippings and brown onion and pepper, stirring until tender. Add chopped tomato; cook and stir lightly for around 5 minutes. Stir in cooked beans, salt and pepper; simmer for around 10 or 15 additional minutes. Remove to serving dish and top with toasted bread cubes and crumbled bacon.

Great flavor!

CANDIED SWEET POTATOES

3 large sweet potatoes, cooked
1 cup light brown sugar,
  packed

1 cup whole milk
4 tablespoons butter
1/2 cup coconut, grated

Peel cooked potatoes and slice. Place potato slices in a buttered casserole dish. Combine the sugar and milk well; pour over potatoes. Cut butter in small pieces and add to top of potatoes. Sprinkle with coconut. Cover and bake at 350 degrees until syrup is thick. Remove cover and lightly brown coconut.

Delightful taste!

CARROT CASSEROLE

1 pound carrots
Salt, to taste
1 small onion, chopped
1 teaspoon prepared mustard

4 saltine crackers, crumbled
1 cup grated Cheddar cheese
1/2 cup mayonnaise

Scrape and slice carrots crosswise. Barely cover the carrots with boiling salted water (1/4 teaspoon salt to 1 cup water). Cook gently until tender. Drain and mash while still hot. Add rest of the ingredients in order given. Spoon into a greased casserole dish and bake at 375 degrees for around 30 minutes or until done.

You will be surprised at the wonderful flavor!

CORN AND TOMATO CASSEROLE

4 cups fresh corn, grated
1/4 cup butter, melted
2 cups water
5 slices bacon, cooked and
  crumbled

2 teaspoons salt
1/2 teaspoon ground white
  pepper
2 fresh tomatoes, peeled and
  sliced

Combine corn and butter; cook and stir for around 5 minutes. Add water, bacon, salt and pepper. Pour mixture into a buttered casserole dish. Arrange tomato slices on top. Bake in a 350 degree oven, uncovered, for around 30 minutes. Serve while still hot.

So good!

CORN AND CHEESE CASSEROLE

2 cups cream style corn
1 cup whole milk
1 large egg, beaten
3/4 teaspoon salt
1/4 teaspoon ground white
  pepper

1 teaspoon granulated sugar
1 cup coarse fresh bread
  crumbs
1/2 cup grated sharp
  American cheese

Combine corn and milk; heat and stir in the beaten egg. Add salt, pepper, sugar, crumbs and cheese and mix thoroughly. Pour into a buttered casserole dish. Bake at 325 degrees for around 30 minutes.

This dish has taste appeal!

CORN CAKES

2 large eggs, beaten
1/2 cup buttermilk
1/4 teaspoon baking soda
1 cup corn, freshly grated
1 cup all-purpose flour

1/2 teaspoon salt
2 teaspoons baking powder
1 tablespoon butter, melted
Vegetable oil

Beat eggs well; add buttermilk, soda and corn. Sift together the flour, salt and baking powder. Add to the egg mixture, blending well. Stir in the melted butter. Drop by spoonfuls and brown on greased hot griddle, turning to brown on other side. Remove to hot serving platter and serve.

Appetizing!

CORN SCALLOP

1 (12-ounce) can whole kernel
  corn
2 large eggs, slightly beaten
1 (16-ounce) can cream style
  corn
2/3 cup evaporated milk
4 tablespoons butter, melted
2 tablespoons minced onion

1/2 teaspoon salt
1/2 teaspoon ground black
  pepper
2 cups saltine crackers,
  coarsely crushed
1 (12-ounce) package Swiss
  cheese, diced

Drain liquid from whole kernel corn and reserve. Beat eggs slightly; stir in the whole kernel corn and 1/4 cup of the liquid. Now add the cream style corn, milk, butter, onion, salt and pepper. Fold in the saltines and cheese. Spoon into a greased casserole dish. Bake at 325 degrees for 1 hour or until set. Serve while still hot.

This will serve as a hearty main dish!

COUNTRY FRIED POTATOES AND ONIONS

6 medium potatoes, sliced
3 medium onions, sliced
Vegetable oil or bacon
  drippings

Salt
Ground black pepper

Pare and slice the potatoes and onions. Heat the oil or drippings until hot. Add the potatoes and onion; cover and reduce heat. Cook slowly, turning as potatoes brown. Remove when all are browned and sprinkle with salt and pepper. Serve hot.

CREAMED CABBAGE

3 cups green cabbage, coarsely
  shredded and cooked
1/2 cup sour cream

1/2 teaspoon caraway seed
Salt and ground black
  pepper to taste

Chop cabbage coarsely and cook in boiling water until tender. Add the sour cream and caraway seed; toss. Season with salt and pepper; reheat just before serving.

Most appetizing!

CREAMED CAULIFLOWER WITH CHEESE

Cold salt water
1 large cauliflower,
  2-1/2 pounds
1-1/2 quarts boiling water
1-1/2 teaspoons salt, divided
3 tablespoons butter
3 tablespoons all-purpose flour

1/8 teaspoon ground white
  pepper
1/2 teaspoon dry ground
  mustard
1-1/2 cups whole milk
1 cup Cheddar cheese, grated
Paprika

Soak cauliflower in enough cold salt water to cover for 30 minutes. Wash head and remove outer leaves. Trim by cutting off base of stalk, if necessary. Break flowerets apart. Drop into 1-1/2 quarts boiling water with 1 teaspoon of the salt and boil just until tender, around 6 to 8 minutes. Do not overcook. Test by piercing with a fork. Cauliflower should be snow white and still slightly crisp. Drain thoroughly. Melt butter and stir in flour, remaining 1/2 teaspoon salt, pepper and mustard. Remove from heat and gradually stir in milk until smooth. Return to heat and cook, stirring constantly until thickened. Lightly blend in cauliflower and reheat. Pour into serving dish; sprinkle immediately with cheese and paprika.

CORN PUDDING

2 cups fresh corn, grated
1 cup whole milk
2 tablespoons butter
2 tablespoons all-purpose flour
1 teaspoon salt

1 tablespoon granulated sugar
1/2 teaspoon ground white
  pepper
3 large eggs

Combine the corn, milk, butter, flour and seasonings, blending well. Beat eggs until light and foamy; add to the first mixture. Pour into a buttered 1-quart casserole dish. Place dish in a pan of boiling water and bake at 350 degrees for 1 hour and 15 minutes or until custard in set.

Really good!

CREAMED GREEN PEAS AND POTATOES

4 cups red potatoes, cubed
1-1/2 cups fresh green peas
1 tablespoon green onion,
  chopped
2 cups boiling water
1-1/2 teaspoons salt

1/8 teaspoon ground black
  pepper
1/2 cup evaporated milk or
  light cream
2 tablespoons butter

Place potatoes, peas and onion in a large saucepan; cover with boiling water and the salt. Bring to a boil; cover and cook for around 15 to 20 minutes or until vegetables are tender. Add pepper, milk (or cream) and butter. Simmer just until slightly thickened.

Oh, so good!

CREAMY POTATO CASSEROLE

10 medium-size red potatoes,
  pared and cubed
1 (8-ounce) package cream
  cheese, softened
1 (8-ounce) carton sour cream
4 tablespoons butter or
  margarine

1/3 cup chopped chives
Salt and ground black pepper
  to taste
Butter, for top
Paprika, for top

Boil potatoes in boiling water until tender. Beat cream cheese until creamy; add sour cream and beat until blended. Now add hot potatoes and beat until all lumps are gone and mixture is smooth. Add butter, chives, salt and pepper to taste; blend well. Spoon mixture into a well-buttered 2 quart casserole. Dot with butter and sprinkle with paprika all over top.

Delightfully different!

EGGPLANT CASSEROLE NO. 1

1 medium to large eggplant,
  pared and cubed
Salt to taste
2 tablespoons butter, melted
1 cup celery, finely chopped
1/2 cup onion, finely chopped

1 large egg, slightly beaten
1 cup milk
1 cup butter-flavored crackers,
  finely crushed
1/2 cup sharp cheese, grated

Cook eggplant in boiling water, seasoned with salt to taste, until tender. Drain well and then add rest of ingredients, except cheese; mix well. Bake at 350 degrees for 1 hour; remove and spread cheese over top. Return to oven and bake until cheese melts. Serve hot.

EGGPLANT CASSEROLE NO. 2

1 large eggplant, pared and
  sliced
Salt and ground black pepper
Bacon drippings or vegetable
  oil
2 medium onions, chopped fine

1 medium green pepper,
  chopped fine
2 cups sharp cheese, grated
2 cups tomatoes, chopped
1 cup bread crumbs

Pare and slice eggplant. Lightly salt and pepper each slice. Heat drippings or oil and brown eggplant. Butter a casserole dish and place a layer of the browned eggplant, then layer with onion, pepper and cheese. Repeat and then pour tomatoes over layers; top with the crumbs. Bake at 350 degrees for 1 hour.

EGGPLANT FRITTERS

1 large (or 2 small) eggplant
1 teaspoon salt
1 large egg
1/3 cup milk
1 tablespoon vegetable oil

1 cup all-purpose flour,
  unsifted
1 teaspoon baking powder
2 teaspoons granulated sugar

Pare and cut eggplant in small cubes; barely cover with water, add salt and cook until tender. Drain well and set aside to cool. Beat egg and then stir in milk and oil. Sift together the flour, baking powder and sugar. Add the flour mixture to the egg mixture, blending well. Fold in the eggplant. Drop by teaspoonfuls into deep hot fat. Brown until golden on both sides. Serve hot.

These will be eaten quickly as they are mouth watering!

FRENCH BEAN CASSEROLE

1 (16-ounce) can French green
  beans
Salt, to taste
2 tablespoons butter, melted

1/2 cup onion, chopped
2 tablespoons all-purpose flour
1 (8-ounce) carton sour cream
Grated Cheddar cheese

Cook beans and salt to taste; drain and set aside. Melt butter and sauté onion; add flour and mix well. Remove from heat and stir in sour cream; fold in beans. Spoon into buttered casserole dish. Sprinkle with grated cheese. Bake at 350 degrees until hot and bubbly and cheese has melted, around 15 minutes.

FRIED CABBAGE

2 tablespoons bacon drippings
  or margarine
1 large head green cabbage,
  coarsely shredded

1/2 teaspoon salt
Ground black pepper

Heat drippings or margarine in large, heavy skillet; add cabbage and sprinkle with salt. Cover and cook over low heat for around 3 minutes on one side. Turn cabbage over and cook for another 3-or 4 minutes. Cabbage should be just lightly browned. Sprinkle with black pepper and serve while still hot. Do not overcook.

Good!

FRIED GREEN TOMATOES

Green tomatoes, sliced 1/2-
  inch thick
Salt
Ground black pepper

Granulated sugar
All-Purpose Flour
Vegetable oil

Slice tomatoes; salt and pepper each slice and sprinkle sugar on one side. Coat each side with flour. Fry slowly in hot oil until brown, turning only once. Carefully remove to serving platter and serve while hot.

FRIED OKRA

Okra, sliced
Corn meal
Salt

Ground black pepper
Hot vegetable oil

Wash and stem okra; cut crosswise into 1/4-inch slices. Combine corn meal, salt and pepper. Add the cut okra and coat with the corn meal mixture well. Place in 1/2 to 1-inch very hot oil. Reduce heat and cook, uncovered, carefully stirring occasionally, until tender. Drain on absorbent towels. Serve hot.

GLAZED CARROTS

10 medium-size carrots
Boiling water
1 teaspoon salt

1/2 cup light brown sugar, packed
1 tablespoon butter

Wash and scrape carrots and cut into 1-1/2-inch pieces. Add boiling water to barely cover and add salt; cover and boil for 10 minutes. Drain carrots and reserve liquid. Place carrots in a buttered casserole dish. Combine 1/2 cup of the carrot liquid, sugar and butter; boil for around 5 minutes and pour the hot syrup over carrots; cover, and bake at 350 degrees for 15 minutes or until carrots are tender. Spoon over glaze 2 or 3 times while carrots are baking.

GLAZED ONIONS

8 small onions, whole
Salt to taste
4 tablespoons butter, melted

1/4 cup light brown sugar, packed

Boil peeled onions in water until tender. Salt to taste. Melt butter and blend in the sugar, stirring to dissolve. Add onions and cook over low heat until onions are covered and glazed, turning over and over.

Great taste!

GOURMET POTATOES

6 medium russet potatoes, baked
1/4 cup butter or margarine, melted
2 cups Cheddar cheese, grated
1-1/2 cups cream cheese, softened

1 teaspoon salt
1/2 teaspoon ground black pepper
1/2 cup green onion, chopped, plus, 1 tablespoon green onion tops, chopped

Scrub potatoes thoroughly and bake at 400 degrees until soft all through when pierced with a fork, around 45 minutes. Cool and then peel and coarsely chop, very carefully. Combine rest of ingredients and fold into potatoes lightly. Turn mixture into a 2-quart buttered casserole. Bake at 350 degrees for 30 minutes.

Irresistible!

GREEN BEANS AND APPLES

1 pound green beans, cut up
Water to cover
Salt to taste
2 tablespoons butter or
  margarine
2 green apples, pared and
  coarsely chopped
1 medium onion, chopped

2 tablespoons all-purpose flour
2 tablespoons granulated
  sugar
1 tablespoon cider vinegar
1-1/3 cups chicken broth or 1
  chicken bouillon cube
  dissolved in 1-1/3 cups
  water

Boil the beans in salted water for around 45 minutes, just until tender. Drain the beans and set aside. Melt the butter; add the apple and onion; stirring often. Cook until the apple is tender. Stir in the flour and add the sugar and vinegar. Gradually stir in the broth and stir constantly until thickened. Stir in the beans; reheat and season with salt again, if necessary.

Different and so delicious!

MARINATED CARROTS

2 pounds carrots, cooked
1 cup tomato soup
1 cup granulated sugar
3/4 cup white vinegar
1/3 cup vegetable oil
1 teaspoon Worcestershire
  sauce

1 medium onion, chopped
1 medium green pepper,
  chopped
1 teaspooon prepared mustard

Scrape and slice carrots crosswise. Barely cover with boiling salted water (1/4 teaspoon salt to 1 cup water) and cook gently until tender but still firm. Remove from heat; drain and let cool. Combine the rest of the ingredients, blending well. Place drained carrots in a large bowl and pour over the marinade mixture. Cover and place in the refrigerator for 24 hours before serving.

A wonderful way to serve carrots!

ONION CASSEROLE

1-1/2 pounds small white
  onions, whole
1 teaspoon salt
3 tablespoons all-purpose flour
1-1/2 cups half and half

2 tablespoons butter, melted
1/2 teaspoon salt
1/2 cup bread crumbs
1 cup grated sharp cheese

Place the whole peeled onions in a large saucepan and cover with water; add salt and cook until tender. Make a sauce of the flour, half and half and butter; add salt and stir into the onions. Pour into a buttered casserole dish and top with the crumbs and cheese. Bake at 325 degrees for around 25 minutes or until lightly browned.

If you like onions, you will enjoy this dish!

PARSNIPS AND TOMATOES

2 medium parsnips, sliced
3/4 teaspoon salt
1/8 teaspoon ground black
  pepper
1 (14-1/2-ounce) can tomatoes,
  mashed fine

1/2 cup onion, chopped
2 tablespoons butter, melted
2 slices white bread, toasted
  and crumbled

Cut parsnips into 1/2-inch slices. Add water to cover and salt; cover and cook until parsnips are tender; around 15 minutes. Add pepper and tomatoes and simmer while you sauté the onion in the melted butter. Now add the onion and butter to the parsnip mixture. Stir in the bread and serve while very hot.

Great dish for parsnip lovers!

POTATO CAKES

2 cups cooked and mashed
  potatoes, seasoned
1 teaspoon onion, grated

All-purpose flour
1/4 cup vegetable shortening

Blend potatoes with the onion. Shape into flat patties of uniform thickness. Coat patties with flour. Heat shortening until almost sizzling hot; place patties in pan. Cook until golden brown; turn very carefully with a spatula and brown other side.

POTATO-CHEESE CASSEROLE NO. 1

4 large potatoes, seasoned and
  mashed
4 large eggs, separated
2 cups Swiss cheese, grated
2 tablespoons chives, finely
  cut

2 tablespoons green pepper,
  chopped
2 tablespoons parsley, chopped
2 tablespoons pimiento, diced
Dash ground black pepper
Paprika

Cook, mash and season potatoes. Quickly beat egg yolks, one at a time, into the hot, mashed potatoes. Combine with the cheese, chives, pepper, parsley, pimiento and black pepper, blending well. Beat the egg whites until stiff. Fold into the potato mixture well. Spoon mixture into a buttered casserole dish. Bake at 375 degrees for around 40 minutes or until golden brown. Remove from oven and sprinkle with paprika. Serve immediately while hot.

POTATO-CHEESE CASSEROLE NO. 2

1/2 cup butter or margarine,
   melted
1-1/2 teaspoons salt
1 (16-ounce) carton sour cream
1 (10-3/4-ounce) can cream of
   chicken soup
1 teaspoon lemon pepper
   seasoning

2 cups grated medium
   Cheddar cheese
1/2 cup onion, finely chopped
2 pounds frozen hash brown
   potatoes

Combine all ingredients, blending well. Spoon into a large buttered casserole dish, Bake at 350 degrees for 45 minutes. 10 to 12 servings.

Quick and tasty!

POTATOES au GRATIN

3 medium potatoes
1 cup whole milk, scalded

1 cup medium Cheddar cheese,
   grated

Pare potatoes and thinly slice in uniform slices. Combine potatoes and hot milk in medium saucepan and heat, stirring, until milk begins to boil. Remove from heat. Arrange layers of potatoes-and-milk in a buttered casserole with a layer of cheese, ending with the cheese on top. Cover and bake at 375 degrees for around 20 to 25 minutes. Remove cover and brown lightly under broiler.

SCALLOPED CORN AND OKRA

2 cups cooked corn
4 cups okra, sliced
4 tablespoons butter or
   margarine, melted, divided
1 teaspoon salt
1/8 teaspoon ground black
   pepper

2 tablespoons all-purpose flour
1 cup whole milk
1/4 pound sharp cheese,
   grated
1/2 teaspoon salt
Bread crumbs, buttered

Prepare corn, cook and set aside. Fry okra in 2 tablespoons butter or margarine for around 10 minutes, stirring often. Place layers of corn and okra in a buttered casserole. Sprinkle each layer with salt and pepper. Combine the remaining butter or margarine, flour and gradually add the milk, until smooth. Add cheese and 1/2 teaspoon salt and heat until cheese melts. Pour over the corn and okra and top with the crumbs. Bake at 350 degrees until the crumbs are browned and the mixture is hot.

OVEN FRENCH FRIES

Potatoes, cut in strips   *Salt*
Vegetable oil

Pare and cut potatoes in strips. Brush with vegetable oil and place on an oiled baking sheet. Place in a 450 degree oven and cook for about 10 minutes; turn to other side with a spatula and brush again with oil. Cook for around 10 to 15 minutes longer or until all are browned. Sprinkle with salt and serve while still hot.

RED BEANS AND RICE

1 pound package dried red
* kidney beans*
2 quarts cold water
1 cup celery, chopped
1 cup green pepper, chopped
1 cup onion, chopped
5 garlic cloves, minced
1 (14-ounce) can tomatoes,
* chopped*
6 cups cold water
1 teaspoon dried red pepper
* flakes*
1-1/2 teaspoons dried thyme
3 bay leaves
1 smoked ham hock
2 pounds any hot smoked
* sausage, slice 1/4-inch thick*
* (optional)*
Hot oil
Salt
Ground black pepper
Tabasco sauce, to taste
Hot cooked white rice
Parsley

Pick over beans and wash well several times. Add cold water and let soak overnight. Next morning, combine the celery, pepper, onion, cloves and tomatoes and add to the 6 cups cold water; drain the beans, rinse thoroughly under cold water; add to the tomato mixture, then add the red pepper flakes, thyme, bay leaves, and ham hock. Bring to a boil, reduce heat and simmer approximately 3 hours, adding more water, if necessary, until beans and ham are very tender. Sauté sausage in small amount of oil; add to the beans, stirring in very gently. Simmer for 20 more minutes. Taste and add salt, pepper and Tabasco. Serve beans over fluffy hot rice. Sprinkle with chopped parsley. 6 to 8 servings.

A famous New Orleans dish and a hearty meal!

RED CABBAGE AND APPLES NO. 1

1 medium head red cabbage,
  2 to 3 pounds, coarsely
  shredded
1 tart apple, pared and
  chopped
3 tablespoons bacon drippings
  or vegetable oil

1/2 cup granulated sugar
1/2 cup water
1/2 cup white vinegar
1/2 teaspoon salt
1/2 teaspoon caraway seed, if
  desired

Combine the cabbage, apple and drippings or oil in a large skillet. Mix together the sugar, water, vinegar, salt and seed; add to cabbage mixture. Cover pan and simmer gently for 30 minutes; check to see if water has evaporated; if not, increase heat and continue to cook until water has evaporated.

Nutritious and really good!

RED CABBAGE AND APPLES NO. 2

1 medium head red cabbage,
  coarsely shredded
3 tablespoons butter or
  margarine, melted
1/2 cup onion, chopped fine

2 tart apples, quartered
1/2 teaspoon salt
1 tablespoon granulated sugar
1/3 cup white vinegar
1/2 teaspoon caraway seed

Coarsely shred cabbage and set aside. Melt the butter; add the onion and cook and stir until onion is tender; add the cabbage and apple; sprinkle with salt. Barely cover with boiling water. Cover and simmer for around 30 minutes. Now add the sugar and cook until most of water has evaporated. Add vinegar and stir until mixed well. Stir in the seed and serve hot.

An elegant dish!

SPINACH CASSEROLE

1 (10-ounce) package frozen,
  chopped spinach
1 (12-ounce) carton cottage
  cheese, creamed
2 large eggs, slightly beaten

1 cup Cheddar cheese, grated
4 tablespoons all-purpose flour
2 tablespoons butter or
  margarine, melted

Cook spinach according to package directions and drain thoroughly. Combine the cottage cheese, eggs, cheese, flour and butter. Now combine with the spinach thoroughly. Spoon into a greased casserole dish and bake at 325 degrees for 1 hour or until set.

Served this way, spinach is not a bore to eat!

SQUASH CAKES

2 medium-size yellow squash,
   or 2 cups
1 small onion, finely grated
1 teaspoon granulated sugar
1 teaspoon salt
1/2 teaspoon ground black
   pepper

1/2 cup all-purpose flour,
   approximately
1/2 teaspoon baking powder
Vegetable oil, for frying

Wash and scrape squash. Grate on a coarse grater to make around 2 cups squash. Add onion, sugar, salt and pepper, mixing well. Now combine the flour and baking powder and stir into squash mixture until it holds together and is right consistency of a fritter batter. You may need to add more flour at this point. Heat 1/2-inch oil in a heavy skillet. Drop by tablespoonfuls into the hot oil. Cook slowly until golden brown, turning to brown other side.

Different way to serve squash and quite good!

SQUASH CASSEROLE NO. 1

3 pounds yellow squash
1/2 cup onion, chopped fine
1/2 cup fine bread crumbs
1 tablespoon granulated sugar
2 large eggs, slightly beaten
1-1/2 teaspoons salt, or to taste

1 teaspoon ground black
   pepper
1/2 cup melted butter,
   divided
1-1/2 cups bread crumbs, for
   topping

Cook squash in boiling water until tender; drain thoroughly and mash while still hot. Add onion, crumbs, sugar, eggs, salt and pepper to taste and 1/4 cup melted butter. Spoon mixture into buttered casserole dish and then drizzle remaining 1/4 cup melted butter over top. Sprinkle with bread crumbs to cover. Bake in 375 degree oven for approximately one hour or until brown on top.

A fine flavored vegetable dish!

SWEET POTATOES, HONEY!

6 medium sweet potatoes,
   whole
1 cup honey

Juice and grated rind of 1
   orange
1 teaspoon salt

Cover potatoes with water and boil until tender. Cool; peel and slice potatoes and arrange in a buttered casserole dish. Mix together rest of ingredients and pour over the potatoes. Bake in a 350 degree oven for around 30 minutes. Serve while still hot.

A nutritious dish and good!

SQUASH CASSEROLE NO. 2

2 cups yellow squash, cooked
and mashed
Salt and ground black pepper
to taste
1 large egg, slightly beaten
1/2 cup evaporated milk

1 tablespoon onion, chopped
1 cup bread crumbs
1 cup sharp cheese, grated
6 tablespoons butter or
margarine, melted

Cook squash in boiling water until tender. Drain thoroughly and add salt and pepper to taste; set aside. Combine the egg, milk, onion, bread crumbs and cheese. Add this to the squash and blend in the butter. Mix together well and bake in a 350 degree oven for around 35 minutes or until set and lightly browned.

This casserole is easy and you and your guests will like it!

SQUASH CASSEROLE NO. 3

8 medium yellow squash
3 tablespoons butter
3 tablespoons onion, grated
2 slices white bread
Milk, 1/4 to 1/2 cup

2 large eggs
Salt and ground black pepper,
to taste
3 slices white bread, grated
1/4 cup butter, melted

Cook squash in boiling water until tender. Drain and mash with butter; add onion. Soak bread in enough milk to soften. Add to squash mixture and beat in 2 eggs, salt and pepper to taste. Pour into a buttered casserole and bake at 350 degrees for 25 to 30 minutes or until squash is set in center and lightly browned around edges. Combine bread crumbs with melted butter and spread over top of casserole. Return to oven and bake until top is golden brown, around 10 minutes. Top will be crunchy.

SQUASH-CHEESE PIE

1 (9-inch) deep dish pie shell,
baked and cooled
8-10 bacon slices
1/2 cup onion, finely chopped
2 cups yellow squash, cooked
and drained

1 teaspoon salt
Ground black pepper, to taste
3 large eggs, slightly beaten
1 cup tomato juice
1 cup Swiss cheese, grated

Bake pie shell and set aside to cool. Cook bacon until crisp; drain, and then crumble over bottom of pie shell. Reserve 2 tablespoons bacon drippings; add onion and cook gently until tender. Stir in the cooked squash, salt and pepper, to taste. Now stir in the beaten eggs and then the juice and cheese. Spoon into the baked pie shell. Bake at 350 degrees for around 1 hour or until set. Slice and serve while hot.

Quick and tasty!

SQUASH-PECAN CASSEROLE

3 tablespoons margarine,
  melted
3 tablespoons onion, finely
  chopped
1 cup whole milk
1 cup dry bread crumbs
Salt and ground black pepper,
  to taste

1/4 teaspoon ground nutmeg
2 eggs, lightly beaten
2 cups yellow squash, cooked
  and mashed
1/2 cup pecans, finely chopped

Melt margarine and sauté onion until tender. Add milk and heat (but do not boil); now pour over the bread crumbs, mixing well. Season with salt and pepper to taste; add nutmeg, blending thoroughly. Stir in eggs, squash and pecans. Grease a casserole dish and spoon mixture into it lightly. Bake in a 325 degree oven for about 35 minutes or until set.

Outstanding taste!

TURNIP GREENS AND DUMPLINGS

Greens:
2 pounds meaty ham bone
4 cups water

1 teaspoon salt
4 pounds turnip greens

Combine meat, water and salt; bring to boil and reduce heat; cover and cook for 30 minutes. Add greens and simmer until tender. Drop dumplings by teaspoonfuls over boiling liquid; do not stir. Boil for 5 to 10 minutes, until dumplings are done.

Dumplings:
1 cup plain cornmeal
1-1/2 cups boiling water

1 tablespoon granulated sugar
1/2 teaspoon salt

Combine all ingredients, blending until well mixed. Drop by teaspoonfuls over boiling liquid. Cook for around 5 or 10 minutes, or until dumplings are done. Serve hot.

STUFFED GREEN PEPPERS NO. 1

4 medium green peppers
3 slices white bread, toasted
  and cubed
2 tablespoons onion, chopped
  fine
2 tablespoons celery, chopped
  fine
2 tablespoons butter, melted

1/2 pound ground beef
1 chicken bouillon cube
1/3 cup hot water
1/2 cup tomatoes, stewed or
  cooked until tender
1/2 cup bread crumbs
Melted butter

Select peppers uniform in size and check to make sure they will stand up straight. Cut a slice from stem end. Remove seed core with kitchen scissors. Do not parboil. Melt butter and sauté onion and celery until tender. Add beef and stir constantly over low heat until all redness is gone. Dissolve bouillon cube in hot water and add to meat; add tomatoes and reheat mixture. Stir in the toasted bread. Fill peppers with meat mixture and top with crumbs. Drizzle melted butter over each one. Fit stuffed peppers snugly together in a greased pan. Bake at 350 degrees for 15 minutes; then turn heat to 400 degrees for 10 minutes until tops are nicely browned.

Really easy and very good!

STUFFED GREEN PEPPERS NO. 2

4 medium green peppers
2 tablespoons butter, melted
2 tablespoons onion, chopped
  fine
1 pound ground beef
1 teaspoon salt
1/4 teaspoon ground black
  pepper

1 large egg, well beaten
1 (8-ounce) can tomato sauce
1 teaspoon Worcestershire
  sauce
1/2 cup sharp cheese, grated
1 teaspoon prepared
  horseradish
1/2 cup quick oats

Select peppers uniform in size and check to make sure they will stand up straight. Cut a slice from the stem end. Remove seed core with kitchen scissors. Do not parboil. Melt butter and sauté onion until tender. Add beef, salt and pepper and lightly brown meat. Beat the egg and blend in the remaining ingredients. Add to the meat mixture. Fill peppers with the mixture and fit snugly together in a greased pan. Bake at 350 degrees for around 45 minutes.

Interesting!

STUFFED POTATOES

6 large baking potatoes, baked
1/4 pound medium Cheddar
  cheese, grated
Salt and ground black pepper
  to taste

1 tablespoon onion, grated
Grated cheese

Bake potatoes in skins at 400 degrees for 1 hour or until done. Scoop out and mash until smooth; add cheese and salt and pepper to taste. Now blend in the onion. Fill potato shells and top with additional grated cheese. Return to oven to brown lightly. Serve while hot.

STUFFED SQUASH

8 to 10 yellow squash
2 tablespoons onion, minced
2 tablespoons butter, melted
2 slices white bread, crumbled
1 teaspoon salt

1/2 teaspoon ground black
  pepper
Grated cheese
Paprika

Barely cover whole squash with water and cook for 10 minutes, or until tender but not soft. Remove from water immediately. Drain and cool. Cut squash in half and scoop out pulp. Combine the onion, butter, bread crumbs, salt and pepper and add to the squash pulp; mix well. Fill the shells with the crumb mixture and pack with a spoon; top with grated cheese and paprika. Bake at 350 degrees for 20 to 30 minutes.

STUFFED TOMATOES

4 large tomatoes, unpeeled
2 large egg yolks, slightly
  beaten
1/2 cup whipping cream,
  unwhipped
2 cups grated medium
  Cheddar cheese
2 tablespoons grated onion

1/3 cup chopped chives
1 teaspoon dry ground
  mustard
1-1/2 teaspoons salt
1/2 cup dry, fine bread crumbs
3 tablespoons melted butter or
  margarine

Wash and halve tomatoes. Scoop out pulp and chop coarsely. Combine egg yolks and cream, blending well. Then add the cheese, onion, chives, mustard and salt. Combine with the tomato pulp. Butter an 8 X 12 X 2-inch casserole dish. Place shells in dish and spoon mixture into shells. Gently toss crumbs and melted butter. Spoon over cheese mixture. Bake in a 350 degree oven for around 25 minutes. Serves 8.

So delicious!

SWEET POTATO BALLS

4 cups cooked sweet potatoes,
  mashed
1/4 cup butter, melted
1/4 cup whole milk
4 tablespoons granulated
  sugar

1/2 teaspoon salt
20 miniature marshmallows
3 cups cornflakes, finely
  crushed

Beat mashed sweet potatoes until smooth; beat in butter, milk, sugar and salt and blend well. Form into balls with marshmallow in center. Roll in finely crushed cornflakes. Place in 450 degree oven and bake until lightly browned.

STEWED TOMATOES

1 (14-1/2-ounce) can tomatoes,
  whole
1 tablespoon granulated sugar
1 small onion, chopped
Salt and pepper, to taste

1 teaspoon crushed red
  peppers, optional
4 tablespoons margarine
2 slices white bread, crumbed

Place tomatoes in a medium saucepan and mash. Add rest of ingredients, except bread, and cook over low heat for around 12 to 15 minutes, stirring often. Turn off heat. Crumble two slices bread and add to the tomato mixture. Serve while still hot.

A very tasty dish that is quick and easy to prepare!

SWEET POTATO CASSEROLE

3 cups cooked sweet potatoes,
  mashed well
1 cup granulated sugar
1 cup melted margarine
2 large eggs, well beaten
1 teaspoon pure vanilla extract
1/3 cup whole milk

1/2 cup light brown sugar,
  firmly packed
1/4 cup all-purpose flour
2-1/2 teaspoons melted
  margarine
1/2 cup chopped pecans

Cook sweet potatoes in boiling water until tender. Cool and peel. Beat until all lumps are gone; add sugar, margarine, eggs, flavoring and milk. Beat until well blended. Set aside and prepare topping. Blend together brown sugar, flour and melted margarine; add the chopped pecans. Spoon the potato mixture into a two quart casserole dish and top with the brown sugar mixture. Bake at 350 degrees for around 25 minutes.

SWEET POTATO SOUFFLÉ

3 cups cooked and mashed
   sweet potatoes
4 tablespoons butter or
   margarine
1/3 cup heavy cream,
   unwhipped
1/2 teaspoon salt

2 large eggs, separated
2 teaspoons freshly squeezed
   lemon juice
1/2 cup crushed pineapple,
   drained
1/2 cup pecans, chopped

Combine cooked potatoes, butter, cream, salt and egg yolks; beat well. Add juice, pineapple and pecans, blending thoroughly. Beat egg whites until stiff and fold into potato mixture. Spoon into a well-greased casserole and bake in a 325 degree oven for around 1 hour.

A delightful dish!

TOMATO CASSEROLE

1 (20-ounce) can whole
   tomatoes, mashed fine
1 large onion, finely chopped
1 cup light brown sugar, firmly
   packed
1-1/2 teaspoons salt

1/2 teaspoon ground black
   pepper
4 slices white bread, crumbled
   in 1/2-inch pieces
1/2 cup butter or margarine,
   melted

Combine tomatoes, onion, sugar, salt and pepper. Cook over medium heat for around 5 minutes. Add the bread and butter. Spoon mixture into a buttered casserole dish and bake at 375 degrees for around 20 minutes.

Measurements and Equivalents

MEASUREMENTS AND EQUIVALENTS

1 gallon. . . . . 4 quarts

1 quart . . . . 2 pints
32 fluid ounces
4 cups

1 pint . . . . 16 fluid ounces
2 cups

1 cup . . . . 8 fluid ounces
16 tablespoons

3/4 cup. . . . . 12 tablespoons
6 ounces

1/2 cup. . . . . 8 tablespoons
2 ounces

1/4 cup. . . . . 4 tablespoons
2 ounces

1/8 cup . . . . 1 fluid ounce
2 tablespoons

1 tablespoon. . . . . 1/2 fluid ounce
3 teaspoons

1 pound . . . . 16 ounces (dry weight)

1/4 pound butter . . . . 1/2 cup

1 ounce baking chocolate . . . . 1 square

1 fluid ounce vanilla . . . . 2 tablespoons

1/2 pint whipping cream . . . . makes 2 cups whipped

1 cup evaporated milk . . . . makes 3 cups whipped

10 graham crackers . . . . makes 1 cup crumbs

1 cup all-purpose flour minus 2 tablespoons equals 1 cup cake flour; sift both before measuring

1 cup vegetable shortening plus 1/2 teaspoon salt equals 1 cup butter.

1 cup whole milk plus 1 tablespoon freshly squeezed lemon juice equals 1 cup buttermilk.

1/2 cup evaporated milk and 1/2 cup water plus 1 tablespoon freshly squeezed lemon juice equals 1 cup buttermilk

1 pound cake flour, unsifted . . . . 4 cups

1 pound cake flour, sifted . . . . 4-1/2 to 4-2/3 cups

1 pound all-purpose flour, unsifted . . . . 3-1/2 cups

1 pound all-purpose flour, sifted . . . . .4 cups

1 pound cheese, grated . . . . .4 cups

1 pound butter . . . . .2 cups

1 pound almonds . . . . .3 cups shelled

1 pound peanuts . . . . .3 to 3-1/2 cups shelled

1 pound pecans . . . . .3 to 4 cups shelled

1 pound walnuts . . . . .4 cups shelled

1 pound brown sugar, packed . . . . .2-1/4 cups

1 pound granulated sugar . . . . .2-1/4 cups

1 pound confectioners sugar, packed . . . . . . .2-1/3 to 2-1/2 cups

WHEN MEASURING...

baking powder, cornstarch, salt, soda, spices, etc., shake the container and dip measuring spoon into the container, fill heaping full and then level off across top with a straight-edge knife.

Measure all liquids by pouring into a measuring cup with the 1-cup line below the rim of the cup. Place on a level surface for accurate measuring. (This can make a big difference).

Always measure flour by sifting once before measuring. Lift flour lightly with a large scoop and fill cup until cup is heaped full; level off with a straight-edge knife without shaking cup. Do not use a measuring cup with 1-cup line below rim of cup.

Helpful Hints

HINTS AND SUGGESTIONS

WHEN DECIDING WHICH FLOUR TO USE

All-Purpose Flour - Made by blending hard and soft wheat flours; excellent for breads, cookies, coffee cakes and pastries.

Cake Flour - Milled from the highest grade of soft wheat and made specifically for making fine cakes.

Self-Rising Flour - Made by combining a soft wheat flour with salt and baking powder and is sifted together many times.

WHEN MEASURING DRY INGREDIENTS

Sift flour immediately before measuring. Use a dry measuring cup and one that can be leveled off with a straight edge knife. Lightly spoon flour into cup and then level off. If other dry ingredients are to be used in the recipe, sift those ingredients along with the flour. For instance, baking powder, baking soda, salt, spices, cocoa.

Brown sugar should be packed into measuring cup or spoon when measuring.

WHEN MELTING CHOCOLATE

Place saucepan over boiling water and allow chocolate to melt; use a rubber spatula to remove all chocolate from pan.

WHEN SCALDING MILK

Pour milk into cold saucepan and place over medium heat; stir constantly so film will not form. When you can feel the heat rise from the milk, remove immediately.

WHEN CARAMELIZING SUGAR

In a heavy saucepan, measure amount of white sugar recipe calls for; turn on low heat and stir with a wooden spoon constantly until sugar turns to a golden brown syrup. Stir in the amount of hot water called for and stir constantly until all sugar is dissolved.

WHEN BEATING EGG WHITES

When separating eggs make sure there is no egg yolk in the whites. Beat until foamy before adding any sugar, then gradually add sugar until stiff peaks form.

WHEN CUTTING DATES, RAISINS OR STICKY FOODS

Use kitchen shears when cutting sticky foods; dip shears into water when shears become sticky.

WHEN BOILING EGGS

Soft Cooked: Have eggs at room temperature. Place eggs in saucepan and cover with cold water; bring to a boil. Remove from heat and cover pan. Let stand for 4 minutes. Cool eggs by running cold water over them.

Hard Cooked: Have eggs at room temperature. Place eggs in saucepan and cover with cold water. Heat until water boils. Remove from heat and cover pan. Let stand for 20 minutes. Cool eggs by running cold water over them.

HOW TO PREPARE FRESH COCONUT

Puncture coconut with a metal skewer or a large nail in the 3 "eyes" on end of coconut. Drain coconut milk by placing over a glass. Coconut milk may be substituted or combined with milk in cake or cookie recipes. Place coconut in a 350 degree oven for 30 minutes or until shell cracks in 2 or 3 places. Remove and cool slightly. Tap coconut with a hammer all around; pry off shell with a sharp knife. pare off brown skin and grate fine or medium fine, as desired. Cover to keep moist and fluffy. Freeze immediately, if you want to use later.

EXTRACTS, HERBS AND SPICES

Experiment with flavorings and spices and your foods will become special. A little cinnamon or nutmeg in your hot oatmeal with cream adds glamor. Don't use too much, just a trace. Try some chives in your creamed potatoes, soups or vegetables. Give your meat, egg and gravy dishes a touch of the oriental with curry. Use some capers in the chicken, fish, potato or green salads that you prepare; or use them as a garnish. Don't forget to add a bay leaf to soups, stews and gravies. Marjoram is a wonderful addition to veal, potatoes, cheese and tomatoes, but use sparingly as it is a potent flavoring. And with any lamb dish you should try mint to make a sauce or try mint jelly. Mint served in tea will delight you with its cool flavor! Just use your imagination and your taste buds to develop your special recipes.

Index

MEET ME IN THE KITCHEN
RE-ORDER BLANKS

Blair of Columbus, Inc., P. O. Box 7852, Columbus, GA 31908, Telephone (404) 563-8787

Please send me _____ copies of MEET ME IN THE KITCHEN, at $15.95 plus $2.00 postage and handling. GA and NC residents, add state sales tax. Enclosed is my check or money order for $. Make check payable to Blair of Columbus, Inc.

Please charge my ( ) VISA/Bank Americard ( ) Master Charge/Interbank No. ( )

_____ Card No. _____
Signature of Cardholder
Card
Expiration date _____ Telephone No. _____
Name _____
Street _____
City _____ State _____ Zip _____

MEET ME IN THE KITCHEN
RE-ORDER BLANKS

Blair of Columbus, Inc., P. O. Box 7852, Columbus, GA 31908, Telephone (404) 563-8787

Please send me _____ copies of MEET ME IN THE KITCHEN, at $15.95 plus $2.00 postage and handling. GA and NC residents, add state sales tax. Enclosed is my check or money order for $. Make check payable to Blair of Columbus, Inc.

Please charge my ( ) VISA/Bank Americard ( ) Master Charge/Interbank No. ( )

_____ Card No. _____
Signature of Cardholder
Card
Expiration date _____ Telephone No. _____
Name _____
Street _____
City _____ State _____ Zip _____

MEET ME IN THE KITCHEN

MEET ME IN THE KITCHEN
RE-ORDER BLANKS

Blair of Columbus, Inc., P. O. Box 7852, Columbus, GA 31908, Telephone (404) 563-8787

Please send me _____ copies of MEET ME IN THE KITCHEN, at $15.95 plus $2.00 postage and handling. GA and NC residents, add state sales tax. Enclosed is my check or money order for $. Make check payable to Blair of Columbus, Inc.

Please charge my (   ) VISA/Bank Americard (   ) Master Charge/Interbank No. (   )

_____ Card No. _____
Signature of Cardholder

Card
Expiration date _____ Telephone No. _____
Name _____
Street _____
City _____ State _____ Zip _____

MEET ME IN THE KITCHEN
RE-ORDER BLANKS

Blair of Columbus, Inc., P. O. Box 7852, Columbus, GA 31908, Telephone (404) 563-8787

Please send me _____ copies of MEET ME IN THE KITCHEN, at $15.95 plus $2.00 postage and handling. GA and NC residents, add state sales tax. Enclosed is my check or money order for $. Make check payable to Blair of Columbus, Inc.

Please charge my (   ) VISA/Bank Americard (   ) Master Charge/Interbank No. (   )

_____ Card No. _____
Signature of Cardholder

Card
Expiration date _____ Telephone No. _____
Name _____
Street _____
City _____ State _____ Zip _____

MEET ME IN THE KITCHEN
RE-ORDER BLANKS

Blair of Columbus, Inc., P. O. Box 7852, Columbus, GA 31908, Telephone (404) 563-8787

Please send me _____ copies of MEET ME IN THE KITCHEN, at $15.95 plus $2.00 postage and handling. GA and NC residents, add state sales tax. Enclosed is my check or money order for $. Make check payable to Blair of Columbus, Inc.

Please charge my ( ) VISA/Bank Americard ( ) Master Charge/Interbank No. ( )

_____ Card No. _____

Signature of Cardholder

Card
Expiration date _____ Telephone No. _____
Name _____
Street _____
City _____ State _____ Zip _____

MEET ME IN THE KITCHEN
RE-ORDER BLANKS

Blair of Columbus, Inc., P. O. Box 7852, Columbus, GA 31908, Telephone (404) 563-8787

Please send me _____ copies of MEET ME IN THE KITCHEN, at $15.95 plus $2.00 postage and handling. GA and NC residents, add state sales tax. Enclosed is my check or money order for $. Make check payable to Blair of Columbus, Inc.

Please charge my ( ) VISA/Bank Americard ( ) Master Charge/Interbank No. ( )

_____ Card No. _____

Signature of Cardholder

Card
Expiration date _____ Telephone No. _____
Name _____
Street _____
City _____ State _____ Zip _____